Marx's Ghost

Marx's Ghost

Conversations with Archaeologists

Thomas C. Patterson

Oxford • New York

First published in 2003 by
Berg
Editorial offices:
1st Floor, Angel Court, 81 St Clements St, Oxford, OX4 1AW
838 Broadway, Third Floor, New York, NY 10003–4812, USA

Berg is the imprint of Oxford International Publishers Ltd.

Library of Congress Cataloguing-in-Publication Data

A catalog record for this book is available from the Library of Congress.

British Library Cataloguing-in-Publication Data
Patterson, Thomas Carl.
   Marx's ghost : conversations with archaeologists / Thomas C. Patterson.
      p. cm.
Includes bibliographical references and index.
   ISBN 1-85973-701-3 (Cloth) – ISBN 1-85973-706-4 (Paper) 1. Marxian
archaeology 2. Archaeology–Philosophy. I. Title.

CC75.7.P39 2003
930.1'01–dc21

                                   2003010059

ISBN 1 85973 701 3 (Cloth)
        1 85973 706 4 (Paper)

Typeset by JS Typesetting Ltd, Wellingborough, Northants.

www.bergpublishers.com

Contents

Preface

This is not the preface I originally wrote for *Marx's Ghost*. Kathryn Earle (my editor at Berg), Bob Preucel (the originally anonymous outside reviewer of the manuscript), Wendy Ashmore (my partner and colleague), Karen Spalding (my friend and frequent co-conspirator during the last forty years), and Carlos Vélez-Ibáñez (my friend and colleague), among others, urged me write something more autobiographical, something that described how I came to write the book. It was important, they said, to write something that described my own intellectual and political formation and explained how I came to think the way I do. Reluctantly, I agreed to do so. My reluctance is based partly on a view that autobiographies can be self-serving and partly out of modesty. In some respects, my life has been a series of "ah ha! now I understand what they are saying" revelations or moments. In other respects, I know that I have changed; fortunately, from my view and those of some people I both cherish and respect, I am no longer the person I was. While some will probably be amused, hopefully others may find this autobiographical account useful.

I was born in Rutland, Vermont, in 1937. My father came from a large rural family on the Gaspe Peninsula in which seasonal wage work was supplemented with farming, fishing, hunting, and woodcutting. My mother's family settled in Montreal after leaving Manchester, England, in the 1890s; her father managed a butcher's shop. My parents moved to Maine around 1940, and I spent all but one of the next twelve years in Portland and Waterville. My father worked variously as a traveling salesman, a chief warrant officer in the Coast Guard during the Second World War, and the manager of a fuel oil distributing company. My mother was a seamstress. My parents had fifth-grade educations; in their view, this limited the kinds of jobs they could get. As a result, they valued education for the opportunities it afforded. Like many anglophone Canadians who came to New England for work and eventually got U.S. citizenship, they were lifelong Republicans, wary of big business and labor unions, and apprehensive of communism and the Soviet Union. A phrase I heard often as a child was, "Behave or the Bolsheviks will get you." My father had a profound sense of fairness, a sentiment that was absent most of the time in my mother's shopkeeper mentality. I attribute this largely to the differences in their class backgrounds and histories; it was an ongoing source of tension throughout their lives.

My father lost his job in July 1952. After several months of indecision, he bought a trailer, loaded my mother and me in the car, and drove West in search of work. In late November, we settled in Pomona, California. My parents soon found work: my mother as a filing clerk in a machine shop, and my father as an expediter at Lockheed. Since both were closed shops, they reluctantly joined the machinists' union in order to work. I came to appreciate the importance of union wages, benefits, and protection a few years later when I began working in a series of non-union jobs, most memorably as a gas station attendant and a draftsman in a guided missile factory owned by General Dynamics.

I enrolled as a sophomore at the town's only public high school, which was a ten-minute walk from the trailer park where we lived. In the school the native-born Anglos, many of whose families were dependent in one way or another on the citrus industry, were becoming a minority as immigrants, mostly from Oklahoma and Mexico, swelled enrollments. At the time, Pomona was undergoing massive social transformation as its rapidly disappearing orange groves were being replaced with equal rapidity by tract homes, shopping malls, and freeways. Even though immigration and new housing developments were transforming the landscape, distinctions between older neighborhoods persisted. The houses and lawns were larger and better maintained north of the tracks; there were more bars and auto-shops and Spanish was heard as often as English on the south side where I lived. The racism and disdain for all but the most mainstream of Protestants were as palpable as they were in New England or in Florida, where I had lived for a year. The slurs were the same, only the ethnicities changed. Later, I learned that, in the 1920s, Pomona was home to one of the largest Ku-Klux-Klan chapters west of the Mississippi River.

In the spring of 1953, when I was fifteen, several of my friends from school and I went to Baja California, Mexico, where we camped for several weeks near a fishing village. We helped the fishermen and their families pull heavy nets onto the beach; in return, they gave us fresh fish and told us about the local fishing industry. In 1955, I enrolled in the newly opened campus of the University of California in Riverside. It was not my first choice, but it was the best of the limited options that were available to me. I majored in the physical sciences, thinking I would graduate and turn a summer job as a draftsman into a career. Fortunately, I discovered after a year or so that I was not particularly interested in either the physical sciences or engineering. I also realized that my job was as mind-numbing as the worst of the blue-collar, assembly-line jobs many of my high-school classmates had taken. The only difference between their jobs and mine was that I wore white shirts with plastic pocket liners. I came to understand why the drafting pool where I worked had one of the highest lost-time accident rates in the plant. Eye injuries were especially prevalent among the draftsmen, who tended to impale themselves with fingers and pencils as they nodded off. They were bored out of their minds by tedious repetition and literally fell asleep while they were drawing pictures of nuts and bolts eight hours a day, five days a week, month after month.

My employment at General Dynamics was terminated in 1958. My boss said it was because of the recession, not because I had complained about losing health benefits or working the night shift. In any event, I wasn't eligible for unemployment benefits. This was also conducive to thinking about what I might do after college. By that time, I needed to fulfill a number of breadth requirements in order to graduate. As a result, I took an introductory anthropology course, not out of any intrinsic interest in the subject but rather because it met at a convenient time. This course, taught by Jack Goins, was the most thought-provoking one I ever took. Other teachers who subsequently helped me hone and refine my interests and skills at UC-Riverside were Bud Winans, and Alex Krieger and Carl Sauer, both of whom were visiting faculty members.

In the process, I remembered and thought about the positive experiences I had had five years earlier in Baja California. This, combined with my recent experience in "big business," underwrote my decision to pursue anthropology as a major, an avocation, and a career. The Black civil rights movement and the anti-capitalist sentiments found in the old labor songs performed by Pete Seeger and others captured my attention in new ways. What I could not comprehend at the time were McCarthyism or the linkages between the Cold War and U.S. imperialism. The process of clarification began slowly and unevenly in the late 1950s when I read in the local newspaper that a classmate from high school had been arrested during demonstrations at House Un-American Activities Committee (HUAC) hearings in San Francisco. I began to ask why.

I enrolled as a graduate student in anthropology at the University of California, Berkeley, in the fall of 1960. The Bay Area was exciting. There were marches and boycotts organized by the civil rights and labor movements; people held strong views about HUAC; the spectrum of political debate and newspapers was much greater than in Riverside, which was then, and still is, more conservative than Orange County; a vocal minority of students pushed the limits of political discourse on campus; and an anti-hegemonic counter-culture was emerging in coffeehouses and working-class neighborhoods around the Bay. In the spring of 1964, protests against U.S. involvement in Vietnam grew louder, and the university administration called in the Alameda County sheriffs to arrest more than seven hundred students protesting a ban on free speech. With the exception of the boycotts and the coffeehouses, my participation was mostly vicarious. I have regretted my inaction ever since; the protesters were right.

I knew I wanted to become an anthropologist, just not what kind. As an undergraduate, I was particularly interested in the historical anthropology of Oceania and intrigued by the implications of the new fossil hominids being discovered in East Africa. Even though some faculty at Berkeley regularly paid lip-service to the holism of the discipline, the balkanization of anthropology had in fact already been institutionalized there by the 1950s. Partly through a process of elimination, I ended up working with archaeologists John Rowe and Ted McCown, who provided me with superb technical skills; in 1962–3, I worked with Ed Lanning on the central Peruvian coast and did a ceramic analysis for my dissertation. René Millon, Gerry Berreman, and Sherry Washburn provoked me to think in new ways. For example, in the spring of 1961, Millon introduced me to Eric Wolf's *Sons of the Shaking Earth*, which was stunning. At the time, I was dimly aware at best that this book was a subtly Marxist analysis of the historical development and transformation of Mesoamerican society. For Wolf, the object of inquiry was always culture and society not archaeology, ethnology, and history.

My experience and growing understanding of Peru in the 1960s had a slow, transformative effect on my future. Three things immediately captured my attention when I went there for the first time in 1961. There was a civil war; there were a few very wealthy people and many more who were poor; and there were lots of anti-American slogans painted on walls. Moreover, the courses I had taken had not equipped me to understand the contemporary reality I was seeing and experiencing. As a result, I began to read what people were writing about the current situation. I slowly discovered with some dismay that journalists writing for leftist newspapers wrote accounts that simultaneously validated my perceptions and explained the social relations of Peruvian society and its political-economic linkages with the United States. I reasoned that, if their work was based in some way on Marx, I should probably begin to read Marx as well. I bought a pamphlet written by Marx at a newspaper stand in Lima. I also realized that I had never read openly leftist authors, beyond the obligatory excerpt or two from the *Communist Manifesto*, in any course I had taken as an undergraduate. While I was fairly clear at that point about the roles McCarthyism and the Cold War played in producing this deficit, it took longer to appreciate fully the consequences and how my work and that of others reproduced the damage.

I also began to ask whether there was anything in Marx's writings that might help me understand the societies whose archaeological remains I had been recording and excavating in central Peru. About this time (the fall of 1963), I met Karen Spalding, who was then framing her dissertation research project on the social history of Peru during the colonial period. Since both of us were concerned with bridging the gap between anthropology and history, our discussions over the next few years eventually turned to the relevance of Marxist social theory for this project and for understanding the societies of the past. We also argued about contemporary politics. At the time, my political views tended toward social reformist; hers did not. The events at the Democratic Convention in Chicago in 1968 led me to conclude that her understanding of the structural constraints inherent in U.S. politics was a lot more perceptive and accurate than mine. In short, she was right and I was wrong. Our conversations and collaboration have continued unabated since then.

I accepted an assistant professorship at Harvard in 1965. I felt out of place almost immediately and resigned three years later. Some of the senior faculty – notably Gordon Willey and George Wald at Harvard and Cyril Smith at MIT – went out of their way to make me comfortable. All of them were towering figures in their fields; however, given my background and insecurities, I avoided interacting with them on anything but the most superficial level. In hindsight that was also a mistake. I was more comfortable talking with students or junior faculty in other departments or universities in the area. Fortunately, Richard Lee, George Cowgill, Mike Moseley, and Jerry Sabloff, among others, were in town and also liked to talk. What I didn't talk about or couldn't articulate clearly were the changes in how I was beginning to understand the world.

I was at Yale from 1968 to 1971, where I continued the pattern of spending more time with students than senior faculty: Richard Burger, Bob and Judy Zeitlin, and Louise Paradis come immediately to mind. I also spent a lot of time with my neighbors; on weekends, I played flag football in a league organized by the city's recreation department. A singular achievement in teaching was that I began to put Marxist authors on reading lists; however, I do not think this was the reason I was denied tenure. My bet instead is on surliness or an ability to provoke arguments by pulling scabs off old wounds. Unfortunately, I still know how to skewer people and make them uncomfortable; fortunately perhaps, I've become more discriminating and aware of when I choose to do so.

I lived with friends in New York City during the 1970s. It was a very active period politically. I participated in a series of Marxist discussion and reading groups that were almost devoid of academics. This was important for a couple of reasons: it not only brought diverse viewpoints to the group but also highlighted the importance of framing arguments in ways that diverse audiences could hear and use constructively. I was working fairly regularly doing a lot of the "nuts and bolts" jobs that make political groups function smoothly and successfully. I handed out fliers, pasted them on walls, sold tickets, collected them, arranged for space and speakers, wrote and produced programs for various events, constructed telephone message trees, did research, and undertook various tasks on security details to ensure that people on the programs or in the audiences were safe.

I became an associate professor at Temple University in 1971; I was tenured two years later and promoted to professor in 1981 or 1982, after the teachers' union mentioned possible legal action and the Dean directed that several anonymous statements in my personnel file should not be considered at all by the members of the promotions committee. One motivation behind the unsigned letters was that I had chosen to live in New York and hence was not part of the "Temple community." This had two effects – infrequent, minimal pay raises during the 1970s and increasingly difficult teaching schedules. At the same time, the cost of the Amtrack commuter rail passes I purchased each month tripled between 1971 and 1980 as the number of trains running between Philadelphia and New York declined steadily. I finally moved to Philadelphia in 1980 but couldn't locate the community imagined by some of my colleagues. It didn't exist in spite of the fact that some of them got together regularly.

In the mid-1970s, I agreed to write a textbook on world archaeology for Prentice-Hall. In my view, what made it different from similar books were some brief but explicit statements about Marxism and its potential relevance for archaeology and some remarks about the behaviorism and reductionism inherent in positivism. The brief sections on Marxist social thought really annoyed the anonymous reviewers. In spite of the fact that their comments delayed publication of the book by a year or more, it eventually appeared in 1981. The contract with Prentice-Hall also called for a workbook on the theory and practice of archaeology. This was the one that really interested me; it appeared in 1983 (Patterson 1983c). The workbook was thoroughly Marxist in conceptioin even though I didn't particularly use the vocabulary or argue the theory except through data or outside the introduction. The problems in the workbook showed that theoretical assumptions can and need to be refined by confrontation with research data. The manuscript sped through the review process, and nothing was said about its theoretical foundations. While I was writing the books, I also learned something important about the process of writing. I began to write interactively with a small group of friends, most notably Karen Spalding, who, at the time, was also rewriting her dissertation for publication. For an entire semester when we were both on sabbatical, we wrote in the morning, shared the manuscripts over lunch, and provided each other with constructive, critical comments over coffee. Writing became a social activity rather than something that should or must be done in isolation.

At Temple, Frank Johnston and I collaborated in launching a biocultural adaptations program that was simultaneously integrative of the discipline and broadly focused on the health and well-being of communities, past and present. After Frank went across town to the University of Pennsylvania, the other participants steadily narrowed the focus of the program and ultimately were looking almost exclusively at the biological realm. The re-balkanization of the faculty that ensued was unfortunate. One bright spot at Temple during this period was that, at least rhetorically, the cultural anthropologists acknowledged the importance of theory. By theory, most of them meant functionalism, structuralism, symbolic anthropology, or empiricism. It seemed appropriate to Peter Rigby and me to talk about Marxism as well. In 1979, we proposed a couple of new courses on "Marxism and anthropology" to the appropriate departmental committee. Critics on the committee balked, arguing that the courses were too narrow and that they did not allow for discussion of all alternative viewpoints. Rigby and I made two points in response. First, the alternate viewpoints, but not Marxism, were either embedded or discussed in every other course offered by the department. Second, if we accepted the logic of our critics, then the biological anthropologists should provide equal time to creationist arguments in all of their courses. This was probably the only time in the history of the department that the biological anthropologists voted unanimously to approve anything that involved Marxist social thought. I was grateful for their support. I would teach versions and updates of these courses over the next two decades to some of the most talented students I have ever met – Rema Hammami, Pamela Calla, Mike Blim, Xiaorong Gu, Lee Baker, Jeff Maskovsky, Jennifer Alvey, Ananth Aiyer, Susan Levine, Niloufer Venkatraman, John Stinson-Fernández, Chris Bernat, David Reichard, Jason Greenberg, Terry Epperson, Kimmika Williams-Witherspoon, and Colleen O'Neill come to mind. Given the diversity of their interests, I had to work hard to keep up with them. I learned a lot from them in the process.

Temple was an interesting place to work. The faculty generally supported trying new ideas. I think my work would have remained more narrowly and traditionally focused if I had not taught there. I attribute this to some terrific colleagues in anthropology and other departments – Judy Goode, Peter Rigby, Tony Ranere, Peter Gran, Kathy Walker, Phil Yannella, and Jim Collins – who were often collaborators, sounding boards, or foils who helped me develop and refine arguments. I also attribute it to the fact that the Temple faculty was unionized and fairly radical, at least during the 1980s. Its members struck on two occasions (1986 and 1990) and were preparing to strike on a third (1984) when a last-minute settlement was reached. These were the moments when the faculty galvanized as a community. I participated in various ways: strike preparations, research, walking picket lines, meeting representatives from the other ten or so unions on campus with varying degrees of regularity, and serving as an elected member of the union executive committee.

My participation in professional meetings was spotty during the 1970s. There were three reasons for this. First, I felt somewhat disenchanted from the American Anthropological Association (AAA), especially after the attack that some members of its Executive Board launched against anti-war activists at the 1971 annual meeting in New York. Second, I was busy, and anthropology was not as central in my life as it had been a few years earlier. Third, given my financial circumstances, I had to make hard decisions about what I would spend money on during the economic collapse and reorganization of the 1970s.

This pattern of intermittent attendance at and participation in conferences changed in 1982, when Richard Burger invited me to participate in a Dumbarton Oaks conference on early architecture in the Andes. I agreed, partly to re-establish connections and conversations with people I had seen infrequently, if at all, since the early 1970s. I noticed two things at the conference: although my acquaintances had all aged considerably, the discourse had not changed that much. This experience, combined with my slightly improved financial circumstances resulting from the promotion, encouraged me to attend other professional meetings. I went to the AAA meetings a month or so later and began to participate regularly in the Council of Marxist Anthropology, where I also renewed old acquaintances and met people I knew only by reputation. I subsequently went to other meetings; I preferred the smaller ones, because it was easier to have extended conversations, and the political spectrum was more progressive. This was particularly true after the AAA made it almost impossible to pass resolutions from the floor of the annual business meetings in the mid-1980s. I got to know a lot of people during this period. The people with whom I collaborated or talked most frequently from 1982 onward were probably Christine Gailey, Karen Brodkin, Elizabeth Brumfiel, Stanley Diamond, Bob Paynter, Alison Wylie, Carole Crumley, Peter Schmidt, Ida Susser, and John Gledhill. They and others mentioned in the acknowledgements of papers published since then were the audience for what I was writing; they helped me to clarify, expand, and extend what I was trying to say. Their comments were always thought-provoking.

With hindsight, not participating in professional activities in the 1970s was a mistake. By isolating myself to a certain extent, I was not sufficiently aware of the activities of others, including archaeologists, who were also trying to incorporate Marxist social theory in their work. More importantly, I didn't really know what they were thinking about. I also never learned how the professional associations operated. This became blatantly apparent in 1985 and 1986 around the World Archaeological Congress. In brief, the British organizing committee of the Congress acknowledged the UN sanctions banning cultural exchanges with South Africa and disinvited participants from that country. Archaeologists from the United States were of two minds about the Congress. They either supported a boycott led by a number of senior scholars in that country or chose not to attend the Congress. I believe that those of us in North America who supported participation in the Congress might have been a more effective counterbalance to the organizers of the boycott if we had had a fuller understanding of the professional associations and how they actually worked. It was an important learning experience for me. Since then, I have held elected offices in two sections of the AAA and served as an elected member of the association's nominations committee. I now have a more complete grasp of how the organization works, its limitations, and the possibilities for constructive engagement and change within it. Not participating in a professional organization like the AAA now appears to me as analogous to not voting in an election and then complaining about the candidates who were elected. This does not mean that I have changed my mind one iota about the limitations inherent in reformist politics, especially when elections in the United States are popularity contests waged by candidates who espouse similar platforms and do the bidding of the same class fractions that support their campaigns.

Preface

The last thirty years or so has involved more than a little change, a lot of work, some discomfort, and occasionally real grief and pain. It has always been product- ive, sporadically amusing, and sometimes truly wonderful. In the late 1980s, Iraida Vargas and Mario Sanoja, my friends and colleagues in Venezuela, made me an offer I couldn't refuse: "Write a book on Mesoamerica for a series we are editing." I wrote the book (Patterson 1997b). Then they wanted pictures of archaeological sites to illustrate it. I had no pictures of Maya sites and thought to myself, "Who might have pictures, and would they let me use them for a publication?" I asked Wendy Ashmore, with whom I had worked in the Archeology Division of the AAA. She had pictures and agreed to let me use them. In gratitude, I invited her to lunch at a Thai restaurant in Philadelphia that was apparently never open for lunch. We had lunch elsewhere; since I really like the food at the Thai restaurant, I suggested dinner there at a later date. She agreed. As Roseanne Roseanneadana, one of Gilda Radner's characters on *Saturday Night Live*, used to say, "one thing led to another." In 2000, we were recruited by the University of California, Riverside. We eventually accepted the offers and started a new life together with her two cats, a mortgage, and a swimming pool described variously as the world's largest feline drinking bowl or an expensive hole in the patio.

Someone recently suggested that I "went home" when we accepted the jobs at UC-Riverside. I disagreed. When I was an undergraduate, there were fewer than a thousand students on the campus, which we (the students) described as the "poor man's Pomona" and which the university administrators now characterize as its "Swarthmore of the West" phase. It currently has more than 16,000 students, and it is definitely not the same institution or place. The trailer park still exists in Pomona. Some of the housing tracts built after I left are now abandoned. Parts of the city resemble the urban wastelands of the South Bronx or Philadelphia and bear silent testimony to the effects of unregulated development that puts profit ahead of human needs. The continual recycling of land is fairly typical of development in this part of Southern California. The vineyards I remember from the 1950s were replaced by dairy farms in the 1960s; these are now covered with gigantic ware- houses built in the 1990s. At one level, the political economy of the region is reasonably clear. At another level, it is textured and complex. It is imperative, I think, to understand this diversity and how it differentially affects the health and well-being of the various groups that live and work here. This is a prelude to forging some viable alternatives to what has happened and is currently taking place in the "edge cities" of Southern California and their environs. I am heartened that a number of my UC-Riverside colleagues see the same problems. They also realize that there are other ways of living than the ones we experience here, and that changing the circumstances of everyday life in this society is still a real possibility.

A number of people provided guidance, both before I began the book and while I was writing it. Their insights, constructive criticism, and inspiration have been invaluable, and I hope that I have not distorted their ideas and words. In addition, I want to thank my colleague and friend, Karen Spalding, who has been there almost since the beginning of the journey. I also want to thank Barbara Bender, Karen Brodkin, Liz Brumfiel, George Cowgill, Carole Crumley, Jonathan Fried-man, Christine Gailey, John Gledhill, Peter Gran, Russ Handsman, Phil Kohl, Mogens Larsen, Mark Leone, Randy McGuire, William Marquardt, René Millon, Chuck Orser, Bob Paynter, Bob Preucel, Mike Rowlands, Jerry Sabloff, Maurizio Tosi, Bruce Trigger, Kathy Walker, Eric Wolf, and Gordon Willey.

I also want to acknowledge the ongoing support of Kathryn Earle, my editor at Berg, whose good advice, sense of humor, and annual dinners are appreciated much more than she knows or than I will ever tell her. I am grateful to Justin Dyer, who helped me remove ambiguities and clarify the argument.

Finally, I especially want to thank Wendy Ashmore – my partner in life – whose high standards of scholarship serve as a model to be emulated and whose steady encouragement, constructive commentaries, and instantaneous feedback are deeply appreciated. She also makes me laugh.

Introduction

For more than seventy years, archaeologists have engaged in a conversation with Marx's ghost. The aim of the book is to explore the myriad dimensions of this conversation. It is seen most easily in the exchanges that have occurred around questions concerned with the rise of civilization, or the origins of states. Like most conversations, the tenor of this one has shifted from time to time. Sometimes the participants have engaged in an open discussion where, while perhaps disagreeing with some of what they hear, they build on other thoughts, creatively incorporating them into their own perspectives and transforming their points of view in the process; as a result, they develop new ways of perceiving and understanding the old problem. On other occasions, the participants resemble trains passing one another on parallel tracks; they talk past one another, not fully grasping what has been said but disagreeing with what they have heard. At other times, they remain silent, either unable or unwilling to acknowledge what has been said to them. In these instances, what is novel bounces off deeply held perspectives; what is threatening to those cherished views is ignored, avoided, or actively repressed. In a phrase, the conversations that archaeologists have had with Marx's ghost have been characterized by genuine dialogue, by backtalk and crosstalk, and by silence, disregard, avoidance, and suppression. The conversations archaeologists have had over the last seventy years with Marx's legacy exemplify all the above.

One thing that makes some conversations so productive is the fact that the participants consciously frame their views in terms of analytical categories – like social class – that derive from the same body of social theory. It is relatively easier to have a productive discussion with individuals who are aware of the shaping effects that particular bodies of social theory have on their views than it is with persons who avoid getting clear on the effects of the implicit and explicit assumptions of their own perspectives or who eschew considering social theory altogether. It is also possible, however, to have a meaningful conversation with individuals who use theoretical frameworks that differ from our own. This is especially true when the participants are familiar enough with their own and with the other theoretical views that they can recast statements in ways that are meaningful in light of those frameworks.

Theoretical traditions – such as Karl Marx's historical materialism, the evolutionism of Lewis Henry Morgan or Herbert Spencer, and the functionalism of Émile Durkheim – shape the ways we understand the world. At one level, the social theory we use helps us to frame questions, to select information that is relevant for answering them, and to organize our answers to those inquiries. At another level, they provide us with a means for evaluating those answers, for determining whether or not we have constructed acceptable or adequate explanations given the evidence we have used. At still another level, theoretical frameworks provide us with ways of using that information to expand or modify existing accounts, to take an old explanation and recast it in innovative ways that provide new insights.

Theoretical traditions are neither homogeneous nor static. Each consists of a series of intertwined strands that continually interrogate and interact with one another. In a phrase, there are subtle and not so subtle differences within each tradition. Attempts to reduce a tradition to a few quotations from foundational works – such as those of Marx or Durkheim – obscure the texture and complexity of the tradition. They conceal the real differences that may exist between the arguments of individuals who use different strands of the same tradition. These traditions are not static, because of the dialectical relationship that exists between theory and evidence. While theory informs our understanding, chains of evidence and the fit between them and what is expected theoretically allow us to elaborate and refine the frameworks we use.

In this book, I am arguing that it is imperative to clarify the distinctions within and between theoretical traditions. This requires getting clear on the implicit and explicit assumptions that buttress these frameworks. At a time when the social sciences are fragmented because of a highly developed technical division of labor, either sharing the same theoretical framework or appreciating the significance of the distinctions between them is the surest way of guaranteeing that meaningful discussions will occur across those historically contingent boundaries. Another reason for getting clear on these theoretical traditions is that they are incorporated into paradigms that both sustain and are sustained by the power relations that exist in the profession and in the wider society. Confusion about these interconnections makes it difficult for us to understand how our research and the statements we make relate to wider social and political-economic currents, and such confusion makes it virtually impossible to investigate the linkages.

Organization of the Book

Chapter 1 explores Marx's legacy to archaeologists and social scientists: his dialectical method, his theory of history and society, and his understanding of ecology. Marx's legacy was informed by his critique of liberal political economy and by his analyses of the development of the capitalist mode of production and its laws of motion. He criticized the political economists for representing the social relations that were peculiar to capitalist society as if they were eternal rather than socially and historically contingent categories. His analyses of capitalism and comparisons with precapitalist modes of production drew attention to the specificity of different kinds of society, their laws of motion, their interconnection with the natural world, and their population dynamics. This exploration of Marx's legacy relies largely on materials that were published before 1932; the exceptions are three letters and the *Grundrisse* and *Ethnological Notebooks,* which appeared in 1939–41 and 1974, respectively. As a result, Marx's published legacy provides a baseline of ideas that readers might have known and drawn upon during the first three decades of the twentieth century. It attempts to answer two questions: What could a well-informed reader reasonably have known, and when could he or she have known it?

Chapter 2 examines how in the late 1920s Australian archaeologist V. Gordon Childe brought together elements of three distinct discourses. Until then, exchanges between archaeologists, sociologists, and Marxists were minimal and largely unacknowledged. The chapter opens with a discussion of the interconnections of the evolutionary sociology forged by Herbert Spencer and the functionalist sociology of Émile Durkheim and then considers their linkages with the evolutionary socialism of Karl Kautsky. Together with Marx and Engels's work, their writings produced a corpus of ideas from which Childe drew selectively to construct his theoretically informed syntheses of archaeological data and historical reconstructions of human social development. The theoretical underpinnings of Childe's reconstructions are then examined. His analyses, rooted largely but not exclusively in Marxist social thought, provoked responses from U.S. archaeologists, sociocultural anthropologists, and historians in the years immediately following the Second World War. Their assessments of Childe's legacy and the alternatives they proposed during the late 1940s and early 1950s are discussed in the third section. The chapter closes with brief considerations of Childe's impact in Latin America and how his theoretical framework was put to use by archaeologists and anthropologists working in the Valley of Mexico.

Chapter 3 analyzes the responses of archaeologists during the 1950s and 1960s to Childe's views concerning the "urban revolution" – i.e. the rise of civilization, the formation of states. Two strands of sociocultural evolutionism shaped archaeological discourse in the 1950s. Both saw societies developing through a linear sequence of stages. The advocates of one strand who built on the economism of the late nineteenth century typically disregarded the connections between their economistic formulations and the evolutionary socialism of the Second International (1889–1914). Proponents of the second strand adopted the positivist formulations of Spencer and Durkheim, whose views also underpinned different conceptualizations of the new (processual) archaeology of the 1960s and early 1970s. The new archaeologists were functionalists concerned with adaptation and with the conditions and forms of social relations that promoted stability. Following Durkheim, they viewed exchange as the means by which the various groups in differentiated societies were bound together. A Malthusian strand of cultural evolutionary thought also emerged in the 1960s. While the proponents of this perspective also viewed the development of exchange relations between areas with diverse resources as unproblematic, they argued, *contra* the new archaeologists, that population growth and warfare were motors of sociocultural evolution. While the majority of archaeologists did not directly engage the legacies of Marx and Childe, a few did. They made explicit use of Marxist concepts such as contradiction and exploitation and indirectly employed other Marxist analytical categories, like mode of production, in their discussions of the rise of civilization.

Chapter 4 considers the emergence of an explicitly Marxist archaeology in the mid-1970s. The advocates of Marxist perspectives in archaeology built on diverse strands of Marxist social thought, which were sometimes at odds with one another. Their elaboration of these perspectives was embedded initially in critiques of processual archaeologists who relied on central place theory, exchange rather than production relations, and systems theory to explain the rise of states. The Marxists focused instead on the different kind of production regimes that flourished in societies manifesting the kin-communal and tributary modes of production, on the various forms of the kin-communal mode of production, on exploitation and the internal dynamics of class and state formation, and on the articulation of mode of production. There were also elaborations of cultural materialist and processual perspectives during this period; both built on the liberal social theory of Spencer and Durkheim, and sought reductionist explanations in order to account for sociological phenomena in terms of psychology, ecology, or systems theory. While the cultural materialists and processualists were critical of each other, neither had much to say about the emergence of an archaeological perspective informed by Marxism. The arenas of discussion between the processualists and the Marxists occurred from the mid-1980s onward in symposia concerned with the rise of chiefdoms, the nature of complex chiefdoms, and the internal dynamics of state formation.

Chapter 5 surveys three arenas of discussion that developed after 1990 between archaeologists who grounded their analyses variously in Marxism and other theoretical perspectives. The first arena involved the historic specificity not only of particular political practices but also of state formative processes and structures. The second focused on issues of heterarchy and social transformation. The third engaged the issue of interregional interaction and examined the ways in which archaeologists have criticized, modified, and extended Immanuel Wallerstein's world systems theory to explain the core–periphery relations manifested by precapitalist world economies and empires as well as capitalist states. The discussions that occurred in the first and third arenas provided theoretical foundations for those historical archaeologists who set out from the late 1980s onward to investigate the interconnections of class, gender, ethnicity, and race as well as the cultural identities constituted by such intersections. The discussions that took place in these arenas also marked the increased porosity or partial erosion of the disciplinary boundaries that separated anthropological and historical archaeology in the United States.

–1–

Marx's Legacy

Karl Marx (1818–83) was a full-time revolutionary who was more concerned with changing society than with interpreting it (Marx 1845/1976:5).[1] He was not an archaeologist, an historian, or a social scientist.[2] Nevertheless his legacy to archaeologists, historians, and social scientists is enormous. For more than a century, they have engaged his ghost and accomplishments in spirited discussions about human societies and their transformation. The reasons for this engagement have been the depth and lasting value of Marx's penetrating insights into the social relations of modern capitalist societies and the processes by which they came into being. More than 130 years after it was written, *Capital*, one of the works for which he is deservedly famous, is still the best single assessment of the dynamics of the capitalist mode of production. Marx's analyses of capitalism and of the struggles taking place in particular countries were always tied to political practice. As an activist whose newspaper was shut down by the Prussian government and who was officially expelled by the Prussians, the French, and the Belgians, he was acutely aware of just how unforgiving the victorious ruling classes could be in political struggles. Consequently, he realized the importance of knowing as accurately, as realistically, and as completely as possible the shifting balance of forces that underpinned class struggles in the industrial countries, in their colonies, and in the noncapitalist states on their margins.

What did Marx and Frederick Engels (1820–95), his friend and collaborator for more than four decades, leave for the generations that succeeded them?[3] What captured the imagination of radical activists for nearly 150 years? What provoked social scientists and historians for more than a century? What has attracted the attention of professional archaeologists for seven decades? Let us examine these questions in terms of the method Marx developed, his theory of society and history, and his analysis of the relation between nature and society.

Marx's Method

Marx developed a distinctive method early in his career, which he honed and refined in subsequent writings. It is a framework – a point of departure – for clarifying problems in order to gain a practical understanding of everyday life in capitalist society. The method is analogous to peeling an onion layer by layer, revealing its internal structure with each successive layer until reaching its core and then reassembling the whole. The technique involves looking behind and beneath superficial appearances; it includes critical examination and abstraction; and it concludes with careful attention to how what has been learned in the process is presented. One moves from the "perceived" concrete by a process of abstraction (breaking the whole into mental constructs) and then back to the "thought" concrete whole but with a greater appreciation and understanding of the unity of the parts and the whole and of its inner dynamics, structure, and contradictions.

This is Marx's "dialectical method." H. T. Wilson (1991) has referred to it as "Marx's critical/dialectical procedure" to emphasize the importance of both critique and the materialist dialectic. Marxist writers differ on which aspect of the method was its most distinctive feature. For Georg Lukács (1923/1971:27), "the category of totality, the all-pervasive supremacy of the whole over the parts," was its essence. For Mao Zedong (1937/1975:311), it was Marx's emphasis on contradictions, which constitute the very essence of totalities. For Bertell Ollman (1993: 26), it was Marx's abstractions. The interconnections of totalities, contradictions, and abstraction will become more clear as we examine the method itself.

The dialectical method addresses the difference between appearances and reality. In the process of clarifying his own thinking, Marx (1861–3/1971:536–7) recalled the story of Cacus, a half-demon who lived in a cave and came out at night to steal people's oxen from their fields. He forced the oxen to walk backwards to mislead the owners when they came to collect their animals the next morning. On the surface, at least, the footprints seemed to reveal that the oxen had walked from the cave and disappeared in the middle of the fields. The point of the story was that the superficial appearance of the footprints obscured what really happened. As Ollman (1993:11) remarked, "to understand the real meaning of the footprints, the owners . . . had to find out what happened the night before." This would require replacing common-sense notions derived from the direction of the footprints with something that linked the processes which took place with a wider set of facts and their interrelations (a totality). It would involve coming to grips with the discrepancy between the appearance of the footprints and the process that actually produced them (a contradiction). It would require the cattle-owners to restructure the way they thought about the world of appearances. Marx believed that adopting a critical, materialist dialectics would have allowed them to proceed with an informed reconstruction of reality.

In the introduction to the *Grundrisse*, a set of notebooks he prepared in 1857–8, Marx (1857–8/1973:100; 1859/1970:206) portrayed the method of the economists in the following manner:

When we consider a given country politico- economically, we begin with its population, its distribution among classes, town, country, the coast, the different branches of production, export and import, annual production and consumption, commodity prices etc.

It seems to be correct to begin with the real and the concrete, with the real precondition, thus, to begin in economics, with e.g. the population, which is the foundation and the subject of the entire social act of production. . . . Thus, if I were to begin with the population, this would be a chaotic conception of the whole, and I would then, by means of further determination, move analytically toward ever more simple concepts, from the imagined concrete toward ever thinner abstractions until I arrived at the simplest determinations. From there the journey would have to be retraced until I had finally arrived at the population again, but this time not as the chaotic conception of the whole, but as a rich totality of many determinations and relations.

The economists' method proceeded from the world of appearances to its simpler, constituent categories and back again to a more profound understanding of that world. While it appeared reasonable on the surface, Marx (1857–8/1973: 100–8) concluded that their procedure was problematic, for a number of reasons. First, in his view, the totalities they were dealing with were not fixed, unchanging entities whose parts equaled the sum of the whole. They were instead dynamic, dialectically structured, and historically determined unities existing in and through the diverse connections, interactions, and contradictions that joined their parts (Mészaros 1991). More importantly, their motion and change (evolution) meant that particular totalities were confined to specific historical periods. Marx and Engels (1845–6/1976:50) captured this dynamic in their discussion of the formation of social totalities in *The German Ideology*.

History is nothing but the succession of the separate generations, each of which uses the materials, the capital funds, the productive forces handed down to it by all the preceding generations, and thus, on the one hand, continues the traditional activity in completely changed circumstances and, on the other, modifies the old circumstances with a completely changed activity.

Thus, in Marx's view, a totality was a "real" concrete unity composed of interacting contradictions. The shifting interactions and mediations (indirect interventions) of its parts were the engines that drove the transformation of objective reality itself.

Marx's second criticism of the economists' method was that it did not adequately deal with the contradictions in their own conceptual apparatus, let alone with the structural and historical contradictions that underpinned capitalist society and its formation. For example, the economists believed that the inequality of people was rooted in human nature. This meant that the social-class structure of a society was constituted by relatively fixed entities whose interrelations were not only unchanging but also harmonious. It implied as well that the members of different classes shared the same goal – the continuation of the society itself. By contrast, Marx argued that social inequality was created by people themselves when the members of one class were to withdraw from production and, to support their leisured existence, to appropriate the goods and labor of the direct producers. The exploitative relation between the idle class and the direct producers meant that their respective members did not share the same interests and goals. In a phrase, their relation was contradictory. Moreover, this opposition was the motor that drove the development of class-based societies in general and of capitalist society in particular (Marx and Engels 1848/1976).

His third criticism of the economists' method was that the abstractions they used were too narrow and their interconnections were not sufficiently examined. Population, for example, remained an abstraction unless it was discussed in relation to the social classes of which it was composed; the class structure itself remained equally abstract unless its foundations – e.g. wage-labor and capital – were also considered; and these foundations in turn presupposed a division of labor and exchange – developments that the economists rarely touched upon. The economists believed that there were things and there were relations, and one could not be subsumed into the other. Marx's abstractions, by contrast, were often extensive, and he frequently subsumed the isolated facts and relations of the economists into a single abstraction. For example, supply and demand, which the economists treated as discrete, Marx (1857–8/1973:83–100) treated as different expressions of the same fact. He often included the relational features of facts and, on occasion, described capital not as a thing but as a social relation.

Marx's fourth criticism focused on the process of abstraction itself. The economists, he argued, were too concerned with the end results. The categories they deployed – money, labor, exchange, or scarcity to name only a few – were not transhistorical but appeared instead in specific historical circumstances. Money, for instance, which was used in the Roman Empire to pay soldiers, did not extend to the rest of the labor force since tribute and taxes were still paid in kind; money gained its contemporary significance only with the development of a particular set of social relations – the monetary system in the sixteenth century – which equated wealth with the possession of money (Marx 1857–8/1973:103). The problem with the economists' account was not so much that their categories "possess a truth for all other societies" but rather that their "historical presentation of development is founded, as a rule, on the fact that the latest form regards the previous ones as steps leading up to itself, and it always conceives them one-sidedly" (Marx 1857–8/1973: 105–6).

Marx wanted to link the "real" concrete world informed by perceptions and appearances with the reconstructed "thought" world informed by theoretical constructs. Thus, he accepted the broad outlines of the economists' method, which proceeded from the perceived "world of appearances" by the process of abstraction to the theoretically informed reconstruction of that world. In important ways, the abstractions Marx deployed were not so different from those of the economists. They did not constitute a "private language" that prevented communication between Marx and the rest of the world (Ollman 1993:27). They were not substitutes for facts. For both the economists and Marx, the abstractions ordered the facts, gave them form, and assigned them relative value.

Nevertheless, Marx was critical of the way the economists abstracted from the concrete world of appearance, of the particular abstractions they used, and of their theoretical reconstruction of capitalist society. These were deficient, in his view, for an adequate understanding of capitalist society – its relations, its processes, its development, and its future. This required different abstractions. The critical way in which Marx's abstractions did differ from those of the economists lay in his concern with a social totality that was continually in flux because of the shifting interactions and contradictions of its constituent parts; as a result, he was concerned with the ongoing process of continual formation and reformation instead of portraying change in terms of the variation between the subject at two distinct moments in time.

What made Marx's abstractions distinctive, as Ollman (1993:26–7, 39) noted, was their extension, level of generality, and vantage point. They were like wide-angle photographs in comparison to the narrow portraits painted by the economists. This was why Marx thought the economists' abstractions were too narrow; they captured neither the identity of the facts nor their connections with other facts that did not appear in the portraits but were clear in the wide-angle photograph. Thus, his abstractions tended to have greater extensions in both space and time. For example, he variously wrote about class, the ruling class, and even the ruling classes in order to encompass, in the latter instance, not only industrial, money, and merchant capitalists but also landlords who derived their income from rent (e.g. Marx 1863–7/1977:884–5; Marx and Engels 1848/1976:482–6).

Marx's abstractions were also distinctive in the sense that they operated at different scales and levels of generality. In some instances, he seemed to use a microscope; in others, he appeared to use binoculars or even a telescope. The economists, whose worldviews were rooted in liberal theory, tended to portray all societies as aggregates of isolated individuals who were bound together by exchange relations. Since they abstracted all societies as being structured in the same manner, the economists were not able to distinguish clearly between different kinds of society, let alone to grasp the particularities of each as well as the peculiar character of capitalist society. Marx's use of abstractions with different scales or levels of generality allowed him to bring into focus and to investigate such differences (e.g. Marx 1863–7/1981:927).

As Ollman (1993:55–8) noted, at the most specific level, Marx wrote about the unique circumstances of particular individuals. At a slightly more general level, he distinguished what was typical of people and their activities because they functioned in modern capitalist society. At an even more general level, he analyzed what was peculiar to people in the class-stratified societies that preceded the appearance of capitalism. At a still more encompassing level, he wrote about the qualities of people and their activities as part of the human condition. At yet broader levels, he recognized the qualities human beings possess because they are part of the animal world, as well as the ones they possess by virtue of being a material part of nature. Each level of generality organized his understanding of the totality in a different way.

Marx's abstractions also had a vantage point or perspective from which to view and analyze society. Ollman (1993:68) wrote that the

> vantage point sets up a perspective that colors everything which falls into it, establishing order, hierarchy, and priorities, distributing values, meanings, and degree of relevance, and asserting a distinctive coherence between the parts. Within a given perspective, some processes and connections will appear large, some obvious, some important; others will appear small, insignificant, and irrelevant; and some will even be invisible.

Perhaps the best known of Marx's vantage points was the perspective of the proletariat. He argued that the conditions in which the various classes live and work provide their members with distinctive perspectives and understandings of their circumstances. In other words, wage workers toiling in factories have quite different understandings of capitalist society from the owners, from the structurally unemployed, or the members of semi-proletarian households who still produce enough to satisfy some of their own subsistence needs. However, Marx's vantage points were not limited just to the understandings of particular classes. For example, he also wrote about the state from different vantage points. For example, in the *Manifesto of the Communist Party*, he and Engels described the state as an instrument of the ruling class (Marx and Engels 1848/1976:486). In *The Eighteenth Brumaire*, he portrayed the state as a machine that responded to the requirements of the economy but also had interests and purposes of its own (Marx 1852/1978:181–97). In the preface to *A Contribution to the Critique of Political Economy*, he depicted the state as the legal and political superstructure of the mode of production (Marx 1859/1970:20). Each vantage point opened up a distinctive line of inquiry.

Finally, Marx paid close attention to how the theoretically informed reconstructions of the "thought" concrete should be presented. There were important differences between his methods of investigation and forms of presentation. His aim was to present the unfolding of capitalist society dialectically, so that his readers could grasp the flux, the continually shifting interactions, the mutually reinforcing processes, and the contradictions in their myriad forms and expressions. He refined this method of presentation over time. Nowhere did he portray the emergence of capitalist society as the end-product of a linear historical development in which the earlier stages were merely stepping stones leading to the latter. In the *Grundrisse*, for example, he began his analysis of the emergence of capitalist society with brief discussions about production in general and about the relations between production, distribution, exchange, and consumption. This was followed by chapters dealing with money, capital, its production process, its circulation process, and the transformation of surplus value into profit. A few years later, in *Capital*, he launched his analysis with a discussion of the contradiction embodied in the commodity – an object that simultaneously satisfies a need and yet is produced to sell. His discussion in the subsequent chapters of *Capital* revealed the centrality of this contradiction and the foundational role it played and continues to play today.

Marx realized that his dialectical method was not a method of historical analysis in the narrow sense. He wrote:

> . . . our method indicates the points where historical investigation must enter in. . . . In order to develop the laws of bourgeois economy . . . it is not necessary to write the *real history of the relations of production.* . . . But the correct observation and deduction of these laws . . . always leads to the primary equations . . . which point to the past lying behind this system. These indications . . . then also offer the key to the understanding of the past – a work in its own right. (Marx 1857–8/1973:460–1, emphasis in original)

As Derek Sayer (1979:149) reminds us, Marx's method

> *opens the way* to a recovery of history. It shows capital's apparently natural and eternal forms rest on relations that are social and historical; relations, in other words, which have been constructed by human beings and are thus capable of being changed by other human beings. It alerts us to a repeatedly suppressed and deeply buried history; beneath all the fictions, the real history of the constant class struggles through which these forms were alone created and alone are maintained. (emphasis in original)

Marx's Theory of Society and History

Marx began to elaborate a theory of society and history in the 1840s.[4] It was part of his critique of the abstractions used by the political economists; it was integral to his dialectical method. He and Engels continued to hone the theory during the next fifty years. Marx (1863–7/1977:759), who distinguished "human nature in general" from "human nature as historically modified in each epoch," started with several observations: (1) human individuals are simultaneously natural and social beings; (2) they are distinguished from animals by virtue of their creative intelligence, productive activity, and sociality; (3) they transform objects of nature to satisfy needs; and (4) they create new needs in the process and thereby transform their own nature. In the late 1850s, Marx refined the theoretical concept of a mode of production that recognized the cooperative, collective relations people enter into as they transform nature. Modes of production were the bare-bones skeletons fleshed out by his analyses of historical process – the basis of his "understanding of the variety of human societies and their interaction, as well as of their historical dynamics" (Hobsbawm 1984:46). From the 1870s onward, Marx and Engels began to look carefully at the ethnological information that was beginning to appear, and they increasingly focused their attention on the precapitalist and noncapitalist societies that either preceded the development of industrial capitalism or existed on its margins. This culminated, for example, in Marx's (1880–2/1974) *Ethnological Notebooks*, Engels's (1884/1972, 1894/1990) *Origin of the Family, Private Property and the State*, and the latter's comparison of "The Peasant Question in France and Germany."

While Marx was interested principally in the sociohistorical development of human society, his enthusiastic but critical endorsement of Charles Darwin's *On the Origin of Species* in 1860 suggested that he was neither oblivious to nor disinterested in the biological processes involved in the evolution of the human species (e.g. Engels 1859/1983; Marx 1860/1985, 1861/1985).[5] Earlier, he and Engels had written:

> The first premise of all human history is, of course, the existence of living human individuals. Thus the first fact to be established is the physical organisation of these individuals and their consequent relation to the rest of nature. Of course, we cannot here go either into the actual physical nature of man, or into the natural conditions in which man finds himself – geological, oro-hydrographical, climate and so on. All historical writing must set out from these natural bases and their modification in the course of history through the action of men. (Marx and Engels 1845–6/1976:31)

Immediately following this was a passage that was deleted in the original manuscript. The crossed-out statement implied that there was a relationship between the diversity of natural conditions, physical variation in the human species, and differences in the trajectories of sociohistorical development (Marx and Engels 1845–6/1976:31).

When Marx examined questions about human nature and history, he typically did so at different scales or levels of generality and framed his answers in materialist terms. At one level, in his view, human beings, like animals, were part of nature. Both lived from nature by maintaining a continuing dialogue with it – a metabolism as he would later call it; both satisfied their needs through their own activity – through this exchange of energy and material with nature. At a different level, human beings in general, while they were still natural beings, were distinct from animals because they were "*human* natural beings" (Marx 1844/1975a:275–6, 337, emphasis in original).

Animals seized and consumed natural objects that would immediately satisfy their own physical needs or those of their young. Animals in general made use of limited arrays of those natural objects – only those things which had physical or chemical properties that met their needs and that could be used or consumed directly. Some animals – ants, bees, and beavers, for instance – even built nests and dwellings; however, they did so in accordance with the standards of the species to which they belonged (Márkus 1978:4). Human beings, by contrast, appropriated and transformed natural objects even when they were free from physical needs. They made use of more environments and a wider array of natural objects, and they did so with more diverse standards, including the "laws of beauty" (Marx 1844/1975a:277). In Marx and Engels's (1845–6/1976:31) words, human beings in general "distinguish themselves from animals as soon as they begin to *produce* their means of subsistence, a step which is conditioned by their physical organiza-tion. . . . The way in which men produce their means of subsistence depends first of all on the nature of the means of subsistence they actually find in existence and have to reproduce" (emphasis in original).

Creative intelligence was the feature that distinguished human beings in general from animals. "Free conscious activity is man's species character" (Marx 1844/ 1964:113, cf. 1844/1975a:276). Marx (1863–7/1977:283–4) described the creative capacity of human beings in the following manner:

Labour is, first of all, a process between man and nature, by which man through his own actions, mediates, regulates and controls the metabolism between himself and nature. He confronts the materials of nature as a force of nature. He sets in motion the natural forces which belong to his own body, his arms, legs, head and hands, in order to appropriate the materials of nature in a form adapted to his own needs. Through this movement, he acts upon external nature and changes it, and in this way he simultaneously changes his own nature. He develops the potentialities slumbering within nature, and subjects it to his own sovereign power. We are not dealing here with those first instinctive forms of labour which remain on the animal level. . . . We presuppose labour in a form in which it is an exclusively human characteristic. A spider conducts operations which resemble those of a weaver, and a bee would put many human architects to shame by the construc-tion of its honeycomb cells. But *what distinguishes the worst architect from the best of bees is that the architect builds the cell in his mind before he constructs it in wax.* At the end of every labour process, a result emerges which had already been conceived by the worker at the beginning, hence already existed ideally. Man not only effects a change of form in the materials of nature; he also realizes his own purpose in those materials. And this is a purpose he is conscious of, it determines the mode of his activity with the rigidity of a law, and he must subordinate his will to it. (emphasis added)

Thus, human beings were characterized not only by the ability to imagine a project and to build it in reality, but also by a corresponding need to do so. It was through labor on the natural world that human beings realized their own species-being and made their own life activity a means to their existence. They exercised their creative intelligence through labor for their own self-realization (Marx 1844/ 1975a:276). Projective consciousness and labor were the essence of human nature; they necessitated social life. The products of labor (or purposive activity) were the labor embodied in the objects which became the objectification of labor as they were transformed and acquired cultural meanings in the process. Culture as purposive action was not separate from labor as objectification; it was "conditioned or expressive of the particular organization of human activity that Marx called a mode of production" (D'Amico 1981:11). As such it not only was the essence of human nature, but it was also "historically modified in each epoch."

Writing in 1876, Engels portrayed the self-realization of human beings from a different viewpoint. In "The Part Played by Labor in the Transition from Ape to Man," he asserted that the decisive step was linked with bipedal locomotion, which freed up the use of the hands. In his view,

[l]abor, after it and then with it, speech – these were the two most essential stimuli under the influence of which the brain of the ape gradually changed into that of man. . . . Labor begins with the making of tools. . . . By the combined functioning of hand, speech organs and brain, not only in each individual but also in society, men became capable of executing more and more complicated operations, and were able to set themselves, and achieve, higher and higher aims. The work of each generation became different. (Engels 1876/1972:255–8)

Marx and Engels believed that human beings had to use their creative intelligence productively and that this was realized through labor. Nevertheless, the ability to express their projective consciousness in creative ways was not the only need of human beings. Elsewhere in their writings, as McMurtry (1978:33–4) pointed out, Marx and Engels made fleeting references to other species needs of human beings in general. These included adequate food, drink, clothing, and habitation; fresh air and sunlight; adequate living and working space; cleanliness of person and surroundings; rest from exertion; variation of activity; time for intellectual development, social intercourse, fulfillment of social functions, free play of the vital forces of the body and mind, growth, development, healthy maintenance of the body, aesthetic stimulation, and play; and meaningful interpersonal and sexual relationships (Marx 1844/1975a:295–6; 1863–7/1977:341, 362, 375–6, 611, 762–802; Marx and Engels 1845–6/1976:38, 417).

Human beings were also social beings; they were communal beings not isolated individuals. The essence of being human was activated in the community. Individuals could not be truly human and live a human life unless they maintained ties with others. Marx (1844/1975a:298) described the sociality of human beings in the following way:

> Social activity and social enjoyment exist by no means *only* in the form of some *directly* communal activity and directly *communal* enjoyment. . . . But also when I am active *scientifically*, etc. – an activity which I can seldom perform in direct community with others – then my activity is *social*, because I perform it as a man. Not only is the material of my activity given to me as a social product (as is even the language in which the thinker is active); my *own* existence *is* social activity, and therefore that which I make of myself, I make of myself for society and with the consciousness of myself as a social being. . . . Above all we must avoid postulating "society" again as an abstraction *vis-à-vis* the individual. The individual *is the social being.* (emphasis in original)

This meant, as George Márkus (1978:16–17) noted, that individuals are human beings only through and because they appropriate and incorporate into their lives and life activities the "abilities, wants, forms of behaviour, ideas etc. which were created and objectified by other individuals of earlier generations or by those contemporary" with them. "Even the human individual in its concrete personality," Márkus continued, "taken in isolation [is] a product of social intercourse and history."

Thus, human sociality was simultaneously communal in character as well as socially and historically determined. "The historically created and objectified material and mental powers can be appropriated by the individual only *within* a human community, through the intercourse with other human beings" (Márkus 1978:18, emphasis in original). Marx and Engels (1845–6/1976:438) summarized the relationship between the individual and society as follows:

> The development of an individual is determined by the development of all the others with whom he is directly or indirectly associated, and that the different generations of individuals entering into relation with one another are connected with one another, that the physical existence of the later generations is determined by that of their predecessor, and that these latter generations inherit the productive forces and forms of intercourse accumulated by their predecessors, their own mutual relations being determined thereby. In short it is clear that development takes place and that the history of a single individual cannot possibly be separated from the history of preceding or contemporary individuals, but is determined by this history.

The sociohistorical circumstances that determined the concrete individual were appropriated, internalized, and turned into constituents of his or her individuality. They were not fetters imposed from the outside on primordial impulses that impeded development of the authentic self. This did not mean that the human personality could be reduced simply to sociological or biological determinants. The individuality of every human being developed through selective activity and its social consequences given the possibilities furnished by the socially and historically determined circumstances in which he or she lived (Márkus 1978: 21–3).

Let us pause briefly to consider the arguments we have just reviewed. R. S. Neale (1985:xvii–xviii) has summarized them in the following way:

> The world is constituted by people with physical and created needs interacting with nature (rather like animals) but endowed with (or developing) a capacity to satisfy those needs through labour as an imagined and constructed, rather than as a random and instinctual activity, and through language. These people are organized into social groups. These groups of people satisfy their needs through labour, and facilitate and understand their activity through language. This labour and productive activity is necessarily social. It always takes place within definite sets of socially produced property relations. . . .
>
> As each cohort of people enters into the pre-existing set of propertied . . . circumstances they also, in satisfying their needs through labour, produce and make themselves, and shape their language. They are also always constrained by the traditions of their dead generations. They work out their own destinies using and developing the range of symbolic forms, including language, available to them. . . . Consciousness and cultural production, although imbricated in the whole productive process, immersed in relations of production, are shaped by it. . .[E]verywhere there is creativity, conscious human labour, trapped and liberated by the relations of production.

Neale's summary is underpinned by the theoretical concept of the mode of production. Marx and Engels portrayed the concept of a mode of production in different ways. In *The German Ideology*, they wrote that the

> mode of production must not be considered simply as being the reproduction of the physical existence of the individual. Rather it is a definite form of activity of these individuals, a definite form of expressing their life, a definite *mode of life* on their part. As individuals express their lives, so they are. What they are, therefore, coincides with their production, both with *what* they produce and with *how* they produce. (Marx and Engels 1845–6/1976:32–3, emphasis in original)

In his most famous description of the mode of production concept, which appeared in the Preface to *A Contribution to the Critique of Political Economy*, Marx (1859/1970:20) wrote:

> In the social production of their existence, men inevitably enter into definite relations, which are independent of their will, namely relations of production appropriate to a definite stage in development of their material forces of production. The totality of these relations of production constitutes the economic structure of society, the real foundation,

on which arises a legal and political superstructure and to which correspond definite forms of social consciousness. The mode of production of material life conditions the general process of social, political and intellectual life. . . . At a certain stage of their development, the material productive forces of society come into conflict with the existing relations of production, or – this merely expresses the same thing in legal terms – with the property relations within the framework of which they have operated hitherto. From forms of development of the productive forces these relations turn into fetters. Then begins an era of social revolution. The changes in the economic foundation lead sooner or later to the transformation of the whole immense superstructure.[6]

This statement has been interpreted in two ways. The more common interpretation argues that the "associated forms of social consciousness" constitute a superstructural level more or less parallel to that of the "legal and political superstructure." This is a reductive argument which means that the forms of consciousness are reflections of the economic foundation of a society. An alternative interpretation of the passage, suggested by Robert D'Amico, is that the associated forms of social consciousness refers to the mode of production as a whole. Thus, "[c]ulture [i.e. the associated forms of social consciousness] constitutes a mode of expression of life conditioned by the form of production or the form of life activity" (D'Amico 1981:12). This interpretation means that culture and economic development are related but relatively autonomous. It allows us to make sense of statements that Marx made in the *Grundrisse* regarding Greek art and myth in classical antiquity and the fascination of the German bourgeoisie with those forms:

> In the case of the arts, it is well known that certain periods of their flowering are all out of proportion to the general development of the society, hence also to the material foundation, the skeletal structure, as it were, of its organization. (Marx 1857–8/1973: 110)

> But the difficulty lies not in understanding that the Greek arts and epic are bound up with certain forms of social development. The difficulty is that they still afford us artistic pleasure and that in a certain respect they count as a norm and as an unattainable model. A man cannot become a child again, or he becomes childish. But does he not find joy in the child's naïveté, and must he himself not strive to reproduce its truth at a higher stage? Does not the true character of each epoch come alive in the nature of its children? Why should not the historical childhood of humanity, its most beautiful unfolding, as a stage never to return, exercise an eternal charm? There are unruly children and precocious children. Many of the old peoples belong to this category. The Greeks were normal children. The charm of their art for us is not in contradiction to the undeveloped stage of the society in which it grew. It is a result, rather, and is inextricably bound up, rather, with the fact that the unripe social conditions under which it arose, and could alone arise, can never return. (Marx 1857–8/1973:111)

Here, Marx argued (1) that there was no simple relation between culture and the economy, and (2) that it was essential to pay attention to the historic specificity of the society. Both culture and labor were forms of objectification, and the causal relation between them was indeterminate. By contrast, Marx sought to explain the relationship between them in terms of the symbolic or meaningful character of action, "expressed in the language of objectification and mediation" (D'Amico 1981:13).

Focusing on the second and longer of Marx's two descriptions of the mode of production, we observe that the two fundamental components of a mode of production were the forces of production and the relations of production. Both the forces and the relations of production of a particular society were the products of particular socio-historical processes and interconnections that developed over time as the members of successive generations worked to gain their livelihoods. In other words, both the forces and relations of production were socially historically contingent and refracted in complex ways the inheritance of the past generations.

The *forces of production*, for Marx, were objectifications of human nature. They were used during the labor process to produce objects that satisfy needs. "The simple elements of the labour process are (1) purposeful activity, that is work itself, (2) the object on which that work is performed, and (3) the instruments of that work" (Marx 1863–7/1977:284). The labor process itself was always mediated by some form of mental activity. Human individuals engage in creative and productive activity (they deploy knowledge and skill and exert energy) by using tools to transform natural materials into objects that satisfied needs. Marx called objects that satisfied needs *use-values*. They included objects that were modified, made, or moved by human beings. The instruments employed in the labor process were also use-values that concretized or embodied the accumulated results of earlier labor processes. The deployment or consumption of use-values – i.e. the satisfaction of needs – underwrote the biological, demographic, and social reproduction of human beings. In Marx's (1863–7/1977:711) words:

> Whatever the social form of the production process, it has to be continuous, it must periodically repeat the same phases. A society can no more cease to produce than it can cease to consume. When viewed, therefore, as a connected whole, and in the constant flux of its incessant renewal, every social process of production is at the same time a process of reproduction. . . .
>
> All other circumstances remaining the same, the society can reproduce or maintain its wealth on the existing scale only by replacing the means of production [i.e. the raw materials and instruments employed to make use-values] that have been used up . . .

With regard to the forces of production, Marx drew a further distinction between subjective and objective factors. The *subjective factors* consisted of the natural capacities of workers and their capabilities to carry out particular tasks; these capacities included their mental and physical abilities (i.e. forms of practical knowledge and know-how), their training, their levels of skill in relation to other members of the society in question as well as technical divisions of labor (specializations of tasks) that occurred within the labor process itself. The *objective* factors of the productive forces included the raw materials provided by nature and the tools, in the broadest sense of the term, that human beings used to sustain life. They were the "external organs" or "extensions of the human body." Marx also referred to the objective factors as the means of production. Both the subjective and objective factors of the productive forces were accumulated through history as successive generations built on the contributions of the ones that preceded them (McMurtry 1978:54–71).

The *relations of production* referred to the relations that existed among the members of a society with regard to control over the productive forces. They were analogous to property relations: Who in the society had the power to use or to exploit the productive forces and to prevent others from doing so? These relations have been modified through history and are manifestations of different modes of production. Thus, in different societies, the relations of production might variously be communal, tributary, or capitalist. In communal societies, the forces of production were held in common by a collectivity, and the members had access to them by virtue of their membership in the group. Tributary societies, like those that existed in Europe during the Middle Ages or the Inca state that existed in the central Andes during the 1400s, had small ruling classes. Their members who had succeeded in separating themselves from the processes of direct production typically claimed ownership of the productive forces and extracted surplus from the direct producers; however, the direct producers retained use rights to the means of production and effective control over their own labor power. In capitalist societies, like the United States today, the means of production are owned privately and access to them is restricted to employees who have sold their labor power in return for a wage. They produce commodities that are subsequently sold in the market. The power to exploit the forces of production to the exclusion of others is simultaneously the power to exploit human beings.

The relations of production correspond to the social division of labor that exists in a society. The social division of labor is an expression of the society's economic relations. It asserts that the forces of production which are owned or effectively possessed by individuals and are thus available for their use coincide with their position in the society. For example, in capitalist societies, members of the working class typically possess only their labor power, which they must sell for a wage, which they use, in turn, to purchase the commodities that replenish and reproduce their lives. Members of the capitalist class, by contrast, own the means of production – the raw materials, factories, tools, and machines, for instance – and use the labor power of the workers they hire to produce the commodities they intend to sell for profit in the market; they keep the money received for those goods less the costs of the raw materials, rent, maintenance, replacement of machines, and wages they must pay to begin a new cycle of production. In this example, the two classes have different relations or connections with the forces of production because of the social division of labor. McMurtry (1978:81) has argued that the relations of production are more "basic" than legal or political relations, because they involve power while the latter involve rights; for example, the economic power of the feudal lords in fifteenth-century Europe enabled them to dispossess peasants by denying them their rights of access to common lands (Marx 1863–7/1977:877–904).

In Marx's (1863–7/1981:927) view, the most distinctive feature distinguishing capitalist society from the various kinds of tributary societies that have existed was the following:

> The specific economic form, in which unpaid surplus-labour is pumped out of direct producers, determines the relationship of rulers and ruled, as it grows directly out of production itself and, in turn, reacts upon it as a determining element. Upon this, however, is founded the entire formation of the economic community which grows out of the production relations themselves, thereby simultaneously its specific political form. It is always the direct relationship of the owners of the conditions of production to the direct producers – a relation always naturally corresponding to a definite stage in the development of the methods of labour and thereby its social productivity – which reveals the innermost secret, the hidden basis of the entire social structure, and with it the political form of the relation of sovereignty and dependence, in short, the corresponding specific form of the state. This does not prevent the same economic basis – the same from the standpoint of its main conditions – due to innumerable different empirical circumstances, natural environment, racial relations, external historical influences, etc., from showing infinite variations and gradations in appearance, which can be ascertained only by analysis of the empirically given circumstances.

The existence of a social division of labor in a society implies the existence of a structure of social classes and of exploitation. Geoffrey de Ste Croix (1984:100) has written that class

> is the collective social expression of the fact of exploitation. (By "exploitation", of course, I mean the appropriation of part of the product of the labour of others; in a commodity-producing society this is the appropriation of what Marx called "surplus value" [which can be roughly translated as "profit"].) Class is essentially a *relationship*. . . . And *a* class (a *particular* class) is a group of persons in a community identified by their position in the whole system of production, defined above all according to their relationship (primarily in terms of the degree of *control*) to the conditions of production (that is to say, to the means and labour of production) and to other classes. The individuals constituting a class may or may not be wholly or partly conscious of their own

identity and common interests as a class, and they may or may not feel antagonism towards the members of other classes as such. Class *conflict* (class struggle . . .) is essentially the fundamental relationship between classes, involving *exploitation* and resistance to it, but not *necessarily* either class consciousness or collective activity in common, political or otherwise, although these features are likely to supervene when a class has reached a certain stage of developments and becomes what Marx once (using a Hegelian idiom) called "a class *for itself.*" (emphasis in original)

Class structures, exploitation, resistance, and class conflict are manifestations of contradictions that emerge from the relations of production. These economic relations of production undergird the legal and political superstructure (i.e. the state) in both tributary and capitalist societies.[7] In Marx's words,

> . . . regulation and order are themselves indispensable elements of any mode of production, if it is to assume social stability and independence from mere chance and arbitrariness . . . . (Marx 1863–7/1981:774)

> . . . every form of production creates its own legal relations, forms of government, etc. The crudity and the shortcomings of the bourgeois conception lie in the tendency to see but an accidental reflective connection in what constitutes an organic union. (Marx 1857–8/1973:88)

It is in the legal and political structure that the economic powers of classes of people are transformed into the rights they possess with respect to the productive forces. In this sense, economic power is more basic than legal and political rights.

The state, the legal and political superstructure of a class-stratified society, consists of those institutions and practices – the police, army, courts, schools, bureaucracy, laws, censuses, and taxes, to name only a few – that have been consciously constructed, wield authority, and protect the ruling-class economic order. These institutions and practices are not independent of the contradictions that exist in the production relations. Their goals are simultaneously to regulate those antagonisms and to express the sentiments of the dominant economic class. As a result, members of the economically dominant class typically control the state apparatus as well. People submit to the state because of the organized force and threats of violence it wields. By protecting the collective interests of the dominant classes and the economic order they control, the state also perpetuates the contradictions and antagonisms that constitute the economic foundations of the society. States are like lids on pressure cookers. They attempt to control volatile, often explosive mixtures by keeping class antagonisms and contradictions in check; they often fail. States are fragile and unstable, because the contradictions that exist in the economic structure, especially those between different fractions of the dominant class, are typically reproduced in the legal and political superstructure.

Marx distinguished a number of modes of production: primitive communism, slave, ancient, feudal, asiatic, germanic, slavonic, and capitalist (Marx 1857–8/1971:471–514, cf. 1857–8/1964:67–120). Since he was mainly concerned with the capitalist mode of production, Marx did not systematically discuss the precapitalist modes of production that preceded it or that persisted on its margins. Nor did he discuss systematically the various forms of tributary societies that manifest these precapitalist modes of production.[8]

Marx's writings in the 1860s were focused mainly on the "laws of motion" that underpinned the capitalist mode of production and distinguished it from precapitalist modes of production. The laws of motion referred to the circulation or exchange of the productive forces that took place between the capitalist class, whose members owned the means of production, and the proletariat or working class, whose members, dispossessed from the means of production, were forced to sell some or all of their labor power in return for wages. The distinctive feature of capitalism as an economic system, in Marx's view, was its concern with the production and sale of commodities – i.e. goods produced for sale rather than use by the people who made them. In precapitalist societies, the circulation of goods was aimed at satisfying needs. In capitalist societies, the goal was making profit, the expansion of money value, rather than the pleasure of using or consuming the commodities acquired through exchange. In precapitalist societies, if money was used at all, it was used to facilitate exchange. In capitalist societies, value was continually being transformed from the money form to the commodity form and then back into a larger sum of money form. Value becomes capital by virtue of the fact that it was involved in the process of expanding or creating additional value. However, there was only one commodity that could create extra value – the human labor power employed by the capitalist to transform raw materials into commodities.

Their incessant drive for profits underpinned the capitalists' continual quest for new markets, new commodities, and the continuous development of the productive forces. They purchased machines and developed ways of organizing production that allowed them to produce more commodities or to produce them more cheaply than their competitors; if the competitors were to remain in business, they were forced to purchase the machines or to invent newer, more efficient ones. Thus, the capitalists were engaged in relentless, never-ending competition with one another. As the machines became more costly, fewer and fewer capitalists could afford them. The number of firms producing that commodity declined, but the ones that survived were larger and had more capital available. Marx referred to these processes as the concentration and centralization of capital. The creation and sale of new commodities – like mass-produced automobiles in the early 1900s or computer software today – initially allowed capitalists greater returns on their investments than other commodities. Once the profit rates in that economic sector evened out, the capitalists sought new, more profitable places for investment to promote economic growth. As the waged workers were replaced by more efficient machines or laid off because of the crises inherent in the capitalist system of production, the unemployed proletariat swelled in size, and their numbers were forced to seek employment in circumstances where few, if any, jobs were available. John McMurtry (1978:91) perceptively noted that "the whole of *Capital*, indeed, may be read as the exposure of a life-and-death struggle between man and capital, in which capital's 'laws of motion' of money growth relentlessly 'suck the blood' of humankind dry . . . ."

The precapitalist modes of production had a different logic from capitalism. Unlike capitalism's industrial proletariat, whose members were dispossessed from the means of production, the direct producers in various forms of tributary societies retained effective possession of their means of subsistence – i.e. they had direct, non-market access to them. To reproduce themselves, the exploiting classes in these societies were forced to appropriate part of the goods produced by the direct producers. They did so by means of various extra-economic forms of coercion – such as tribute, tithes, or threats. As long as this relationship persisted, there were no incentives for the exploiting classes to dispossess the direct producers from the means of production or to improve the efficiency of the productive forces. There were, however, incentives under certain conditions for the direct producers to increase their productivity (Brenner 1986).

The most distinctive features of societies manifesting the primitive communist mode of production were (1) collective ownership of the primary means of production, and (2) the absence of a social division – i.e. a class structure – in which the members of one group permanently appropriated the social product or labor of the direct producers. The social relations were not exploitative in the sense that one group did not extort product or labor from another. Engels (1884/1972:233) wrote that "production was essentially collective, just as consumption proceeded by direct distribution of the products within larger or smaller communistic communities." Eleanor Leacock (1982:159) has argued that there was no exploitation in primitive communal societies because of the unity of the production process and the direct participation of all adults in the production, distribution, circulation, and consumption of social product. This meant that each individual was dependent on the group as a whole. It also implied that there were no structural differences between producers and non-producers. Such a distinction existed only from the perspective of an individual who was too young, too old, or not a participant in a particular production process. However, the distinction disappeared when the focus was extended beyond the particular individual and a single labor process. It became inverted from one labor process to another, as the direct producer in one became a consumer in the next.

Primitive communal societies, Engels noted, lacked hereditary status and gender hierarchies. In a commentary on the Iroquois, he wrote: "There cannot be any poor or needy – the communal household and the gens know their responsibilities toward the old, the sick, and those disabled by war. All are equal and free – the women included" (Engels 1884/1972:159). Individuals were leaders by virtue of their age, life status, kin connections, gender, or life experience, and they could be removed from the position by their kin. Engels was aware that the ability of an individual or group to withdraw from direct labor and to rely on the labor of others depended on maintaining the continued goodwill of the community.

> The lowest police officer in a civilized state has more "authority" than all of the organs of gentile [i.e. tribal] society put together; but the mightiest prince and the greatest statesman or general of civilization might envy the humblest of the gentile chiefs, the unforced and unquestioned respect accorded him. For the one stands in the midst of society; the other is forced to pose as something outside and above it. (Engels 1884/ 1972:230)

A central thesis of Engels's (1884/1972:137–46) *Origin of the Family, Private Property and the State* was that the subordination of women, the creation of a gender hierarchy, was inextricably linked with the rise of social stratification and the origin of the state. Marx (1880–2/1974:329) viewed the state not as the highest stage of social development but as an "excrescence of society." Such abnormal outgrowths were characteristic of class-stratified societies and mediated the relations within and between the classes. The important questions for Marx and Engels were how and why social classes appeared, and what processes were involved.

The common thread of human society, as Lawrence Krader (1976:223) has suggested, was life in the community, where the opposition between the private and the public was non-existent or poorly developed. This thread was broken, however, with the appearance of social classes – i.e. when a class of new men began to pursue individual or individual-class interests in the context of the continuing institutions of the community. These institutions and the community itself were distorted, transformed, and dissolved when, and if, their extortions were successful. The constitution of the state was connected with the appearance of the conditions for the constitution of the class structure and for the reproduction of the dominant class as real economic class relations developed.

The agencies of the state subsumed the administration of justice, the conduct of war and diplomacy, and other activities that were previously carried out by the community. They did this in the interest of the state and of the society as a whole. This, however, was the basic contradiction of civil society. The state was simultaneously the representative of the class in whose interests it was organized and the mediator of the oppositions between individuals of that class and between the opposing classes of the society as a whole. The state stood above society only when the economic class relations of appropriation had become dominant. This involved the ideological objectification of individual human beings, which means that they ceased to exist as real people and began to appear as formal entities – legal or civil personalities – in the eyes of the state. This was difficult to achieve in tributary societies, where communities, not individuals, retained rights and exercised effective power over the means of production.

When pressed about the possibilities of social change, Marx and Engels repeatedly asserted that people made their own history under conditions not of their own choice. The forms and traditions of past generations shaped the present, which, in turn, had the capacity to limit or channel what might happen in the future. But accidents happened, and people did occasionally make history. This occurred especially when people were able to conceive of new ways of seeing the world around them, and were able to merge theory with practice.

Marx's Ecology

Marx refined his views on the interconnections of nature, society, and population in his ongoing critique of political economy and in his discussions of capitalist agriculture and industry.[9] In the mid-1840s, he made two important points in this regard. The first was that "[m]an *lives* from nature, i.e. nature is in his *body*, and he must maintain a continuing dialogue with it if he is not to die. To say that man's physical and mental life is linked to nature simply means that nature is linked to itself, for man is part of nature" (Marx 1844/1975b:328, emphasis in original; cf. 1844/1975a: 276). In the late 1850s, Marx (1857–8/1973:489; 1863–7/1977:283) began to characterize the "continuing dialogue" between human beings as a "metabolic exchange" that was mediated, regulated, and controlled by labor. For our purposes here, the implication of this perspective was that human societies, along with soils, animals, plants, climate, geography, and so forth, were constitutive of the larger totality we call "nature" (Levins and Lewontin 1985:137–42, 278–85).

Marx's second point in the 1840s was that both labor and nature contributed to the production of wealth (Burkett 1999:26). "The worker can create nothing without *nature*," he wrote (Marx 1844/1964:109, emphasis in original). Thirty years later, he restated this conclusion: "Labour is *not the source* of all wealth. *Nature* is just as much the source of use values (and it is surely of such that material wealth consists!) as labour, which itself is only the manifestation of a force of nature, human labour power" (Marx 1875/1989:81, emphasis in original). In the intervening years, Marx (1863–7/1977:131) pointed out that certain things – like air, for instance – whose utility to human beings was not mediated by labor were also use values.

As he launched his studies of the genesis of capitalist agriculture and industry in the late 1850s, Marx became increasingly aware of conditions that had altered the metabolic exchange between human society and nature. The development of capitalist agriculture had, in his view, provoked "an irreparable rift in the inter-dependent process of social metabolism, a metabolism prescribed by the natural laws of life itself" (Marx 1863–7/1981:949). He observed:

> It is not the *unity* of living and active humanity with the natural, inorganic conditions of their metabolic exchange with nature, and hence their appropriation of nature, which requires explanation, or is the result of a historic process, but rather the *separation* between these inorganic conditions of human existence and this active existence, a separation which is completely posited only in the relation of wage labour and capital. (Marx 1857–8/1973:489)

Marx's studies of capitalist production led him to change lenses and to examine the metabolic rift at two different levels of generality. In both instances, the issue was no longer that "man was part of nature," which was true, of course. At the more general level, he was concerned with how the conditions necessary for human production had "diverged from those required for a reproduction of and evolution of nature unaffected by human intervention" (Burkett 1999:29–30). At the less general level, he was concerned with the specificity of the "metabolic rift" created by capitalist production. Thus, in the early 1860s, Marx integrated his materialist conception of nature with his materialist conception of society as "historically modified in each epoch" (Foster 2000:141–77).

From the 1860s onward, both Marx and Engels repeatedly commented on the depth of this metabolic rift and the extent to which human societies had transformed the natural world in which they lived. Engels (1873–82/1940:172, cf. 1873–82/1987:511) vividly portrayed the impact of human societies on nature:

> There is damned little left of "nature" as it was in Germany at the time when the Germanic peoples immigrated into it. The earth's surface, climate, vegetation, fauna, and the human beings themselves have continually changed, and all this owing to human activity, while the changes of nature in Germany which have occurred in the process of time without human interference are incalculably small.

Marx and Engels also realized that the metabolic rift created by capitalism was different from the ones forged by precapitalist modes of production. Marx (1863–7/1981:949) described the shift in the following way:

> Small-scale landownership presupposes that the overwhelming majority of the population is agricultural and that isolated labour predominates over social; wealth and the development of reproduction, therefore, both in its material and its intellectual aspects,

is ruled under these circumstances, and with this also the conditions for rational agriculture. On the other hand, large landed property reduces the agricultural population to an ever decreasing minimum and confronts it with an ever growing industrial population crammed together in large towns. . . .

Large-scale industry and industrially pursued large-scale agriculture . . . are originally distinguished by the fact that the former lays waste and ruins labour-power and thus the natural power of man, whereas the latter does the same to the natural power of the soil.

Engels later (1876–8/1939:195; cf. 1876–8/1987:164) referred to the destruction of soil in the waning years of the Roman Republic when small-scale peasant farms were replaced by large estates that used slaves to raise livestock: "Italy was brought under cultivation chiefly by peasants; when in the final period of the Roman Republic, the great estates, the *latifundia*, displaced the small peasants and replaced them with slaves, they also replaced tillage with stock-raising and, as Pliny realised, brought Italy to ruin."

From the early 1860s onward, Marx's studies of capitalist agriculture and industry revealed important dimensions of the metabolic rift that developed with the advent of capitalism. Simply put, capitalist development was a two-fold process that involved the simultaneous development of a proletariat whose members needed to sell their labor power and an internal market for the commodities they had to purchase to satisfy their subsistence needs. The former was accomplished by enclosure acts which drove them from their lands; the latter by the establishment of factories in places, usually near sources of water power, that attracted ever-increasing numbers of people in search of work. This was the origin of the dichotomy between town and countryside. Marx described metabolic rift in terms of the contradiction they engendered. In *Capital*, he wrote:

Capitalist production collects the population together in great centres, and causes the urban population to achieve an ever-growing preponderance. This has two results. On the one hand it concentrates the historical motive power of society; on the other hand, it disturbs the metabolic interaction between man and the earth, i.e. it prevents the return to the soil of its constituent elements consumed by man in the form of food and clothing; hence it hinders the operation of the eternal natural condition for the lasting fertility of the soil. . . . But by destroying the circumstances surrounding that metabolism . . . it compels its systematic restoration as a regulative law of social production, and in a form adequate to the full development of the human race. . . . [A]ll progress in capitalist agriculture is a progress in the art, not only of robbing the worker, but of robbing the soil; all progress in increasing the fertility of the soil for a given time is progress towards ruining the more long-lasting sources of that fertility. . . . Capitalist production, therefore, only develops the technique and the degree of combination of the social process of production by simultaneously undermining the original sources of all wealth – the soil and the worker. (Marx 1863–7/1977:637–8)

Marx's ecology was influenced by two writers in the 1850s (Foster 2000:144–54). One was soil chemist Julius von Liebig (1803–73); the other was political economist and farmer James Anderson (1739–1808). Liebig discovered that fertility of the soil was determined by the nutrient that was in least supply; this has been called "Liebig's law of the minimum." Anderson observed that soil fertility could be maintained or increased by judicious applications of animal and human wastes, and that circumstances which deprived the soil of these manures decreased its fertility. Anderson also noted that the emigration of people from the countryside to the industrial cities, like London, deprived agricultural soils of these nutrients. Human wastes were carried instead into the Thames River, where they added nothing to the fertility of the soil but adversely affected the lives of people, workers and capitalists alike, who resided or made their livelihoods downstream. When steam power became a substitute for waterfalls in the nineteenth century, the capitalists in the manufacturing towns were forced to seek new locations for their factories in order to avoid clogging the boilers, pipes, and vents of the new power supply with the effluents carried by the highly contaminated rivers which flowed through the industrial cities. The factory owners turned again to the clean waters that flowed upriver from or in the rural areas outside of the industrial cities that they had helped to establish a few generations earlier (Marx 1861–3/1968:144–9; 1863–7/1981:195). In Marx's view, Anderson also had a much better grasp of the theory of rent and population than either David Ricardo (1772–1823) or Thomas Malthus (1766–1834), the pre-eminent political economists of the early nineteenth century.

Ground-rent, according to Marx, appeared when capitalist farming became separated from ownership of the land that was being cultivated; differential rent reflected the fact that landowners received more income from labor invested in fertile lands than they did from similar quantities of labor invested in equal amounts of marginal land. Anderson and Marx believed, *contra* Ricardo and Malthus, that rent had nothing to do with the absolute productivity of agriculture, because soil fertility could be continuously improved with the addition of nutrients. They believed that rent was determined by the price of the crop, and that the cost of cultivating the least productive field was at least as expensive as that of cultivating the most fertile field, which, of course, produced the greatest profits (Marx 1861–3/1968:147–8).

That Anderson was also a critic of Malthus's theory of population did not escape Marx's attention. Malthus (1798/1926:13–6) claimed, but never demonstrated, that the growth of the human species was outstripping the amount of food that could be produced, and that the shortages of food were felt most strongly by the lower classes. He further argued that it was impossible to alleviate the widespread poverty that prevailed among the working classes of Britain, because of the relative inelasticity of food production with respect to population growth. Malthus's views appealed to the landed gentry and the state, both of whom wanted relief from subsidies provided by the Poor Laws to the industrial proletariat; they outraged the factory owners, who wanted the subsidies to their workers to continue (Meek 1953/ 1971:3–15). Anderson, by contrast, argued that soil fertility could be improved by adding nutrients, and that food production could be increased under a judicious system of management. He implied that the plight of the poor was not rooted in nature but could be alleviated by increasing food production. But as Marx observed repeatedly, there was nothing rational about capitalism. In his words, "The moral of the tale, which can also be extracted from other discussions of agriculture, is that the capitalist system runs counter to a rational agriculture, or that a rational agriculture is incompatible with the capitalist system (even if the latter promotes technical development in agriculture) . . ." (Marx 1863–7/1981:216). Anderson also demonstrated, to Marx's (1861–3/1968:145) satisfaction, that the agricultural productivity of a country rose and fell in tandem with the growth and decline of its population.

This reinforced one of Marx's longstanding critiques of the political economists – their tendency to represent bourgeois relations of production as eternal categories. Engels (1865/1987:135–6) captured this sentiment clearly when he wrote:

> The so-called "economic laws" are not eternal laws of nature but historical laws that appear and disappear, and the code of modern political economy, insofar as the economists have drawn it up correctly and objectively, is for us merely a summary of the laws and conditions in which bourgeois society can exist. . . . For us, therefore, none of these laws, insofar as it is an expression of *purely bourgeois relations*, is older than modern bourgeois [capitalist] society; those which have been more or less valid for all previous history, are thus only an expression of such relations as are common to all forms of society based on class rule and class exploitation. (emphasis in original)

The objects of Engels's criticism were Thomas Malthus and his theory of population. Malthus, of course, argued that his law of population operated in the same manner at all times and places. By contrast, Marx developed his theory of population in the context of a discussion of the general law of capitalist accumulation. He focused on the rapidity with which new machines and technical processes appeared in diverse spheres of production, replacing the workers who had previously toiled in those factories. He wrote that

> [t]he working population therefore produces both the accumulation of capital and the means by which it is itself made relatively superfluous; and it does this to an extent which is always increasing. This is a law of population peculiar to the capitalist mode of production; and in fact every particular historical mode of production has its own special laws of population, which are historically valid within that particular sphere. An abstract law of population exists only for plants and animals, and even then only in the absence of any historical intervention by man. (Marx 1863–7/1977:783–4)

Thus, the distinctive feature of Marx's theory of population was its historical specificity: different modes of production had their own laws of population.

Marx and Engels were adamant over the years about the irrationality of capitalism. "The development of civilization and industry in general," from Marx's (1863–7/1981:322) perspective, "has always shown itself so active in the destruction of forests that everything that has been done for their conservation and production is completely insignificant in comparison." Marx (1863–7/1981:195–8) recommended re-using the massive amounts of refuse produced by capitalist industry and agriculture: iron filings, cloth, rags, the unused fibers discarded by textile mills, the waste products of the chemical industry, and the tons of human excrement pumped daily into the Thames.

Perhaps the most irrational feature of capitalism, in Marx and Engels's view, was the separation of industrial from agricultural production – the creation of the division between town and country. Engels (1876–8/1987:277) portrayed the effects: "The first great division of labor, the separation of town and country, condemned the rural population to thousands of years of mental torpidity, and the people of the towns each to subjection to his own individual trade. It destroyed the basis of intellectual development of the former and the physical development of the latter." He urged the

> abolition of the antithesis between town and country. It has become a direct necessity of industrial production itself, just as it has become a necessity of agricultural production, and, besides, of public health. The present poisoning of the air, water and land can be put an end to only by the fusion of town and country; and only such fusion will change the situation of the masses now languishing in the towns, and enable their excrement to be used for the production of plants instead of for the production of disease. (Engels 1876–8/1987:282)

Ending the separation of town and country would require abolishing the social division of labor and revolutionizing the old methods of production. It would entail redistributing people and industries across the landscape and associating certain activities that shared raw materials – such as beet farming with beet-sugar manufacturing and the distillation of schnapps. It would entail associations of producers, rather than private property in the means of production; it would make use of economies of scale. Most importantly, it would eliminate the capitalist mode of distribution (Engels 1876–8/1987; Marx 1875/1989; Marx and Engels 1848/1976). Thus, Marx and Engels's ecological project for transcending the alienation of human beings from nature was the same as their political project of transcending the alienation experienced by human beings under the capitalist mode of production.

In the next chapter, we will begin to analyze how archaeologists in particular and social scientists and historians more generally drew on the various aspects of Marx's legacy.

V. Gordon Childe and the Opening Dialogue

Australian archaeologist Vere Gordon Childe (1892–1957) was arguably the most influential archaeologist of the twentieth century as well as a political activist of the Left for his entire life (Gathercole 1989; Green 1981; Peace 1992; Trigger 1980).[1] He was also *the* pivotal figure in the formation of the discourse that linked Marxist social thought and archaeology. From the 1930s onward, Childe juxtaposed the findings of archaeologists and functionalist sociologists influenced by Émile Durkheim (1858–1917) and Herbert Spencer (1820–1903) with the sociohistorical perspectives forged by Marx, Engels, and their successors. Until then, Marxism, archaeology, and sociology had been distinct, relatively independent discourses; the archaeologists and sociologists had insulated themselves from one another and from the Marxists by "mutual disregard" or "collective misrepresentation" (Bottomore 1981; Llobera 1981). Any cross-fertilization that occurred was largely unacknowledged and was mediated by references to Charles Darwin's theory of evolution by natural selection, as we shall see below. Childe's contribution was the dialogue he launched; it took account of the theoretical perspectives of Marx, Engels, and the evolutionary socialists, like Karl Kautsky, who followed them on the Left as well as the liberal views elaborated by Durkheim, Spencer, and their followers.

What aspects of Marx's legacy did Childe find useful? How did he deal with the critiques of Marx's views and those of his successors that were implicit in the writings of sociologists like Durkheim and Spencer? How did he take up and assess the alternatives to Marx's theory of history and society that were proposed by his successors and by the sociologists? How did he incorporate their perspectives into his archaeological writing? Let us examine these questions in terms of the contradictory theoretical viewpoints that flourished from the 1890s through the early 1930s, how Childe brought them into a dialogue with Marxist social thought, and the debates his views provoked in the archaeological profession.

"Mutual Disregard" and Critique

The period from 1890 to 1914 was an exceptionally fertile one. It witnessed the elaboration of Marxist social and economic theory as Marx and Engels's successors examined transformations in capitalist society that they had sensed but had not lived long enough to analyze in detail; these included the published and widely translated accounts of evolutionary socialists, like Karl Kautsky (1854–1938). The period also marked both the heyday and the rapid decline of Herbert Spencer's influence. Moreover, it saw the appearance of alternative explanations for the rise of industrial society, including those of Durkheim and Max Weber (1864–1920).

Herbert Spencer, a contemporary of Marx and Engels, wrote continuously and voluminously from the early 1850s to the mid-1890s; in fact, Spencer's writings continued to appear for several decades after his death.[2] In *Social Statics*, his earliest book, he simultaneously adhered to the *laissez faire* economic doctrines of utilitarian writers like Jeremy Bentham and rejected their ethical theory. In his view, the utilitiarians, who saw morality as based on enlightened self-interest or mutual need, treated it as a constant; by doing so, they failed to recognize the diversity of ethical systems and the fact that these varied from one society to another. Furthermore, they did not take into account the natural rights of individuals (Spencer 1851/1995:3–30, 86). In Spencer's view, a theory of morality must recognize the diverse forms of moral intuition and ethics that have existed in different societies, that morality is mutable rather than fixed, and that individuals do indeed have natural rights.

Spencer also elaborated his theory of development in the 1850s; by 1857, he conceptualized development as progress and later as evolution in terms of a highly abstract, universal formula: the cosmos, life, human and social cognition, and human society were propelled by the same inherent progressive tendencies (Spencer 1857). Progress, from this perspective, was a slow, gradual process that resulted from repeated differentiations of structure. On the one hand, it was marked by continuous movement from an initial, undifferentiated, homogeneous structure to steadily more differentiated, heterogeneous structures that were composed of distinct but functionally interrelated parts. On the other hand, it was also a continuous process involving increasingly complex forms of organization and modes of integration of the constituent parts.

Spencer's theory of societal evolution was more textured than is commonly portrayed, since he sought to elaborate additional principles that explained differentiation – i.e. the building of structure – and that accounted for the diversity of societies. In his view, the inherent instability and oppressive conditions of homogeneous societies underpinned their disruption as well as the differentiation and the crystallization of more heterogeneous structures that followed. He also argued that the process of building structure transformed the circumstances in which the members of a society found themselves, and that these circumstances in turn had myriad effects which changed the institutions, behaviors, and beliefs defining their interrelations (Spencer 1862/1880:347, 373, 397). Thus, in Spencer's view, societal evolution was shaped by a number of factors. He emphasized the environment, the size of the society, the physical traits and knowledge possessed by its members, and derived factors. The latter included population size and density, the degree of social differentiation and specialization of tasks, increased productivity, and increased modes of contact with other societies (Spencer 1874–96/1898, 1:10–14). In his words:

> The pre-established environing influences, inorganic and organic, which are at first almost unalterable, become more and more altered by the actions of the evolving society. Simple growth of population brings into play fresh causes of transformations that are increasingly important. The influences which the society exerts on the nature of its units, and those which the units exert on the nature of society, incessantly co-operate in creating new elements. As societies progress in size and structure, they work on one another, now by their war-struggles and now by their industrial intercourse, profound metamorphoses. And the ever-accumulating, ever-complicating super-organic products, material and mental, constitute a further set of factors which become more and more influential causes of change. (Spencer 1874–96/1898, 1:14)

Spencer's theories of societal evolution drew inspiration from diverse sources. Like Charles Darwin (1809–82), he was influenced by Malthus and wrote:

> From the beginning pressure of population has been the proximate cause of progress. It produced the original diffusion of the race. It compelled men to abandon predatory habits and to take up agriculture. It forced men into the social state; made social organization inevitable; and has developed the social sentiments. It has stimulated progressive improvements in production, and increased skill and intelligence. It is daily pressing us into closer contact and more mutually-dependent relationships. (Spencer 1852:267)

Thus, the aggregation of individuals required organization, and that organization involved differentiation, coordination, and integration. The demographic growth of these societies promoted further differentiation, including the emergence and eventual separation of regulatory, political structures from operative, socio-economic structures and distributive structures concerned with communication and transportation (Turner 1985:21–2).

Spencer classified societies in two ways, each of which took account of a different facet of his theory.[3] In one scheme, the motor for societal evolution (growth) involved the successive aggregation of smaller communities into a larger one (compounding, in his terms) combined with the emergence of distinct regulative, operative, and distributive structures, and the concomitant internal differentiation of these structures (Turner 1985:86–92). Compounding usually occurred through war, conquest, and political alliance into successively larger units. He wrote:

We saw that societies are aggregates which grow; that in the various types of them there are great varieties in the growths reached; that types of successively larger size result from the aggregation and re-aggregation of those small sizes; and that this increase by coalescence, joined with interstitial increase, is the process through which have been formed the vast civilized nations. (Spencer 1874–96/1898, 1:469)

He discerned five societal types in terms of the degree of compounding – simple without leaders, simple with leaders, compound, doubly compound, and trebly compound. Ethnographically, these correspond roughly to bands with temporary leaders, tribal societies with permanent leaders, societies with hierarchies of chiefs, bureaucraticized states, and the modern political state (Turner 1985:88).

With regard to his second scheme, Spencer suggested that the regulative structures of societies oscillated back and forth between centralized (militant) and decentralized (industrial) forms. This meant, he wrote, that

[w]e are class societies, then, in two ways; both having to be kept in mind when interpreting social phenomena.

First, they have to be arranged in the order of their integration, as simple, compound, doubly-compared [i.e. doubly-compound], trebly-compared [i.e. trebly-compound]. . . . Omitting the lowest types which show no differentiation at all, we have but few exceptions to the rule that each society has structures for carrying on conflict . . . and for carrying on sustenations; and as the ratios of these admit gradation, it results that no specific classification can be based on their relative developments. Nevertheless, the militant type, characterized by the predominance of the one, is framed on the principle of compulsory co-operation while the industrial type, characterized by the predominance of the other, is framed on the principle of voluntary co-operation, the two types when evolved to their extreme forms, are dramatically opposed. (Spencer 1874–96/1898, 1:574)

There was a second dimension to Spencer's argument about societal evolution. In his view, societal evolution also underpinned cognitive development or evolution. His theory of psychological evolution combined associationism with the acquisition of learned characteristics. Associationism was the reigning psychological doctrine of the nineteenth century; it claimed "(1) that complex mental phenomena are formed from simple sensations, and (2) that this occurs by means of habit" (Young 1963:275). Spencer (1904, 1:470) wrote: "The familiar doctrine of association here undergoes a great extension; for it is held that not only in the individual do ideas become connected when in experience the things producing them have repeatedly occurred together, but that such results of repeated occurrences accumulate in successions of individuals." Hence, the theory of association was extended from the individual to the group. These accumulations of "repeated occurrences" in "successions of individuals" involved the transmission and inheritance of traits that were learned and used. In fact, Spencer (1887:74) thought this process of change and mode of inheritance were more important than evolution by natural selection in the later stages of societal evolution that witnessed the rise of civilization. In a phrase, even though he publicly accepted Darwin's theory of evolution by natural selection and referred to the concept of natural selection in his own work, Spencer's evolutionism remained resolutely Lamarckian (Peel 1971: 141).

Spencer's concern with morality, his theory of societal evolution, and his functionalism foreshadowed by several decades Émile Durkheim's (1893/1964) exploration of these issues in *The Division of Labor in Society* (Lukes 1977:86; Turner 1985:21–2). The appeal to Darwin as well as the Lamarckian underpinnings of Spencer's theory were echoed from the late 1880s onward in Durkheim's work as well as in the evolutionary socialism of Karl Kautsky.

Durkheim was concerned with the moral basis of modern industrial society and with the conditions required to establish a new morality that would promote social order or social stability.[4] He contrasted the individualism that lay at the core of the collective conscience of industrial societies, like France, with the circumstances that existed in socially undifferentiated, primitive societies. In these homogeneous communities, the life experiences of each individual were virtually identical, and individuals had similar feelings and attitudes that manifested themselves in webs of shared beliefs, values, symbols, and rules that they adhered to with a religious-like fervor. These shared beliefs stressed the primacy of the group over the individual. By contrast, in modern industrial societies, few sentiments were held in common because of the complex division of labor and the diversity of individual experience. Those that were shared emphasized the differences between individuals and their mutual interdependence. Whereas primitive society had universal moral codes, highly differentiated societies had ethical codes that applied only to the members of particular segments of the society.

Durkheim (1886:61–9) believed that religion, morality, and law were the three important control mechanisms of society. They dictated the sentiments and ideas of a group and regulated the actions of its members. While morality allowed people to live together by adapting individuals to one another, religion stood at the core of the entire institutional apparatus of society.

> Religion contains in itself from the very beginning, even if in an indistinct state, all the elements which in dissociating themselves from it, articulating themselves, and combining with one another in a thousand ways, have given rise to the various manifestations of collective life. From myths and legends have issued forth science and poetry; from religious ornamentations and cult ceremonials have come the plastic arts; from ritual practice were born law and morals. (Durkheim 1898:ii)

The solidarity of a society was constituted by the moral exchange and symbolic communication that took place among its members. The particular form of that solidarity was shaped by the degree of social differentiation in the society. Social differentiation – i.e. the division of labor – modified religion, morality, and law. Durkheim (1893/1964) provided an evolutionary account of the effects of increasing social differentiation in *The Division of Labor in Society*, using ethnographic and historical information to explore the crisis of modern society and how religion – that "essential and permanent aspect of humanity" – was transformed in the process (Durkheim 1912/1965:13).

Like Spencer, Durkheim construed social evolution as a directional tendency from undifferentiated, primitive (segmented) societies to highly differentiated, modern ones with complex structures and forms of organizations. Since "social life . . . [was] an uninterrupted series of transformations," change was gradual and continuous (Durkheim 1895/1938:134). The motor driving social differentiation was the concentration of people in a confined area, like a city, which intensified interactions between individuals and increased moral density. At this point, Durkheim (1893/1964:266, 276) evoked population growth and Darwin's "struggle for existence" to explain why social differentiation occurred. In his view, as primitive bands encountered one another with increasing frequency, they began to compete for scarce natural resources; however, the social differentiation resulting from occupational specialization allowed them to coexist since the various groups used different natural resources.

Social order was maintained in primitive bands, because their members participated in the same activities, cooperated, and shared natural sentiments (Durkheim 1885/1978). These shaped their interpersonal relations. Morality was rooted in friendship and in shared beliefs and sentiments. Moreover, it was underpinned by religious beliefs and practices. In Durkheim's (1893/1964:135) words: "Religion comprises all, extends to all. It contains in a confused mass, besides beliefs properly religious, morality, law, the principles of political organization, and even science, or at least what passes for it." He called this form of social order "mechanical solidarity." It broke down when the primitive bands aggregated into larger tribes and acquired their own distinctive features – territory, specialized functions, political authority, and sacred ancestors – in the process. Further social differentiation occurred when tribes came together to form a confederacy in which each group assumed a particular function within the larger unit – e.g. the Levites became priests in the ancient Israelite confederacy. The formation of confederacies laid the foundations for the increasing separation of the gods from everyday life as well as for a rudimentary division of labor – i.e. functionally interdependent units. Because "classes and castes . . . arise from the multitude of occupational organizations being born amidst the pre-existing family organizations," the members of each class or caste developed their own morality (Durkheim 1893/1964:182; 1887:123).

Structural differentiation and functional interdependence increased further with the emergence of the ancient city-state, which was an aggregate of clans, tribes, and confederacies. The principal subdivisions in the city-state were territorial rather than kinship groupings. Social and political unity was vested in the state rather than in either family or tribal groups or in the religious cults they maintained. The domestic religious cults – typical of the tribes and confederacies – were subordinated to a state religion that was simultaneously more abstract and less pervasive in its control of everyday life; in order to incorporate the diverse population that resided in the city, the symbols of the state religion were also more general than those of the kin-based cults (Durkheim 1893/1964:156–62, 181–6). Thus a new form of social cohesion – "organic solidarity" – developed with the rise of the city-state. It was based on the emerging social differentiation, specialization, functional interdependence, and individuality of the city-dwellers. It downplayed tribal loyalties, stressing instead the importance of place over kin. In a phrase, the state and the civic morality it promoted were intimately bound up with religion and religious beliefs.

Two changes occurred in medieval society, the stage that preceded the development of the modern industrial nation. The first involved the emergence of specialized institutions that were concerned with government, religion, education, and economics. The second involved inter-regional differentiation in the European economy, which produced an international division of labor. Under these conditions, Christianity became even more abstract and less tied to particular beliefs and practices (Durkheim 1893/1964:288–91). By allowing more individual reflection, voluntary action, and rational investigation, it facilitated the secularization of the state and the economy (Durkheim 1893/1964:163–4).

Modern industrial states were thus freed from the territorial constraints of the city-state and medieval society. They had large-scale, functionally specific institutions concerned with government, education, manufacturing, and commerce that operated across the state. These institutions were interrelated and subordinated to the state, which established, through procedural and restitutive laws, the conditions for their cooperation (Durkheim 1893/1964:212–29). Moreover, the division of labor in modern society promoted individuation, differentiated personalities, and the growth of a market economy; this ultimately pitted one individual against another when they sought to buy or sell the same item.

For Durkheim, the state was the central organ that coordinated the functions of the various parts of the social whole. By virtue of its central role, it was more able than individuals to grasp the significance of the whole and to make it function (Durkheim 1893/1964:113). As society advanced, the state became a source of social control by virtue of its regulation of the moral exchange and communication that occurred between diverse individuals and groups. In other words, the state determined the normal functions of the different parts of the social whole and their interrelations with one another.

However, the problem with modern industrial society, in Durkheim's view, was that the division of labor had produced less solidarity instead of more social cohesion. This was an abnormal development, a pathology, rather than an integral feature of advanced society. It occurred because the economy had become separated from the social whole. The relations between capital and labor were unregulated and, hence, existed in a state of anomie. The inequalities resulting from unequal exchanges in the market imposed a forced division of labor that reflected wealth and family position rather than a natural distribution based on the talents and abilities of individuals. To overcome this pathology, the state needed to promote the formation of secondary organizations – such as professional or occupational groups – that had been destroyed by the rise of modern industrial society, which operated on a national rather than local or regional scale. These secondary groups would link individuals directly to the state and "drag them, this way, into the general torrent of social life" (Durkheim 1893/1964:28).

Thus, in modern society, the state was no longer merely the moral regulator of society, as it had been in the ancient city or in medieval times. It had become a representation of the collectivity and a moral community that forged rules and inspired loyalty. It had the capacity to create the conditions for instituting a new morality, one that necessarily involved secondary groups in the regulation of economic life and that dealt with the contradictions between the social norms of equality before the law and the inequalities and injustices arising from the inheritance of property and differences in talent.

Karl Kautsky, editor of *Die neue Zeit* from its inception in 1883 to 1917, was arguably one of the leading theoreticians of the world socialist movement in the years preceding the First World War.[5] Like Spencer and Durkheim, he was familiar with the ethnographic and historical accounts of the day, and wrote about ethics and societal evolution among many other topics. Kautsky had read Darwin and was influenced by his writings during the 1870s. By the 1880s, he saw Darwin as a major figure in the development of a materialist view of nature; however, in spite of his respect for Darwin's accomplishments, Kautsky (1927/1988:46) remained a lifelong Lamarckian, who believed in "the acquisition and hereditary transmission of new characteristics through the influence of new conditions . . . and that change of the environment, then, remains always the most important factor in the evolution of organisms."

Kautsky distinguished evolution in the organic world (i.e. nature) from societal evolution; from 1885 onward, he believed that societal evolution could not be explained by the same laws that governed evolution in nature except in the most general way. Like plants and animals, human societies adapted to their environment, but the kinds of adaptations were different. The adaptations of plants were passive; those of animals were active because they possessed volition, cognition, and locomotion. However, when human societies adapted to their environments, they changed not only themselves, as plants and animals did, but also their environments by creating new tools and forms of organization "to solve newly appearing problems" (Kautsky 1927/1988:462). In his view, there were physical and chemical laws that operated on nature under some conditions and not others; there were sociohistorical laws that applied to human society in general; and there were sociohistorical laws that applied only to particular forms of human society, such as capitalism (Kautsky 1927/1988:477). He also noted the differences between his materialist conception of history and that of Spencer, which "recognize[d] only general natural laws governing all societies," as well as its mirror image, which claimed that "society is [not] governed by any natural law at all" (Kautsky 1927/1988:478).

There also was a sense in which Kautsky was a societal evolutionist like Spencer and Durkheim. He believed in the inevitability of socialism (Kautsky 1906/1918:206). In his view, primitive societies – i.e. those without social class divisions – had existed for 800,000 years, whereas class-stratified societies, by contrast, had existed only during the last 10,000 to 15,000 years of human history; they were products of the conquest of one group by another (Kautsky 1927/1988:250).

> The advances made by civilization, especially since the emergence of the state, have fragmented the mass of the population into an enormous number of occupations; they have caused great differences in the educational levels of different strata; they have, in war and peace, thoroughly mixed the very diverse races. . . . This continuously progressing differentiation . . . meets in industrial capitalism. (Kautsky 1927/1988:523)

What distinguished capitalist society from its class-stratified predecessors, in Kautsky's view, were the facts that its means of production had

> become so enormous, that they burst today the frame of private property [and that] the productivity of labour is grown so huge that today already a considerable diminution of labour time is possible for all workers. These grow the foundations for the abolition not of the division of labour, not of the professions, but for antagonism of rich and poor, exploiters and exploited, ignorant and wise. (Kautsky 1906/1918:205)

Because of this development, "[t]he capitalist social system has run its course; its dissolution is now only a question of time. Irresistible economic forces lead with the certainty of of doom to the shipwreck of capitalist production. The substitution of a new social order for the existing one is no longer desirable, it is inevitable" (Kautsky 1892/1971:117).[6]

What Kautsky's view of societal development shared with those of Spencer and Durkheim was the sense of inevitability; the outcome of change was written, as it were, into the whole fabric of human history. It also distinguished Kautsky's view from Marx's emphasis on the importance of agency and of contingency: the idea that people occasionally do make their own history under circumstances not of their own making, and that, in those instances, they do transform social structures and relations.

Childe's Engagement with Marxist and Liberal Social Theory[7]

It is difficult to pinpoint precisely when V. Gordon Childe became acquainted with the writings of particular authors or with particular texts. There are several reasons for this. One is the style of bibliographic citation that prevailed at the time; another is concerned with what was presumed to be knowledge shared by an informed reading public which therefore did not warrant citation. Nevertheless, it is possible to sketch broadly when he became aware of the authors mentioned earlier. Childe's biographers have indicated that he read Marx and Engels as an undergraduate at the University of Sydney in the 1910s. They have also mentioned that he discussed their work, and probably that of Kautsky as well, with his longtime friend Rajani Palme Dutt, who was a founding member and the leading theoretician of the British Communist Party in the early 1920s. Childe certainly became knowledge-able about the writings of Durkheim and, through him, Spencer in the mid-1920s, when he translated Alexandre Moret and Georges Davy's (1926) *From Tribe to Empire* for the publisher Kegan Paul Ltd. Moret, an Egyptologist, collaborated with Davy, a sociologist who had studied with Durkheim, "to produce a Durk-heimian interpretation of the development of ancient Egyptian civilization" (Trigger 1989:251). They drew heavily on Durkheim's *Division of Labor in Society*, which in one sense is a commentary on Spencer, and on his *Elementary Forms of Religious Life*.

Of course, one sure-fire way of demonstrating Childe's awareness of particular texts and authors and their influence, beyond quotations and citations, is to consider what he actually wrote. Did particular ideas and views originate with him? If not, where might they have come from? In this section, let us consider briefly the intellectual milieu in which Childe worked, the theory of society and history he honed and refined from the mid-1930s onward, and then what he had to say about the relations between society and nature.

Childe labored in an intellectual milieu shaped by liberal, Marxist, and neo-Kantian thought. He incorporated all three currents to varying degrees into his views about archaeology and ancient cultures and societies. For example, he adopted the neo-Kantians' distinction between the natural and human sciences (Benton 1977:104–10). Archaeology, for Childe, was a human science concerned with the historical study of ancient peoples. In his view, the differences between archaeology and the natural sciences involved both subject matter and method.

Consequently, "the concepts of natural sciences could not be applied without modification" (Childe 1935:2). Nevertheless, he also believed that archaeologists could learn a great deal from the investigations of natural scientists – such as their reconstructions of past environments from pollens and soils, their statistical analyses, and their development of absolute dating techniques, to name a only few he mentioned (Childe 1956). Thus, unlike Spencer, he was not concerned with elaborating natural laws that applied equally to the organic world and to the evolution of human society. In this regard, Childe's views resembled those of Marx, Engels, Durkheim, and Kautsky. They were certainly different from those of his logical positivist contemporaries, who, from the late 1920s onward, championed the development of a unified science and scientific methodology (Kolakowski 1966/1969:169–200).

The concept of culture occupied a central place in Childe's theory of society and history. In 1929, he described an archaeological culture as a complex of "certain types of remains – pots, implements, ornamentation, burial rites, house forms – constantly recurring together" (Childe 1929:v–vi). However, from the mid-1930s onward, Childe (e.g. 1935:2; 1947:52) regularly deployed an expanded notion which depicted culture as "observable facts," as a "social tradition," and later as the "whole life of a community": "The traits of a culture are thus presented together to the archaeologists because they are the creations of a single people, adjustments to its environment approved by its collective experience; they thus express the individuality of a human group united by common social traditions" (Childe 1935:3).

By 1946, Chile (1946a:243) portrayed a society as an "association of men and women" with a common culture, and hinted at their interconnections with Marx's notion of a mode of production: "Marx . . . asserted that the mode of production in the long run determines the ideological superstructure. Here 'mode of production' means the means of production together with the property relations that permit of their full utilization, and 'ideological superstructure' includes social, religious, legal, and aesthetic institutions, beliefs, and conventions" (Childe 1946a:250). In this passage, Childe seemed to imply that material culture (i.e. the means of production) belonged to the economy or economic foundations, while the symbolic, signifying aspects of culture, equated with the "ideologue superstructure." A year later, he restated the interconnections of the two analytical categories in slightly different terms: ". . . it is not the forces of production that immediately constitute the determinant, but the mode of production, the economy within which these forces can function" (Childe 1947:59).

Three features of these passages are significant. First, Childe clearly located the motor for sociohistorical change and development in the contradictions between the forces and relations of production and how they manifested themselves in the superstructural elements (law, politics, ideology, and associated forms of social consciousness) of the mode of production. Second, he was clearly attempting to integrate society, culture, and mode of production as interconnected parts of an active, larger social totality. Third, his use of "ideology as culture" was a more inclusive category than that of "ideology as false consciousness," which is popular today. In Childe's usage, ideology was the worldview characteristic of a particular class or group, and included what Raymond Williams (1981:26) later termed the "formal and conscious beliefs" as well as the "less conscious, less formulated attitudes, habits and feelings, or even unconscious assumptions, bearings and commitments."

Childe's concept of culture, as Bruce Trigger (1980:40–4; 1989:163–7) observed, had obvious roots in the conceptual framework used by Gustaf Kossinna (1858–1931) in his *Die Herkunft der Germanen* (The Origins of the Germans), which appeared in 1911. However, Childe's formulation of culture as well as that of Kossinna also had roots in wider issues raised by the neo-Kantians, who were concerned with the philosophical foundations of the human sciences. Wilhelm Dilthey (1833–1911), a founder of this school of thought, had written earlier about "lived experience" and "understanding as imaginative identification":

> Every single human expression represents something in common to many and therefore part of the realm of objective mind. Every word or sentence, every gesture or form of politeness, every work of art and every historical deed are only understandable because the person expressing himself and the person who understands him are connected by something they have in common; the individual always experiences, thinks, acts, and also understands in this common sphere. (Dilthey quoted by Outhwaite 1975:26–7)

As Ted Benton (1977:106) put it: "Inter-subjective 'understanding' is possible only on the condition that the subjects between whom the understanding takes place share a common culture." This was the point of Childe's concept of culture, and of Kossinna's for that matter. It was also a point made in different words by Marx and Engels, as we saw in the preceding chapter: The members of a society are constrained by its traditions; they work out their destinies using and refining the material and symbolic forms available to them. Culture is thus the arena in which they live and experience everyday life.

From 1936 onward, Childe (1936/1983, 1942, 1946b, 1950/1972, 1954) turned his attention increasingly toward examining the dynamic forces of human society – those that promoted historical development as well as the contradictory ones that impeded sociocultural change. He discerned two major transformations in human history. The first – the Neolithic Revolution – was a consequence of technological innovations that transformed the mode of subsistence. The second – the Urban Revolution – involved the rise of civilization – i.e. the formation of class-stratified, state-based societies and the exploitation of the direct producers by a class whose members had withdrawn themselves from the production process.

His basic premises in these works were that "human needs are not fixed and immutable," and that "an individual apart from society would not be human" (Childe 1954:38–9). The members of human society cooperate, communicate with language, and use tools to transform natural materials into objects that satisfy culturally determined needs. They also transform themselves in the process as they create new needs and acquire new knowledge of the worlds in which they live. Childe (1954:40) continued, indicating that the "supply of food available to support a human population is determined not only by the fertility of the environment but by the techniques for extracting food and, further, by the system of redistributing product. The latter factors provide bases for classifying societies into groups. . . . Let us term the way in which a society secures its food 'the basic economy.'" He discerned three broad types of societies: those with "food-gathering" (foraging) economies, those with "food-producing" (neolithic) economies, and those whose basic economy involved the extraction of tribute from classes of direct producers by a ruling class (Childe 1950/1972:50; 1954:40–4).

Childe's (1936/1983:37–50) most detailed discussions of foraging communities typically juxtaposed descriptions of various Paleolithic societies with ethnographic data. He acknowledged the diverse "modes of life" of the societies with "food-gathering" economies resulting from adjustments to different natural circumstances. The members of these communities used tools, communicated through language, and cooperated with one another as they acquired food; transformed natural objects into clothing, shelter, and other items that fulfilled needs; and gained a more profound knowledge of their environment. Although they were economically self-sufficient, the communities were not necessarily isolated from one another. They had "some form of social organization beyond the simple family," and the later ones at least were large enough to undertake communally organized activities, like animal drives during certain seasons of the year (Childe 1936/1983:40, 46). The members of these communities also engaged in aesthetic or magico-religious endeavors, like art, that were not immediately practical economic activities.

Childe (1950/1972:45) portrayed the social organization of the food-gathering societies in the following way:

> Now in any Stone Age society, . . . everybody can at least in theory make at home the few indispensable tools, the modest cloths and the simple ornaments everyone requires. But every member of the local community, not disqualified by age, must contribute actively to the communal food supply by personally collecting, hunting, fishing, gardening or herding. As long as this holds good, there can be no full-time specialists, no persons nor class of persons who depend for their livelihood on food produced by others and secured in exchange for material or immaterial goods or services. . . .
>
> Social division of labour, save those rudiments imposed by age and sex, is thus impossible. On the contrary community of employment, the common absorption in obtaining

food by similar devices guarantees a certain solidarity to the group. For co-operation is essential to secure food and shelter and for defence against foes, human and subhuman. This identity of economic interests is echoed and magnified by identity of language, custom and belief; rigid conformity is enforced as industry in the common quest for food. But conformity and industrious co-operation need no State organization to maintain them.

Earlier, Childe (1946b:32–3) had applied the label of "primitive communism" to this form of social organization. His repeated emphasis on the importance of cooperation and sharing imply that he saw the relations of production operating at the level of the local community rather than at the level of the individual household. This means, for example, that every individual is dependent on the multi-family group. It also means that individuals who may not have participated in one episode of food production will nevertheless receive shares of that activity because of the expectation that they will be involved in future episodes since food production is an ongoing activity. Childe's repeated remark over the years that these local communities were not isolated in spite of their economic self-sufficiency suggests that certain activities, like large-scale game drives, may have involved the cooperation of members from several different local communities during particular seasons of the year. In other words, the relations of production and reproduction may even have extended beyond the local community.

While Childe's accounts of foraging societies viewed archaeological and ethnographic information through the lens of Marxist social thought, his views about the significance of Upper Palaeolithic cave paintings in France and Spain drew inspiration from Durkheim. Durkheim, as you will recall, argued that religion, manifested in ceremonies, rituals, and beliefs, was the glue that bound together the members of primitive societies into a seamless whole. Childe (1936/ 1983:48) suggested that the cave paintings "were doubtless connected with other magical ceremonies," and that "[t]he artist-magicians were experts, specially trained for their task. As such they must have enjoyed respect, and even authority, in whatever social organization then existed. But they can hardly have been specialists in the sense of being exempted from participation in the food-quest of the group." In sum, these and other products of palaeolithic art imbued with meaning and possessing ritual significance functioned to reaffirm interpersonal relations and reinforce shared beliefs and sentiments.

Childe recognized the existence of prosperous food-gathering societies, like the Kwakiutl of the Northwest Coast of North America or the Upper Paleolithic hunters of Western Europe, that developed elaborate spiritual cultures and lived in areas with rich hunting grounds and well-stocked rivers. As a result, they were able to produce food surpluses and, hence, had the capacity to support artist-magicians who "may have been liberated from the exacting tasks of the chase to concentrate on . . . ritual," and whose economic claims to a share of the proceeds were based on "socially sanctioned superstitution" (Childe 1942:41). They were the first specialists, and, despite what their kin and neighbors may have thought, their actions contributed little materially to the success of the food quest. In Childe's view, many of the prosperous food-gathering cultures of the Upper Paleolithic disappeared because of their inability to cope with the waning resources and new conditions that emerged at the end of the Ice Age.

Elsewhere, the members of these kin-based communal societies continued to eke out an existence as their ancestors had despite their new environmental circumstances. In a few places, like the Near East, some of them succeeded in domesticating plants with edible seeds or fruits and animals. This was a slow process. Initially, it may have meant little more than the addition of a new activity or two to the more traditional ones of their food quests: women perhaps planted a few seeds, or men culled adult males or juveniles from a herd of sheep (Childe 1942:57–8). However, little if anything was changed in the patterns of cooperation and sharing passed down by their ancestors, who were buried under house floors in many neolithic communities (Childe 1936/1983:62–4, 76–7; 1942:60, 64). The communities continued to manifest primitive communism – i.e. what Eric Wolf (1982:88–100) would later call the "kin-ordered" or communal mode of production – and typically lacked chieftains (Childe 1936/1983:76).

While the transformation occurred slowly, it was ultimately revolutionary in the structural changes it wrought. The food-producing revolution was manifested differently in different regions and often in different parts of the same region as the members of local communities applied its principles in diverse ways according to their local circumstances (Childe 1942:56). Nevertheless, what they shared was that land, animals, or both were gradually transformed during the process from objects of production to means of production. The members of these communities no longer just collected wild fruits and seeds from the land; instead, they tilled it, planted seeds or tubers, tended the crops, and waited for them to ripen in order to harvest them at right time. They milked the cows and goats they domesticated and sheared the sheep each year for their woolly fleece. Farming, stockbreeding, or some combination of both as a basic economy required the production of a surplus. Minimally, the communities had to have breeding stock, and they had to reserve a certain portion of one year's harvest to provide seed for the next crop and food until that crop ripened; however, as Childe himself (1942:60) pointed out, beyond this, "a neolithic economy offers no material inducement to the peasant to produce more than he needs to support himself and his family and provide for the next harvest." Nevertheless, he was aware that the annual yields could outstrip the needs of the community and support population growth or rudimentary trade (Childe 1936/1983:63). He was equally aware that droughts, storms, diseases, and other events beyond people's control could destroy crops and herds, spelling "famine and annihilation for the self-contained and isolated community" (Childe 1942:68).

In Childe's (1942:60) view, the neolithic communities were economically self-sufficient; their members grew the food and made the items they needed from locally available materials. This did not mean that they were isolated from one another; in fact, he argued that intercourse between neighboring groups was frequent and vital for progress. They traded for non-essential goods that were not locally available; they also exchanged ideas, knowledge, and even thoughts about something as seemingly mundane as how pottery should be decorated. These inter-community exchanges ultimately provided the foundations for development of "intercommunal specialization" within the same region (Childe 1936/1983:66; 1942:61–3). This kind of exchange and specialization implied the existence of ongoing social relations between the members of the various local groups. Given the small size of the local communities, this perhaps entailed little more at first than the matrimonial mobility of men and women. Later, however, it involved full-time craft specialists who broke out of their local communities and supported themselves by moving from village to village plying their wares (Childe 1950/1972:46).

Childe linked the food-producing revolution with the appearance of new technical divisions of labor; this was perhaps more apparent among the members of mixed farming communities, where some individuals tended crops while their kin and neighbors herded livestock in distant mountain pastures (Childe 1936/1983:61). It was also apparent for the itinerant craftsmen who were slowly severing connections with their local communities. And it was probably also true for communities involved in specialized production and regional exchange networks. The backdrop against which these new divisions of labor occurred were communities in which there was little if any specialization, and craft goods were the products of collective traditions rather than individual innovations. Cooperative activities – like farming, herding, and even making pots – dominated everyday life, and "found outward expression in social and political institutions . . . [that] were consolidated and reinforced by magico-religious sanctions, by a more or less coherent system of beliefs and superstitions, by what Marxists would call an ideology" (Childe 1936/1983:74). Following Durkheim's lead, Childe suggested that this was the realm of the magico-religious specialist who toiled on behalf of the community and who received a portion of its surplus in return (see above); however, the neolithic ideologies they produced, especially when these were well developed, actually impeded the growth of scientific knowledge by curbing the exchanges of ideas between communities (Trigger 1978:105–6).

The era of primitive communism preceding the rise of states and stratified societies was, for Childe (1936/1983:172–80), the truly creative epoch of human history. This was especially true in areas, like Mexico or the Near East, where neolithic worldviews were weakly developed and did not impede further techno-logical innovations. The members of these communities developed the first food-producing economies. They increased productivity through irrigation; the selective breeding of plants, livestock, and pack animals; and other technological and organizational innovations, such as copper and bronze metallurgy and water transport, that saved both time and effort. These innovations allowed the communities to produce surpluses. Other innovations – the production of metal implements or woven textiles – coupled with growing surpluses, increasingly dense technical divisions of labor, and inter-village exchange, occasionally underwrote the transformation of what had been exotic luxury goods into objects that satisfied needs of steadily growing numbers of people. They also transformed the lives of the expert craft specialists who produced these goods as they became separated from the production of their own food.

> As long as such things were accepted as luxuries, their use did not destroy the fundamental self-sufficiency of the Neolithic group. As long as they remained luxuries, their provision would offer a very unreliable livelihood for their makers and purveyors. Few would risk becoming full-time specialists; most remained farmers or hunters or fishers who secured a more varied diet and enhance prestige by plying a handicraft or by trading. (Childe 1954:45)

While the Urban Revolution – the rise of states – rescued these workers from a potentially semi-nomadic existence, it had other equally important consequences for their everyday lives (Childe 1950/1972:46).

The crystallization of social class structures, the most visible expression of exploitative social relations – rather than cities, writing systems, long-distance trade, or monumental buildings – marked the onset of Childe's second revolution. The appearance of ruling classes halted technological progress in the early civilizations and transformed direct producers – both farmers and craftsmen – into serfs who produced the surpluses appropriated by the rulers to satisfy their own needs and desires and to ensure the continued reproduction of their kind (Childe 1942: 123–4). They used violence or the threat of it to control subordinated groups and to ensure the regular extraction of surplus labor time and goods. They also relied on the reactionary forces of religion and superstition to bolster their position and to inhibit the development of rational science. In Childe's (1936/1983:172–80) view, the appearance of class-stratified, state-based societies marked a slowdown in the rates of technological innovation and social progress. Under these circumstances, as Trigger (1978:112) noted, only a limited expansion of the economy was possible: "Luxury goods were sold to the ruling classes of less advanced neighbouring states in return for raw materials. The conquest of adjacent regions increased the internal wealth and purchasing power of victorious states and spread the wealth among a new class of professional soldiers" (cf. Childe 1942:116–7).

Childe suggested that social class structures and the early state appeared in three forms: the temple city, the use of war captives, and the tributary state. What the various forms had in common was the fact that the social relations of the neolithic community which had been based on cooperation and sharing were distorted and ultimately dissolved as some members of the community withdrew from direct production and began to support themselves with labor and goods appropriated from their neighbors. What distinguished one form of the early state from the others was the way in which their ruling classes extracted surplus goods and labor from the direct producers. In the first of these, "[f]irst-fruits in the form of grain can . . . be used to support a priest – a full-time specialist in conciliating the imaginary powers – or indeed a whole college of priests. If sufficiently abundant, they may then be used to support full-time smiths and other specialists" (Childe 1954:47). In the second, prisoners taken in battle were enslaved and incorporated by their captors into the subsistence economy. They enriched their owners by producing food and goods above and beyond what they consumed. The slaveowner/war leaders used the surplus to support craft specialists or to enhance their own positions in the local community (Childe 1954:47–8). In the third, the nascent ruling class claimed ownership of the community's land and extracted tribute in the form of taxes or rent from the peasants who effectively possessed and worked the soil (Childe 1954:53).

Childe (1936/1983:130) understood the dialectic of class and state formation: It was "propagated by violence and imposed by the force of imperialism." It involved not only what Stanley Diamond (1974:1) later characterized as "conquest abroad and repression at home" but also resistance to those processes. In a discussion of the relations between state-based societies and the kin-ordered communities on their margins, Childe (1954:57) wrote:

> To resist the well-armed forces of civilized states the barbarian victims must organize their economy to secure regular supplies of metal, at least, and the service of competent metal-workers. At the same time, the authority of any chief who led the resistance movements would be consolidated. He could, and indeed, must, become a concentrator of social surplus and so his court would become a new centre of demand for raw materials. In these ways civilization . . . was bound to spread, and spread it did. (cf. Childe 1934/1953:243–4)

Within the state-based societies themselves, Childe (1950/1972:48–9; 1936/ 1983:140) described the "priests, civil and military leaders and officials [who] absorbed a major share of the concentrated surplus" and whose number kept meticulous records "for practical business and administration" and ensured that the taxes, tribute, and rent owed by the producing classes were paid in a timely manner.

Childe (1936/1983:172–80) argued that early state-based societies were wracked by contradictions. The internal contradictions resulted from the social class structure, which expressed exploitation. Their ruling classes appropriated goods and labor from the producing classes, whose share of the wealth was minimal. The direct producers were degraded not only in an economic sense but also in an intellectual sense. External contradictions resulted from the fact that early states – at least those in the Near East – were no longer self-sufficient, because they relied "for essential raw materials on imports from regions occupied by different societies" (Childe 1936/1983:176). These came to the fore as societies on the margins of the early states adopted elements of civilization – e.g. metal weapons – and regained control of raw materials that were being removed from their territories. This in turn undermined the economic foundations of the state. Thus, in Childe's view, the early states were unstable. When they disintegrated, "wealth was returned to general circulation, ideas (or what Childe called cultural capital) survived, and freedom from superstitions and political control of entrenched social systems facilitated [new] technological innovations and their practical application" (Trigger 1978:124–5).

The early states also stifled the creativity of their producing classes. In the kin-ordered communities that antedated their appearance, the men and women who had engaged in direct production repeatedly applied scientific principles to improve their lives; irrigation, wheeled vehicles, fermentation, and metallurgy were only a few of the labor-saving innovations that appeared before the crystallization of the first states. After states appeared, there were few contributions of comparable importance – perhaps the decimal notations and alphabets used to record censuses and economic transactions. The reason for the relative absence of innovations that increased productivity in the early states was that their ruling classes "had no need to bother about labor-saving inventions," since their wealth rested on their ability to extort labor and goods from the producing classes rather than in improving productivity (Childe 1936/1983:175).

Thus, by the early 1940s, Childe had formulated an explicitly Marxist perspective on the rise and fall of ancient civilizations. He recognized not only changes in the productive forces but also the appearance of exploitation, oppression, and class struggle. His view implied that the rise of civilization was a mixed blessing that brought a rising standard of living for the small ruling classes and increased immiseration for the vast majority of the population. It implied that the interests of the rulers and the direct producers were opposed in fundamental ways to one another.

Childe never wrote systematically about the interconnections between societies and the natural worlds they inhabited. His comments on the subject were scattered throughout his writings, mostly in passages dealing with changes at the end of the Ice Age or with the rise of food production. It is clear, however, that he realized local communities were embedded in their environments and that they subsisted by appropriating raw materials and transforming them through labor into objects that satisfied culturally determined needs.

Childe also believed that there was a dialectical connection between the local communities and their environments. On the one hand, he repeatedly portrayed foraging societies as parasitic on nature, because they had not transformed plants, animals, or land from objects of production to means of production. This left the members of these communities at the "whims of the environment" (Childe 1928:2). This was particularly true for the prosperous foraging societies that occupied rich habitats at the end of the Pleistocene. These groups had the capacity to produce foodstuffs and other goods beyond what they consumed and used the surplus they produced to support magico-religious specialists, who withdrew from the production process itself. These specialists afforded no real help to their neighbors, which allowed them to cope with diminishing food resources at the end of the Ice Age. As a result, the cultures of prosperous foraging groups "decayed" (Childe 1938/1983:47–50).

On the other hand, Childe (1942:48) portrayed food-producing communities in a very Kautskyian manner as "active partners with nature" who had emancipated themselves from the "whims of the environment" by creating new forms of production and cooperation to solve new problems. By transforming land, plants, and animals into means of production – by making them implements rather than objects of labor – the members of these communities were able to "control their own food supply" and to "augment the supply according to demand" (Childe 1935:7). In the process, they adapted "their economy and equipment to a strictly specialized and localized environment. The latter would offer each society its own distinct opportunities for discoveries and inventions" (Childe 1942:62). Furthermore, Childe (1942:68) was also aware that droughts and other calamities often spelled disaster for these communities, especially the more isolated ones.

It is difficult to discern in Childe's writings the impact that food-gathering and food-producing societies had on their environments – e.g. soil exhaustion, overfishing, or the depletion of forests for firewood or building materials. In this regard, his concept of the interconnections between nature and society bears more similarity to that of the political economists, who were criticized by Marx for viewing nature as a larder to be stripped of its resources by humankind or to be conquered and transformed into a means of production. What was clear in Childe's writings, however, was Marx and Engels's notion of metabolic rift. The first rift occurred with the advent of food production; the second was associated with the rise of states and the concentration of population in cities. These rifts were forged by people, not by the natural worlds that they inhabited. They not only paved the way for population growth, but also marked alterations in the ways that peoples understood their worlds (e.g. Childe 1950/1972:44–7).

Childe thus built generally on the work of Marx and Engels. He was familiar with at least the broad outlines of Lewis Henry Morgan's *Ancient Society*, which had been the point of departure for Engels's *Origin of the Family, Private Property and the State.* Childe (1946a:251) cited both works. He also incorporated views that Durkheim expressed in *The Division of Labor in Society* and in *The Elementary Forms of Religious Life*; however, as Trigger (1978:36) suggested, Childe probably became familiar with them through his translation of Moret and Davy's *From Tribe to Empire.* He used comparative ethnological data derived partly from Durkheim and partly from anthropologists – e.g. Franz Boas and Bronislaw Malinowski – to flesh out his characterizations of the social relations found in food-gathering and early food-producing communities. From his days as librarian at the Royal Anthropological Institute, he may also have been familiar with Spencer's *Descriptive Sociology* (1873–1934) – a comparison of different societies in sixteen volumes hailed as the intellectual precursor to the Human Relations Area Files (Turner 1985). Neither Spencer's social theory, beyond an occasional use of the analogy between society and an organism, nor the evolutionary socialism of Kautsky seems to have left much of an imprint on Childe's views and writings.

Childe was concerned with discerning the motors of cultural progress and refining his understanding of the forces that promoted and impeded development. To do so, he examined how they were manifested in different, historically and socially specific settings. As a result, there was a continuous interplay in many of his writings between what was typical of all human societies and what was particular to one or a few.

Early Postwar Responses to Childe

Childe was at the height of his career when the Second World War ended in 1945. His biographers have documented his friendships with anthropologists in the United States and their attempts to find employment for him. The impact of his writings was most apparent at the University of Chicago in the years immediately following the war. Trigger (1978:126–7) pointed out that Childe's writings received extensive coverage in *Human Origins* – which was prepared by the anthropology faculty at the university as "an introductory, self-study syllabus for ex-soldiers who were coming back into the university as mature undergraduates." As a result, his views soon became widely known by students of anthropology in the United States.

The Chicago anthropologists – e.g. Robert Redfield and Robert Braidwood – engaged Childe's theoretical perspectives as well as his interpretations of the archaeological record. They developed Durkheim's functionalist theory of change as well as his views about the structure of society and the effects of social differentiation. Durkheim's use of the organic analogy led them to view change as a slow, gradual, and continuous process. Redfield embraced this perspective and criticized Childe for calling the beginnings of food production and the formation of states "revolutions." This implied, in Redfield's view, that the transitions marked by the neolithic and urban revolutions occurred rapidly rather than slowly and incrementally over extended periods of time. Adopting the language of gradualism, he referred to them instead as "the great transformations of humanity" (Redfield 1953:24).

Redfield (1953:11–21) also criticized Childe's ideas about cooperation. They were too narrowly utilitarian in his view, since the incentives and motivations to work in primitive communities were largely social rather than economic: "They arose from tradition, from a sense of obligation coming out of one's position in a system of status relationships, especially those of kinship, and from religious considerations and moral convictions of many kinds" (Redfield 1953:11). Redfield then drew a distinction between the moral and technical orders of society. The *moral order* bound men and women together because of shared beliefs in "what is right" or "what constitutes the good life" (Redfield 1953:20–1). The *technical order*, in contrast, did rest not on such convictions. It bound individuals together through "mutual usefulness," "deliberate coercion," or from "mere utilization of the same means" (Redfield 1953:21). Redfield proceeded to point out that the moral order was dominant in primitive or folk societies, while the technical order dominated civilized life in state-based societies. In a most Durkheimian passage, he suggested that

> the great transformations of humanity are only in part reported in terms of the revolutions in technology with resulting increases in the number of people living together. There have also occurred changes in the thinking and valuing of men. . . . Like changes in the technical order, these changes in the intellectual and moral habits of men become themselves generative of far-reaching changes in the nature of human living. (Redfield 1953:24–5)

It was important, Redfield argued, to understand the relationship between the two orders. He thought that Childe placed too much emphasis on the technical order and had not paid enough attention to the moral order and its transformation during the passage from primitive or folk society to civilization.

Redfield thus resurrected Durkheim's arguments from *The Division of Labor in Society*. Religion, morality, and law were the three most important control mechanisms of society; they dictated the sentiments and ideas of a community and regulated the actions of its members. Social differentiation increased because of the concentration of people, which intensified the interactions between individuals, enhanced communication, and increased the moral density of the community. It also broke down the mechanical solidarity of the constituent parts of the community as they slowly acquired their own distinctive features and specialized functions – e.g. territory, authority, activities, and ancestors.

The primitive or precivilized folk society, in Redfield's view, was the village community in which there were no specialized priests and all of the members shared the same essential beliefs about nature and the purpose of life. However, as social differentiation increased, "the folk society . . . gave rise, within itself, to a civilization, the moral order accordingly developed an aspect of public management by an elite, or class, who carried forward a specialized speculative expansion of some of the ideas of the native tradition . . ." (Redfield 1953:72). One implication of Redfield's statement is that class formation and the emergence of class structures were natural features of human society rather than historically and socially contingent processes. Childe would not have agreed with this conclusion.

Braidwood also couched his analysis of the rise of civilization in Durkheimian terms. Civilization, in his view, appeared not as a result of the increased efficiency of the early food-producing communities, but rather because of the elaboration and "further development of social, political, moral, and religious forces that made possible the integration of the growing population into a functioning civilization" (Braidwood 1952:6). It was the new social institutions, the new forms of thought, and the appearance of a less folk-like moral order that underwrote the rise of civilization after permanent agricultural villages, temples, and market towns were established in both the hilly flanks and riverine areas of the Near East. Braidwood contrasted this with what he perceived to be Childe's emphasis on economic foundations of life. To borrow Marx's "base–superstructure" architectural metaphor for a moment, while Braidwood located the motor for change in the superstructure, Childe situated it in the mode of production upon which the entire superstructure was built. Although Braidwood may have viewed Childe as an economic determinist, he was not an economic determinist in the same way as Julian Steward, for example.

Anthropologists and archaeologists were not the only University of Chicago scholars to deploy Durkheim's views on the rise of civilization. Ancient historian Albert T. Olmstead argued that civilization was progressive and represented the highest stage of social development. For Olmstead, human agency was found in the civilized elites of the towns and not among the uncivilized peasants, nomads, and tribal peoples who inhabited the hinterlands surrounding the urban centers. He described the process in this way:

Near the end of the paleolithic period, men of our own species were inhabitants of the Near East. Cattle, sheep, goats, and pigs were domesticated; barley, wheat, and flax were cultivated. Thereafter the inhabitants of the Near East were divided, some as wandering nomads, some as settled villagers. While the nomads remained essentially the same, civilization grew in the villages. Walls were built to protect the prosperous from the less fortunate or from the nomads, and a "king" was chosen to lead the village levies in war. Specialization of function increased as life became more complex. That the soil might give freely of its products, there was worship of the powers of fertility, which became defined as true gods and goddesses . . . . (Olmstead 1948:3)

Social differentiation transformed society and undermined the mechanical solidarity of the primitive communities surrounding the towns. The agents of change were found among the civilized villagers. They were the elite, whose innovations trickled down, first to the rest of the townspeople and then more slowly to the uncivilized peasants, nomads, and tribal peoples in the countryside. The urban elite exerted their influence through the political-juridical and moral-religious institutions which they controlled. This is essentially the same argument that Redfield (1934/1962, 1954/1962) made in his theories about the "folk-urban continuum" and "the cultural role of cities." Childe, as you will recall, argued that the ruling classes were not especially innovative nor did they particularly encourage innovations among the direct producers.

From the late 1930s onward, Leslie White had been the leading exponent of cultural evolutionism in anglophone anthropology.[8] He drew variously from the social theoretical perspectives of Marx, Spencer, Durkheim, Morgan, Kautsky, and Childe. As a result, there were similarities and differences between his views and those of Childe. For example, both emphasized the importance of culture as a totality. White wrote:

Culture is an organization of objects (tools, utensils, ritual paraphernalia, materials of art, etc.), acts (patterns of behaviour, customs, rituals, institutions), ideas (beliefs, knowledge, lore), and sentiments (feelings and attitudes) that is dependent upon the use of symbols. A symbol is a thing – object, art, colour, etc. – whose meaning is determined by those who use it; articulate speech is the most important and characteristic form of symbolic behaviour. Man alone is capable of behaviour . . . . (White 1976:38)

Culture was the "extrasomatic" means that people employed in the "struggle for existence" (White 1943/1949:363). White distinguished three subsystems of culture – the technological, social, and ideational.

The technological system is composed of the material, mechanical, physical, and chemical instruments, together with the techniques of their use, by means of which man . . . is articulated with his natural habitat. Here we find the tools of production, the means of subsistence, the materials of shelter, the instruments of offense and defense. The sociological system is made up of interpersonal relations expressed in patterns of behavior, collective as well as individual. In this category we find social, kinship, economic, ethical, political, military, ecclesiastical, occupational and professional, recreational, etc. systems. The ideational system is composed of ideas, beliefs, knowledge, expressed in speech or other symbolic forms. . . .

These three categories comprise the system of culture as a whole. They are, of course, interrelated; each reacts upon the others and is affected by them in turn. But the influence of this mutual interaction is not equal in all directions. . . . The primary role is played by the technological system. (White 1943/1949:364–5)

For White, culture enveloped a "base–superstructure" model of society. The base was constituted by the technological system, which he defined largely in terms of the forces and means of production that people used to transform the raw materials of nature into objects that satisfied needs. Childe was also familiar with this model; however, in his perspective, the base was constituted by the mode of production – the forces and means of production *and* the relations of production which underpinned political and ideological superstructures. The difference led Childe (1946a:250) to characterize White's view as "technological determinist." A further distinction between them was that White saw culture as a product of "symbolling," while Childe saw it more as a consequence of labor (Fluehr-Lobban 1986).

White was aware of Marx's "metabolism" between human communities and the natural worlds they inhabited. He focused on the amounts of energy they were able to extract from nature and how they did so. As a result, the "agricultural revolution" marked a major turning point in human history. It changed the relationship between human communities and nature by extending "cultural control over the lives of plant [and animal] species" (White 1959:286). The results were larger food supplies, the increased productivity of human labor, and growing population numbers. An important question for White (1959:292) was "what will cause a people to produce more food than they need?" His answer was coercion resulting either from the conquest of one group by another, as Kautsky argued, or from social differentiation within the community itself, as Spencer and Durkheim suggested. Social differentiation, the appearance of distinct occupations, marked the subordination of kinship to other forms of organization as well as new forms of distributing goods in the community. This culminated with the appearance of civil society – "higher cultures" that were organized on the basis of property relations (White 1959:329).

White championed Spencer's view that biological and cultural systems were becoming more internally differentiated and organized. In the case of cultural systems this was achieved by putting energy to work more efficiently as their technologies improved. This constituted what White (1943/1949:368–9) called the basic law of cultural evolution: "Other factors remaining constant, *culture evolves as the amount of energy harnessed per capita per years is increased, or as the efficiency of the instrumental means of putting energy to work is increased*" (emphasis in original). White did not argue that this advance was continuous. Chronic warfare and commerce underwrote class formation, dividing "societies of the post-Agricultural Revolution era into a small, wealthy, powerful, ruling class on the one hand and a large class of peasants, serfs, or slaves on the other" (White 1943/1949:380). The social system created by the agricultural revolution created conditions that "contained" the technological process and brought innovations and cultural progress to a standstill. The reason was, that in class-stratified societies, technological innovations that increased efficiency were not perceived as advantageous by the ruling classes, whose wealth derived from exploiting the labor or goods of the direct producers (White 1943/1949:382). In this regard, of course, White's views echoed those of Childe and Marx rather than those of Spencer and Durkheim.

On several occasions in the mid-1940s, White (1945a, 1945b) drew a distinction between the processes of development that characterized societal or cultural evolution in general and the trajectories of development that characterized particular peoples or states. He wrote, for example:

> The Boas school has confused the *evolution of culture* with the *culture history of peoples*. The evolutionists worked out formulas which said that a culture trait or complex B has grown out of trait or complex A, and is developing into, or toward, trait or complex C. In other words, they describe a culture process in terms of stages of development. They say nothing about peoples or tribes. . . .
>
> But the Boas school has tried to apply these formulas that describe a process of cultural development to the culture history of a people. Naturally the attempt failed; the cultural formulas have nothing to do with [the histories of particular] peoples. (White 1945a:343, emphasis in original)

In these instances, it seems to me that White was attempting to deal with two issues originally raised by Marx: the existence of structural contradictions which are characteristic of all class-stratified societies; and historical contingency. For White, the evolutionist, contradictions were an aspect of what happened when social differentiation occurred; they were an integral aspect of a developmental process that affected the evolution of culture as a whole. Historical contingency reflected what happened in the historical development of particular cultures or societies. Marx, as you will recall, suggested that people made their own history under circumstances they themselves did not choose. In some instances, they succeeded in making history – i.e. resolving the contradictions; in others, they failed, and the contradictions persisted.

Steward's theory of cultural evolution, which he and others elaborated from 1948 onward, was adapted from one proposed in 1946 by the influential Peruvian agrarian capitalist and *aficionado* of archaeology, Rafael Larco Hoyle (1948), whose views were derived from and simplified those of Childe (Willey 1946; cf. Bennett 1948). Larco was an economic determinist who argued that the cultures of the north coast of Peru had evolved through a series of stages, and that the motor driving this development was the expansion of the agrarian productive forces, most particularly the development of irrigation systems.

Steward modified and expanded Larco's conceptual scheme and terminology to order to deal with the evolution of early civilizations in the New World; he quickly extended this framework in "Cultural Causality and Law: A Trial Formulation of the Development of Early Civilizations" to deal with the rise of early civilizations in both hemispheres (Steward 1948, 1949, 1953). Steward's evolutionary framework was adopted in its broad outlines in the mid-1950s by Gordon Willey and Philip Phillips (1958:67–71) in their influential *Method and Theory in American Archaeology*.

Steward also thought that the adoption of agriculture by foraging bands marked a major turning point in human history. The era of incipient agriculture, in his view, was long, and relatively few technological advances occurred until settled village life was established. This laid the foundations for a series of "formative era" developments: the intensification of agricultural production with the advent of community-level irrigation systems, population growth, the expansion of people into previously unoccupied areas, an increased technical division of labor as craft specialization took hold in the villages, the construction of religious edifices, and the appearance of a social division of labor toward the end of the era as a share of the total product was set aside for the ruling class. Thus, small local communities whose members were linked together by kin relations were slowly transformed into multi-community states with ruling classes and religious leaders who controlled the irrigation systems (Steward 1949, 1955a:191–3, 1955b:59–64).

This set the stage for the emergence and development of culturally distinct regional states. Irrigation works were enlarged, which increased the amount food produced; the surplus food production released a larger portion from agriculture and allowed them to pursue arts, crafts, and intellectual interests that emerged toward the end of the formative era. While the old technologies were elaborated and fine art was produced by highly specialized, full-time artisans, no new technologies were developed in these increasingly competitive theocratic states with their priest and warrior classes. Monumental architecture dedicated to the upper classes, increased trade, and the beginnings of persistent warfare were the hallmarks of this era (Steward 1955a:195–6). In 1950, Steward wrote:

> The rise and decline of the kingdoms in the ancient centers of civilization in Egypt, Mesopotamia, India, China, Meso-America, and the Andes is often described as the rise and fall of civilization. It is true that the particular kinds of societies found in these centers did not survive, but most of the basic cultural achievements, the essential features of civilization, were passed on to other nations. In each of these centers both culture and society changed rather considerably during the early periods, and everywhere the developmental processes were about the same. At first there were small communities of incipient farmers. Later the communities cooperated in the construction of irrigation

works and the populations became larger and more settled. Villages amalgamated into states under theocratic rulers. . . . Finally culture ceased to develop, and the states of each area entered into competition with one another. (Steward 1950:103)

. . . an era of cyclical conquest followed. The conquests conformed to a fairly stable pattern. . . . Each state began to compete with others for tribute and advantages. One or another state succeeded in dominating the others, that is, in building an empire, but such empires ran their course and collapsed after some . . . years only to be succeeded by another empire not very different from the first. (Steward 1950:103–4)

For the historian this era of cyclical conquests is filled with great men, wars and battle strategy, shifting power centers, and other social events. For the culture historian the changes are much less significant than those of the previous eras when the basic civilizations developed or, in the Near East, those of the subsequent Iron Age when the cultural patterns changed again and the centers of civilization shifted to new areas. (Steward 1950:104)

The industrial revolution brought profound cultural change to Western Europe and caused competition for colonies and for areas of exploitation. Japan entered the competition as soon as she acquired the general pattern. The realignments of power caused by Germany's losses in the first world war and by Italy's and Japan's in the second are of a social order. What new cultural patterns will result from these remains to be seen. (Steward 1950:104–5)

During the 1950s, the cultural evolutionists typically held that culture and nature were conceptually distinct spheres. They saw people exploiting or using natural resources in order to achieve certain ends; the appropriation of nature occurred in the context of various institutional arrangements that structured the organization of work and the use of tools. In Steward's (1955a:37) words, they were concerned with those cultural features that were "most closely involved in the utilization of the environment in culturally prescribed ways." That is, they focused on the cultural core – that constellation of social, political, and religious patterns most closely related to subsistence activities and economic arrangements, rather than on those secondary features less closely tied to the core that gave cultures with similar cores the outward appearance of distinctiveness. They argued that economic arrangements resulting from the relations of production had potent shaping effects on other aspects of social organization.

The cultural evolutionists were less concerned with adaptation or with the interactions between a society and its natural environments than they were with technology and productive arrangements, both of which were, in their view, historically determined (Steward 1955a:39–42). From their perspective, change and development occurred when new technologies and institutional forms appeared as a result of either independent invention or borrowing.

The cultural evolutionists were functionalists who accepted the distinction between synchronic and diachronic forms of analysis. Their goal was diachronic: to study how cultures changed. Their perspective was regional and comparative rather than particular or universal. To accomplish their goal, they separated the study of change or growth from the study of history. In Steward's words, they were concerned with *evolutionary* rather than *historical* changes. The former were cumulative, reflecting the natural growth or unfolding of the potential inherent in the culture type itself, the gradual and continuous accumulation of small incremental shifts. When the evolutionary potential of the type was finally exhausted, a new, qualitatively different cultural type with its own distinctive economic, political, and social arrangements emerged. Historical changes, on the other hand, were conceptualized in terms of unique events, accidents that impinged on the normal growth and development of culture.

In the 1950s, neither Steward nor any of the U.S. archaeologists advocating cultural evolutionism discussed exploitation, class struggle, or the oppressive character of class and state formation in their analyses. To the extent that these conditions were mentioned at all, they were portrayed as natural or necessary outcomes of the rise of civilization itself.

Childe's work was also appreciated by archaeologists and students in Latin America in the years immediately following the war. For example, Childe had corresponded regularly since 1928 with Pedro Bosch Gimpera, a Spanish Civil War exile who resided in Mexico after 1938. One student, José Luis Lorenzo, travelled to London in the late 1940s to study with Childe at the Institute of Archaeology before returning to Mexico in the early 1950s. Pedro Armillas, another Spanish Civil War exile in Mexico, discussed Childe's work in the courses he taught at the university. Julio C. Olivé Negrete's MA thesis, which dealt with Childe's contributions to archaeological theory, was published in 1958 (Olivé Negrete 1987).

Central European refugees and veterans of the Spanish Civil War residing in Mexico – Armillas, Angel Palerm, and Pedro Carrasco – brought with them textured appreciations of Marx's social theory. They also recognized the subtleties and nuances of Childe's arguments. In the late 1940s and early 1950s, they collaborated with other refugees and U.S. scholars – most notably Eric Wolf and René Millon – who brought their own understandings of Marxism and Childe to these international collaborations.

Examinations of their writings reveal the depth of the influences from Childe and Marx. For example, in describing cultural development in Mesoamerica, Armillas (1948, 1951) spoke about the development of the productive forces, asked how the labor required to build the great pyramids was organized, and alluded to the extortion by the ruling classes preceding the destruction of Teotihuacán. Millon's (1954:178) early work at Teotihuacán was concerned with whether the valley was "large enough in and of itself to make possible the development of a class society based on production by means of irrigation." Wolf's (1959) *Sons of the Shaking Earth* was an extended analysis of the dialectics of class and state formation in Mesoamerica, first of the autochthonous processes and then of the processes that came into play as the region's peoples became enmeshed in colonial and capitalist social relations after 1500.

The publications of Childe as well as those of his critics and commentators were read widely and struck resonant chords for a number of archaeologists from the 1950s onward. We will examine in the next chapter how archaeologists drew on this legacy as well as the one established by Leslie A. White.

–3–

Disregard, Engagement, and Dialogue, 1945–1980

Archaeologists dealt with Childe's Marxist analyses in various ways after the Second World War. This was the time when they began to incorporate social evolutionary thought into their writings – cautiously at first and then more explicitly from about 1960 onward.[1] They drew inspiration from various sources: Durkheim and Spencer, classical political economists such as Adam Smith or Thomas Malthus, contemporary anthropologists – notably Julian Steward and Leslie White – and even Childe himself. The archaeologists who treated Childe as a sociocultural evolutionist either avoided confronting his Marxist legacy altogether or dealt with it only indirectly. Even though the archaeological discourse was relatively insulated from explicit encounters with Marxist social thought, however, the barrier separating them was never complete in the postwar years. By the late 1960s, the porosity of that barrier and even its erosion were already apparent. Furthermore, the cross-fertilization that occurred was no longer mediated by references to Darwin.

How did archaeologists deal explicitly and implicitly with the legacies left by Marx and Childe in the postwar years? What aspects of those legacies did they find useful? How did they articulate those features with commentaries on and critiques of Marx's and Childe's work? How were other theoretical perspectives incorporated into the discourse on societal and cultural evolution? Let us examine these questions in terms of the diverse theoretical perspectives that emerged after 1945 and the debates they provoked.

Cautious Disregard: Eras of Sociocultural Evolution

The idea of sociocultural evolution intrigued archaeologists in the United States during the 1950s. Contemporary writers – V. Gordon Childe, Robert Redfield, Julian Steward, and Leslie White – informed their views in different ways. A decade or so later, new editions of classic works by Herbert Spencer and Lewis Henry Morgan would add fresh dimensions to our understandings of the processes involved. The renewed interest in societal evolution in the postwar years was merely one manifestation of a wider concern with economic growth and the conditions that underwrote development and modernization (Patterson 1999a: 113–21).

Through the late 1950s, a number of U.S. archaeologists took as their primary task the delineation of sequences of units of sociocultural development that they variously called eras, levels, or stages. (e.g. Beardsley *et al.* 1957; Braidwood 1960a, 1960b; Collier 1955; Krieger 1953a, 1953b; Strong 1948; Willey and Phillips 1958). Childe's influence was immediately apparent in the sense that all of the sequences they proposed distinguished with varying labels between a pre-agricultural "era of food-collecting," on the one hand, and a succeeding "era of incipient farming or food-production," on the other. All of them also recognized something akin to the Urban Revolution, which they equated with the rise of civilization – the appearance of social stratification, the state, and large, densely populated settlements. They were less comfortable, it seems, with Childe's use of the term "revolution" and its implications in Cold War America; they preferred instead, for example, to view the Neolithic Revolution as Redfield (1953:5) did: a transformation that took place gradually and cumulatively over an extended period of time and that began at different times in different parts of the world (Haury 1962:117; cf. Greene 1999).

While the archaeologists discerned varying numbers of developmental stages (four to six), some of which were further subdivided, the defining characteristics of the stages were remarkably similar from one proposed sequence to the next. Alex Krieger's was simultaneously one of the simpler and more elegant. It built on the succession of developmental eras outlined by Julian Steward (1949) a few years earlier, which was discussed in the preceding chapter. In Krieger's (1953b:247–8) view, a stage was "characterized by a dominating pattern of economic existence." He distinguished four stages. The earliest was the Paleo-Indian stage, which included peoples who lived in the Americas toward the end of the Wisconsin Ice Age and derived their livelihood in part by hunting large mammals, many of which are now extinct. This was followed by a food-gathering, or "archaic," stage in which peoples added the harvesting and preparation of plant foods, fishing, and shellfish gathering to their subsistence activities. The third food-producing stage involved domestication and the appearance of agricultural practices; it was most developed in the Andes and Mesoamerica and appeared later in less developed forms north of Mesoamerica. Krieger (1953b:249) felt that population pressure may have underwritten the invention of agriculture by "forcing man to increase the yield of nature to survive." The fourth stage, "urban life," was marked by "very large settlements, complex stratified society, a high degree of division of labor, and extensive trade" (Krieger 1953b:250). This level of development was attained only in the Andes and Mesoamerica, a matter that Krieger believed warranted further consideration.

Gordon Willey (1953:378) noted that archaeologists who dealt with historical-developmental parallels in the Central Andean and Middle American areas focused on a slightly different set of issues. They were concerned primarily with the rise and growth of sedentary agricultural communities during a "formative" stage. This was followed by a "classic" or "florescent" stage marked by technical and aesthetic innovations and the appearance of diverse regional specializations that expressed themselves in well-defined styles. The third major stage, he wrote, was more difficult to define, since its "common-denominator qualities are more difficult to abstract" and the criteria shift.

> Whereas the criteria for the first two [stages] recapitulate technological and artistic trends, the third stage is not essentially characterized by these factors. In some regions there is an apparent aesthetic decline, although this is a subjective impression difficult to measure. Certainly, there is no technical falling-off, and in some places, such as the Central Andes, there are continued technological advances. The single unifying characteristic is, rather, the evidence for widespread, social, political and religious disturbances. . . . Terms such as "Expansionist" or "Militarist" have, accordingly, been applied to this third stage. (Willey 1953:378)

Willey was certainly correct that the political-economic criteria he used to define the stages shifted. He viewed the formative stage primarily in terms of the productive forces of the economic base. He understood the classic or florescent stage mainly in terms of technological innovations that affected the forces and means of production and of a new division of labor that involved both occupational specialization and social differentiation (class and state formation). The rise and fall of states was clearly the defining characteristic of the militarist or expansionist stage. What was not clear in Willey's writings at this time, however, were the historical motors that drove development from one stage to the next.

Willey and Philip Phillips addressed the issue of historical causality in their *Method and Theory in American Archaeology*, which appeared in 1958. They noted that the units employed by archaeologists to construct time-space frameworks worked best for describing cultural change and development on local or regional scales; however, they believed they lacked an adequate foundation for "a synthesis New World archaeology as a whole" (Willey and Phillips 1958:61). They argued:

> For larger syntheses, another type of formulation must be resorted to, one that is free from strict limitations of time and space yet has a general historical validity in the widest sense. The only possible kind of scheme that meets these requirements, so far as we can see, is a series of cultural stages in what we have chosen to call a historical-developmental sequence. These stages will of course be founded on common participation in important historically derived traditions, but their formulation is a procedure distinct from the

methods of systematic historical (spatial-temporal) integration. . . . The historical-developmental sequence remains, however, as we shall attempt to demonstrate, essentially on the descriptive level of organization. (Willey and Phillips 1958:64)

In sum, Willey and Phillips asserted that the succession of developmental stages they would propose later in their book was classificatory and descriptive. They further contended that the sequence of stages they defined, unlike the one proposed by Steward, did not constitute an evolutionary scheme, because they had deliberately sought to eliminate historical causality from their definitions. They suggested that Steward's scheme was explanatory, whereas they were "classifying cultures in a sort of theoretical twilight" (Willey and Phillips 1958:71).

Despite indicating that they would eschew discussion of historical causality, Willey and Phillips quickly returned to the subject.[2] They saw

two broad divisions of a fundamental technological and economic nature: hunter-gatherers and agriculturalists. . . . As in the Old World, these two general patterns of life have a sequence relationship with the hunter-gatherers preceding the farmers. And, as is also the case in the Old World, there is a considerable chronological overlap, with hunting-gathering cultures persisting in some regions into periods of contemporaneity with farming cultures. It should be recognized that no other differentiation between stages . . . has the same profundity and significance as this one. In this we are in agreement with Robert Braidwood [1952] and Robert Redfield [1953], who see the Old World "urban revolution," or "dawn of civilization," as something that was made possible by the establishment of agriculture several millenniums earlier, but not as marking a technological and economic shift as profound as the one from food-gathering to food production. . . . The criteria for dividing pre-agricultural stages are essentially technological. . . . The criteria for dividing stages above the threshold of agriculture take reference in much more complex data. They pertain to social and political organization, religion, aesthetics – to the whole of what Redfield has termed the "moral order." (Willey and Phillips 1958:72–3)

Three features stood out in Willey and Phillips's discussion of historical causality. First, they pointed out that pre-Columbian America was a mosaic of different cultural types and that this diversity was a manifestation of uneven cultural, sociopolitical, and economic development. Second, they rooted the rise of food-producing villages in technological and economic changes that were enveloped by and in new organizational forms and ways of understanding the world. Third, their emphasis on the importance of the "moral order" in socially differentiated, post-agricultural societies contrasted with Redfield's suggestion that the rise of civilization was underwritten by the steadily increasing importance of the "technical order" and the simultaneous crystallization of a less folk-like moral order. Let us consider each point in more detail.

Willey and Phillips (1958:74–6, 144) dealt with the issue of uneven development in terms of two different kinds of "cultural lag": temporal and marginal. In their view, temporal lag was a consequence of persistence without change. Marginal lag, however, was either a consequence of one-sided or incomplete change from the standpoint of the developmental criteria employed, or a result of developmental regression. Three examples they cited included (1) food-producing cultures that moved into unfavorable areas and regressed to pre-agricultural modes of production; (2) advanced hunting-fishing-gathering cultures, like those on the Northwest Coast, that presumably lacked the potential for demographic increase that agricultural production normally provided; and (3) relatively undifferentiated formative cultures that were suddenly enmeshed in the tributary relations of states and became more socially differentiated as a consequence of their incorporation into a wider configuration.[3]

Willey and Phillips quickly added that the succession of developmental stages they described did not constitute a natural system. In their words,

> There is nothing inevitable about five stages; there might as well be four, or even eight. Nor is there any law, evolutionary or otherwise, that says that all New World cultures must pass through these stages one after the other in their proper order. . . . As we have previously stated, our basic theoretical position is that culture is not an independent order of phenomena (the "cultural superorganic"), and from this it follows that there are no universal, irreversible processes of cultural development. . . . In a general sense the sequence is historical as well as developmental, but the individual stages can have no correspondent historical unity or reality. (Willey and Phillips 1958:77)

Two years later, Marshall Sahlins (1960) addressed, and perhaps clarified, Willey and Phillips's distinction between historical and developmental interpretations, even though the words he used were different. Sahlins distinguished specific from general evolution. Specific evolution, in his terms, was marked by an historical sequence of forms in a particular cultural tradition, one form giving rise to the next. General cultural evolution, in contrast, was marked by the successive emergence of new levels of development – such as the rise of feudalism or capitalism – in cultural traditions that were often unconnected or only partially linked.

The tension between culture-historical and developmental interpretations was a frequent characteristic of Willey's work from the mid-1950s onward.[4] It is most evident in the synthetic concepts – such as "Nuclear America" or the "Pacific Littoral Tradition" – that he elaborated to capture hints about the developmental relations and similarities of diverse arrays of archaeological assemblages (Willey 1955, 1960a, 1960b, 1971:488). In a sketch of the main outlines of cultural development in the Americas, he wrote:

In Nuclear America the town and eventually the city had its beginnings in the settled farming village. A centralizing factor in this development was undoubtedly the temple. . . .

Although the cities and civilizations which developed in Middle America and Peru in the 1st millennium A.D. were unique in their own right, it is obvious that they also drew upon a common heritage or culture which had begun to be shared by all of Nuclear America at the level of village-farming life. (Willey 1960a:83–4)

Willey concluded the article with a brief mention of the mound-building Middle Woodland cultures of eastern North America with essentially archaic subsistence economies, and suggested that the correlation between village life and agricultural production might not exist in every instance. He implied that the interplay of general features and local factors underwrote the particularities of such cases.

Willey subsequently expanded the argument that he and Phillips had made earlier which linked the appearance of food production with technological and economic changes wrapped in new organizational forms and systems of knowledge. By the mid-1960s, he was also beginning to portray the origins of agricultural food production in terms of "the interaction of climate, natural resources, man, and his culture" (Willey 1964:386).[5] He further cautioned that this statement should not be interpreted reductively as a claim for either environmental or climatic causation. Like Steward, Childe, and Marx who wrote before him, Willey distinguished the realm of human beings from the natural world and focused attention on the metabolism that linked one to the other. In a phrase, the human realm existed in and was partly constitutive of a larger totality he viewed as the natural world. This natural realm was subject to and shaped by different forces from the one constituted by diverse human communities studied by archaeologists. Implicit, I believe, was the idea that the connections between them were dialectical; however, Willey neither reflected upon the nature of the relationship nor elaborated this view.

Willey and Phillips emphasized the increasing importance of the moral order in socially differentiated, post-formative agricultural societies. This contrasted with Redfield's view that the rise of civilization – i.e. the formation of class-stratified, state-based societies – was underwritten by the growing importance of the technical order, the erosion of the traditional moral order, and the emergence of a new, less folk-like moral order more attuned to the new circumstances. For Willey and Phillips (1958:182), the classic stage marked "the threshold of civilization in so far as 'civilization' is defined as city life." It was also characterized by

such qualities as excellence in the great arts, climax in religious architecture, and general florescence in material culture. . . . The attributes of civilization in the commonly accepted sense of the term – outstanding public architecture, great art styles, class differentiations, codified intellectual systems (preserved in writing), and some knowledge of science, formal hierarchies of deities, widespread trade in raw materials and luxury goods – are there. . . . In the Classic cultures of both Middle America and Peru there is evidence of strong social class distinctions and of heavy pomp and dignity surrounding the ruling classes. . . . [I]t is also noteworthy that a strong regional ethnocentrism is reflected in sharply differing art and architectural styles. (Willey and Phillips 1958:182–4)

This portrait of the societal type characteristic of the Classic era contrasted with their description of the Postclassic stage several pages later.

The Postclassic stage in Middle America and Peru is marked by the breakdown of the old regional styles of the Classic stage, by a continuing or increased emphasis upon urban living, and inferentially, by tendencies toward militarism and secularism. . . . In the Postclassic we see the wide, interregional transferences of total art and architectural styles. The mechanisms behind these transferences are debatable, but it is reasonable to interpret many of them as actual movements of large groups of people accompanied by military force. These trends toward militarism and large-scale warfare are reflected . . . [by] increases in fortifications and fortified communities. . . . The implications for a gradually increasing secularization of culture and society in the Postclassic are less direct. We would, however, argue that a decrease in the number, size, and elaboration of pyramid mounds and other kinds of religious structures is one clue to the waning of religious authority. Another is the aesthetic decline from Classic standards which characterizes much of Postclassic art . . . [accompanied by] standardization and mass production of objects. (Willey and Phillips 1958:193–4)

In brief, the native city of the New World had large population aggregates either within residence or within reach, was the seat of politico-religious power, served as an economic center, and maintained complex and diverse divisions of labor among its citizens. (Willey and Phillips 1958:194)

Willey and Phillips, and subsequently Willey himself, typically characterized civilization in terms of the florescence of art styles and religion. These elaborations occurred in cities, broadly defined. The urban communities were marked by social class structures and by occupational specialization. They were also seats of power, religious at first and then increasingly secular or military. Culture and power emanated from the cities and flowed into the countryside. The cultural dynamics implied by this perspective were identical to those found in Redfield's "folk–urban continuum" model. While acknowledging that class and state formation were integral features of classic era society, Willey and Phillips did not discuss the significance of the two processes and their connections with cultural elaboration.

Unlike Childe, Willey and Phillips did not view the rise of civilization and urban life as a political-economic process marked by contradictions. They also placed less emphasis on the "culture core" than Steward did. In their view, the motor of change shifted from one stage to the next in the development of human society. The appearance of new economic relations and technological innovations during the Formative Era were relatively unencumbered by cultural and religious considerations at least at the onset of the stage. Cultural and religious elaborations were the motor of change during the Classic stage and occurred against a backdrop created by social differentiation and the rise of the theocratic state. For reasons unspecified, this motor waned at the end of the Classic, and a new political-economic motor emerged during the Postclassic stage as power shifted away from the religious cults to civil or military authorities and as standardized, mass-produced goods replaced the aesthetically pleasing items produced by skilled artisans.

Willey and Phillips shared the positive valuation placed on the role of the state by Durkheim, Redfield, and Steward. This view derived from various strands of liberal social theory. In this perspective, the state secured and maintained the conditions required for life, liberty, and the pursuit of happiness or property. It also provided the conditions necessary for creativity. Childe, as you will recall, argued against this view. He suggested that the most creative period in human history preceded the rise of civilization and that states, in fact, suppressed creativity because of the oppressive and exploitative social relations they sustained.

While Willey and Phillips and Krieger sought to apply their developmental schemes on a continent- or hemisphere-wide basis, other archaeologists had more limited aims. Donald Collier (1955) and William Strong (1948) devised frameworks that reflected the processes of change and stages of development that occurred in the Virú Valley on the north coast of Peru. The schemes they proposed afforded a window from which to view cultural evolution on the coast of northern Peru and then across the entire central Andean region. Since they defined the developmental stages they used on the basis of archaeological evidence from Virú and its environs, there was a close correspondence, to use Willey and Phillips's distinction, between their historical and developmental interpretations at least on the north coast. However, efforts to apply the developmental stages further afield – e.g. the south coast of Peru – confronted the fact that the sequences of change and development in these regions differed from those in Virú. Consequently, the cultural characteristics used to define particular developmental stages did not always cohere and constitute units of cultural similarity that resembled those on the north coast. The debate that ensued revolved around cities and when they developed in particular regions.

John Rowe (1962, 1963) challenged the claims of Collier, Strong, and other Peruvianists who employed developmental schemes based on the Virú Valley data. He claimed that cities – which he defined narrowly as a settlement type rather than more broadly as process like Childe's urban revolution or the rise of states – appeared much earlier in other parts of the central Andes than they did on the north coast. This meant that the sequences and timing of particular developments in these regions – such as the appearance of cities – diverged from those on the north coast. Thus, in his view, historical interpretations of what actually transpired in those regions were at odds with interpretations of the more general processes that affected everyday life across the entire Andean region. While Rowe's definition of the rise of cities differed significantly from what Collier, Strong, Willey, and others actually meant by the phrase, his point about the need to demonstrate more clearly the connection between specific and general evolution was well taken. It was important to demonstrate the linkages and to show clearly how developments in particular regions were manifestation of wider processes. Robert Adams (1960c), who was more sympathetic to evolutionist arguments, made the same point.

Other writers from the late 1950s onward focused less on the stages of development than on the motors of change themselves. Richard S. MacNeish was one of the more prominent. MacNeish (1958:146–9, 201) applied the ideas of Steward, White, and Childe in his study of cultural evolution in the Sierra de Tamaulipas in northern Mexico. He argued that the motor driving cultural evolution in the region was a marked increase in agricultural production that occupied during the Laguna Phase. Agriculture was the least labor-intensive and most productive subsistence activity. It provided about 75 percent of the calories consumed by the members of these communities. It afforded them the time and surplus product that underwrote their elaboration of other dimensions of their culture. It also accounted for permanent settlements, population growth, and social differentiation.

In the wake of the intensive archaeological-botanical project in the Tehuacán Valley, MacNeish couched his conclusions about the origins of agriculture and its consequences in a new series of theoretically laden statements. Gone was the idea of the "neolithic village" postulated by Childe, Braidwood, and Steward, among others. In MacNeish's view, the early farmers no longer necessarily lived in permanent villages, and the traits reputedly associated with the formation of these settlements did not necessarily appear at the same time in the archaeological record. Agriculture was adopted slowly instead of rapidly transforming the subsistence economy, and, initially, horticulture was not even the most productive subsistence activity of the incipient farmers. In his words, he began to "think more in terms of Neolithic 'evolution' than 'revolution'" (MacNeish 1964:37).

He further argued that there were diverse trajectories of social development in regions with different environmental settings or microenvironments. Consequently, at any given moment, Mesoamerica was a patchwork or mosaic of local cultures with different economic bases. Regarding the formation of these diverse, unevenly developed local cultures, he wrote:

> One gets the impression that the development of civilization and more effective food production in Mesoamerica is due not to a single evolution of developmental stages of

culture and subsistence, but that a series of concomitant developments of rather different ecological zones are interacting with and interstimulating one another in such a manner as to bring about cultural development and increasingly effective food production. . . . Or to put it another way, was not the development of effective food production and the concomitant cultural growth in Mesoamerica in no small part owing to the fact that there were contiguous environments or ecological zones that were exploited agriculturally in different ways, and evolved through different cultural stages, and their geographic closeness allowed the varied subsistence developments to interact and interstimulate one another? (MacNeish 1967:309)

Thus, interaction and exchange were now seen as the glue that bound together these unevenly developed cultures and gave the mosaic as a whole its momentum. Simply put, MacNeish had shifted his views regarding the motor of social evolution from production to exchange relations. Not only was exchange the cement that bound together communities from different regions, it was also the engine that drove slow but steady cultural development.

Archaeologists were not the only anthropologists stimulated in the postwar years by Marxist, Childean, and evolutionist accounts of the rise of civilization and the formation of states. Sociocultural anthropologists – notably Robert Carneiro (1967b, 1970), Morton Fried (1960, 1967, 1975), Irving Goldman (1955, 1960, 1970), Marshall Sahlins (1961, 1963), and Elman Service (1962/1971, 1975) – added to the discussions of the era fresh, diverse perspectives as well as alternative understandings of the developmental stages and processes involved. The impact of their work will be considered in more detail in subsequent sections of this and later chapters.

Disengagement: The New Archaeology, Adaptation, and Exchange

Criticisms of the empiricist perspective that dominated archaeology appeared in the 1960s. The new, processual archaeology – launched by Lewis Binford, Kent Flannery, and others in the United States and by Colin Renfrew in Britain – built more explicitly on Spencer and Durkheim in ways that were different from the evolutionists and empiricists of the preceding decade. Joseph Caldwell (1959) introduced the term "new archaeology" to describe trends he saw transforming American archaeology; these included growing interests in ecology, settlement patterns, and neo-evolutionary views that not all aspects of culture had equally important roles in bringing about change. The new archaeology as it developed in the United States consisted of several autonomous strands of thought that ultimately are theoretically incompatible (Gándara 1980, 1981).

In two early polemics, Binford (1962/1972, 1965/1972) set out a theory of culture that contrasted with those employed both by traditional archaeologists who conflated artifact typologies and culture and by the cultural evolutionists. Binford (1962/1972:22, 24–5) viewed culture as an integrated system and "the extra-somatic means of adaptation for the human organism." It "functions to adapt the human organism, conceived generically, to its total environment both physical and social." The technological subsystem interfaces with the physical environment; the social subsystem "functions as the extrasomatic means of articulating individuals with one another into cohesive groups capable of efficiently maintaining themselves and of manipulating technology." The ideological subsystem is composed of "items which signify and symbolize the ideological rationalizations for the social system and further provide the symbolic milieu in which individuals are enculturated, a necessity if they are to take their place as functional participants in the social system."

Since culture was internally differentiated, individuals did not share culture as much as they participated in it differentially, presumably because of age, gender, experiential, or class differences. The complexity of a cultural system, in Binford's view, was a function of its internal structural differentiation and the specificity of its various subsystems. Following White and Durkheim, he argued that "the degree to which all the participants share common ideational preferences should vary inversely with the complexity of the system as a whole" (Binford (1965/1972:199). That is, the members of simple, internally undifferentiated societies have shared beliefs and understandings, while those of complex, structurally differentiated societies occupy diverse social positions and have different beliefs and under-standings of their social milieu as a result of that diversity.

Cultural changes, in Binford's (1968/1972:436ff.) view, were initiated in communities by external factors – such as alterations in the natural environment or the relations with neighboring groups – that disturbed the existing adaptation. Such disturbances had the potential, at least, to unleash new behaviors and innovations that would ultimately return the cultural system to some equilibrium condition with regard to the field in which it operated. They could affect the technological, social, and ideological subsystems of the culture, resulting in their extinction, reorganiza-tion, or the emergence of more complex forms because of increased structural differentiation (Binford 1972:107). In other words, Binford's conceptualization of change differed significantly from that of Steward, for example, who viewed the economic core as determinant, both in structuring other aspects of the culture and as the motor of technological change and progress. Binford's theory of change was, in reality, a theory of how social order or stability was disturbed and disrupted.

Binford then turned his attention to questions of testing methodologies and explanation in the late 1960s, and these – along with a concern for understanding the formation of archaeological deposits, explaining the genesis of the archaeo-logical record, and decoding its significance – became central concerns from the mid-1970s onwards (Binford 1977, 1978). He called this "middle-range theory."

Over the years, he and others adopted a theory of science and explanation that was ultimately rooted in the tenets of logical positivism (Kelley and Hanen 1988; Watson, LeBlanc, and Redman 1971, 1984; Wylie 1982). This meant that the methodological procedures of the natural sciences could be adapted to archaeology, and that explanation should be causal, subsuming individual cases under more general laws. This implied that the phenomena of human subjectivity, volition, and will provided no barriers to treating human social conduct as an object, and that explanations which attempted to account for facts in terms of intentions, goals, or purposes should be either rejected or transformed into causal explanations.

The form of explanation demanded by this underlying theory of science had several implications. First, the explanations were transhistorical in the sense that they lacked reference to particular historical episodes; consequently, the processual archaeologists retained both the distinction that the cultural evolutionists had made between the study of cultural process and the study of history; they further believed that only the study of process constituted a genuine scientific activity. Second, when they eliminated intentionality from explanations, people were transformed from active agents making their own history under circumstances not necessarily of their own choosing into passive consumers or recipients responding to processes and events beyond their control; if one word was characteristic of processual archaeology, it was *adaptation* – the activities of a society changed in response to and to keep in step with changes in the natural and cultural environments. Third, when intentionality was not completely removed from their explanations, reference was made to underlying forms of motivation or to qualities presumed to be inherent in the object of inquiry – such as the natural tendency of societies to move toward equilibrium or to exhibit optimizing or maximizing behavior.

While Binford turned his attention to middle-range theory, Flannery and Renfrew addressed the issues of social and cultural change. Flannery was concerned with the development of early food production in Mesopotamia and Mesoamerica, with the ways in which inter-regional exchange was subsequently used to sustain structurally differentiated societies in Mesoamerica, and finally with evolution of civilization itself. He saw the beginnings of food production in both areas as protracted processes that unfolded over several millennia and that were preceded by "a flexible, 'broad spectrum' collecting pattern, keyed to the seasonal aspects of the wild resources of each environmental zone, with perhaps a certain amount of seasonal migration from zone to zone" (Flannery 1965:1250). The transition to food-producing economies in Mesopotamia was underwritten by mutations and changes in gene frequencies of particular species – wild wheat, barley, and sheep. It occurred after these and other species, removed from their natural habitats and shielded from natural selection by communities of broad-spectrum foragers, underwent genetic changes in their new environments. The "favorable changes were emphasized by the practices of the early planter and herder" (Flannery 1965:1255). Following Binford's (1968/1972) lead, Flannery (1969) subsequently suggested that population growth in optimal environments ultimately forced some foraging populations to move into marginal areas. They adapted to the new conditions by bringing familiar resources that had flourished in the optimal environments but were scarce or absent in their new homelands. By doing so, they unwittingly subjected the old resources to different selective pressures, and ultimately recognized the advantages of the new forms.

Flannery used the idiom of systems theory to describe the shift from a food-collecting economy in Mesoamerica to one based on the incipient cultivation of wild grasses.[6] He characterized the transition "as one of gradual change in a series of [food] procurement systems, regulated by two mechanisms called seasonality and scheduling. I would argue that none of the changes which took place during this period arose *de novo*, but [they] were the result of expansion and contraction of previously-existing systems" (Flannery 1968a:68). The motors underwriting the changes in the food procurement systems – and hence shift from a food-collecting to a sedentary agricultural economy – were

> a series of genetic changes which took place in one or two species of Mesoamerican plants which were of use to man. The exploitation of these plants had been a relatively minor procurement system . . ., but positive feedback following these initial genetic changes causes one minor system to grow all out of proportion to the others, and eventually to change the whole ecosystem. (Flannery 1968a:79)

Other food procurement activities – deer-hunting, for instance – were re-scheduled, and new activities – such as planting and harvesting and the procurement of wild waterfowl – were initiated as the cultural systems adapted to these new circumstances.

Flannery (1972:399) then explored the cultural evolution of civilizations – that is, states or those "human societies [that] have evolved to levels of great sociopolitical complexity." After describing antecedent forms of sociopolitical organization – bands, tribes, and chiefdoms – he portrayed the state as a form of sociopolitical organization with a centralized government, a professional ruling class, social stratification, occupational specialization, monopoly of force, rule by law, and economic structures controlled by elites and characterized by reciprocal, redistributive, and market exchanges. In Flannery's (1972:408, 414) view, states appeared because of the complex relationships and feedback between a series of variables or prime movers. State formation was a long, slow process that involved increased internal differentiation and specialization of the cultural subsystems and denser linkages between the various subsystems and the highest-order controls of the society. He believed that "the mechanisms and processes [by which states emerge] are universal, not merely in human society but in the evolution of complex systems in general. The *socio-environmental stresses* [which select for those mechanisms] are not necessarily universal, but may be specific to particular regions and societies" (Flannery 1972:409, emphasis in original).

Thus, when socio-environmental stresses impinge on the adaptive milieu, evolutionary mechanisms such as promotion and linearization are unleashed. In promotion, an institution assumes a new position at a higher level in the control hierarchy. In linearization, lower-order controls are bypassed by higher-order controls; however, promotion and linearization can promote stress and instability and trigger social pathologies – usurpation, meddling, and hypercoherence – that resemble Durkheim's (1893/1964:353–74) description of anomie. The evolution of civilizational systems was a protracted, continuous process of internal responses and adaptations, first to external socio-environmental stresses and then to the social pathologies that developed. The effect was that the components of the cultural system were the optimal or best-compromise solutions at any given moment to the problems produced by the natural and social environments. Thus, the culture/ nature opposition of the cultural evolutionists was eliminated, and the productive forces and relations typical of a particular type of society were stripped of their historically constituted specificity.

In the early 1970s, Renfrew (1972/1984:275–6) also adopted systems thinking and the idea that culture was composed of a number of interrelated subsystems – subsistence, technological, social, cognitive, exchange, and demographic – to explore trajectories of culture and social change. He argued that growth occurred only as long as there was change in one subsystem which induced further change in other subsystems. Building on Walter Rostow's (1960) notion that certain conditions were required for take-off and sustained growth, he suggested that, for civilization to emerge, change had to occur in at least two of the subsystems he identified.

One of the problems of the systems theory approaches used by Flannery and Renfrew was that the issue of political power was not adequately conceptualized. When they mentioned it at all, they treated power as "the ability to exercise control or command over others" (Renfrew 1984:24). This perspective missed several essential points. First, by conflating power with authority, they do not deal adequately with coercion, force, or resistance to the actions of the states. Second, they do not deal adequately with the questions: Where did power come from? Was it the product of other social transformations, such as in technology, or the result of changes of a different order, like population growth or environmental change? Was it a universal feature of human society, as some postmodernists claim, or did this historical phenomenon arise with the formation of social classes and the state and represent the organized use of force by the members of one class to subordinate those of another?

At the same time as they were promoting systems approaches as a means for understanding the evolution of civilization, Flannery and Renfrew also published important articles on the role of inter-regional exchange relations. Flannery (1968b) drew on the ethnographic literature to construct a model that would clarify the linkage between the Olmec and the Valley of Oaxaca. He wrote that

> a special relationship exists between consumers of exotic raw materials and their suppliers, especially when the suppliers belong to a society which is only slightly less stratified than that of the consumers. First, it seems that the upper echelon of each society often provides the entrepreneurs who facilitate the exchange. Second, the exchange is not "trade" in the sense that we use the term, but rather is set up through mechanisms of ritual visits, exchange of wives, "adoption" of members of one group by the other, and so on. Third, there may be an attempt to adopt the behavior, status trappings, religion, symbolism, or even language of the more sophisticated group – in short, to absorb some of their charisma. (Flannery 1968b:105)

One inference Flannery (1968b:106–8) drew from the model was that highland societies that were already stratified or were on the verge of being internally stratified were more receptive to Olmec status paraphernalia and could fit more easily into existing structures than their less stratified neighbors. In the process, the highland elites began to emulate the behavior and symbolism of the coastal elite.

Whereas Flannery viewed inter-regional exchange as a means of maintaining status hierarchies, Renfrew emphasized its role as a potential motor of change. He argued that "systems of trade or exchange form only one component in the aggregate of systems which constitute a culture" (Renfrew 1969:153). Trade accomplished several things: (1) it was a source of wealth and potential surplus; (2) it led to more specialized and hence efficient production; (3) it promoted contact and the exchange of ideas; and (4) it created new demands and the production of new commodities. In the Aegean world, trade played the major economic role in the intensification of culture during the Early Bronze Age. Renfrew (1969:159–60) wrote:

> Metal was an obvious form of wealth, . . . and the development of fortification may be related to this and to the increase in seafaring. In any case, the intensification of culture at this time has as two causative factors the economic upsurge produced by the invention and production of a new commodity and the striking increase in communication within the Aegean. These were certainly more important than any increase in agricultural efficiency and population brought about by the introduction of metal tools.

Flannery's and Renfrew's emphasis on exchange raised several interrelated questions. What role did exchange play within a community? What role did the circulation of goods between communities play? And what role did trade play in stimulating economic growth and class formation? Exchange was clearly an important process, and it was clearly not limited to products that satisfied needs related to physical survival. It is also clear that exchange did not occur because of environmental differences within and between communities, even though it might have allowed the specialized production of different groups to complement one another. Exchange occurred because of the social relations that existed within and between communities. It served to create, cement, and reproduce those relations. Exchange was, and still is, an essential intermediate step between the production of goods, on the one hand, and their distribution and ultimate use or consumption, on the other; it can take a variety of forms within and between communities.

This perspective focuses attention on the division of labor that existed within a society and on the labor processes involved in the production of goods. Were particular goods produced for immediate use, for circulation within the community, or for transfer to another group? Were the rights of use to those goods held by the community as a whole or by some particular category of its members? If a particular good was to be exchanged, was it produced exclusively for transfer, or was it actually produced for use within the community with only a portion to be transferred to outsiders? Did the exchange transaction involve the transfer of goods of mutual advantage to both groups, or did it involve the circulation of commodities – i.e. goods that were produced for sale at a profit in the market? Unlike other forms of exchange, commodity exchange has the potential for making consumption increasingly dependent on the sale rather than direct use of the goods produced. As a result, it has the ability to dissolve old social relations and to increase the importance of money in the circulation process. Under these conditions, trade no longer makes use just of surplus production; instead, as Marx (1863–7/1981:448) observed, the capacity it has "gobbles up production itself and makes entire branches of production dependent on it."

Flannery and Renfrew had largely synchronic views of the role of exchange. What they did not explain were the conditions that underpinned the emergence of inter-regional exchange (Adams 1974:242–3). This raised the general question of the role of exchange as a motor of socioeconomic development. For growth to occur, there must be development of the productive forces with accompanying changes in the labor processes and their organization. By themselves, the exchange relations that existed within a society or between societies were not automatic motors of development. Since exchange created, cemented, and reproduced social relations within and between groups, it was essential, as Flannery implied, to focus on the relations of production that existed within the communities themselves. These relations were the ones that promoted or inhibited real economic growth. They promoted growth if the trade items were incorporated into existing processes of production with new or expanded labor processes of if they led to the development of new means of production; they inhibited growth if the trade goods were used or consumed immediately, if they were hoarded, or if they were restricted to certain social classes or strata within the community. In a phrase, change was linked not with exchange but rather with the development of the social relations of the community.

Engagement: Symbiosis, Exchange, Population, and Warfare

From the mid-1950s onward, other archaeologists focused their attention increasingly on ecology and demography. They sought to explain the rise of civilization in terms of underlying ecological and demographic motors. William T. Sanders (1956:115) wrote: "The study of settlement patterns is a study of the ecological and demographic aspects of culture. Settlement pattern is, in effect, human ecology, since it is concerned with the distribution of population over the landscape and an investigation of the reasons behind that distribution." Sanders proceeded to argue that the development of civilization in Mesoamerica refracted the enormous ecological diversity of the area. Habitats where different crops and goods were produced were often located in close proximity to one another. Thus, a trip of thirty or forty kilometers often involved a complete shift not only in climatic conditions but also in the crops that were grown.

This ecological diversity was manifested in geographical regions, like Central Mexico. The inhabitants of its various subregions had already been farming for several millennia by the time Europeans arrived in the early sixteenth century. As a result, the region as a whole was densely populated, and the communities residing in the different subregions were bound together by commerce. They existed in "an internal economic symbiosis" and, taken as a whole, constituted a "symbiotic region" (Sanders 1956:115). That is, the villages were associated with each other in mutually beneficial ways. Sanders (1956:126) further suggested that the complex zoning of environments in Central Mexico which underwrote elaborate commercial relations and dense population also underwrote the development of "huge" urban centers – Teotihuacán and Tenochtitlán – on two different occasions in pre-Columbian times; he described them as "religious and administrative centers, with large, resident, non-food-producing, economically specialized populations and completely urban settlement patterns" (Sanders 1956:126).

Sanders elaborated his views in the 1960s. He asserted that "the environment should be considered as an active, integrated part of the cultural system not as a passive extra-cultural factor" (Sanders 1962:34–5). Borrowing Arnold Toynbee's notion of "challenge and response," he argued that each environment offered a different set of challenges, and that the diversity of environments found in regions like Central Mexico further complicated the challenges they posed. From neo-classical economists, he borrowed the idea that communities behave efficiently in ways that allow their members to optimize or maximize particular outcomes; as he put it, "in responding to such challenges, cultural response tends to take the path of greatest efficiency in the utilization of the environment" (Sanders 1962:34). Sanders also refined his views about civilization and the conditions that underwrote its development in Central Mexico. Civilization was a particular type of cultural growth characterized by technological achievements that were "always the product of a *large organized human society with marked occupational specialization and social stratification.* . . . [Civilization was] thus one kind of solution to the problem of adjustment to a physical and biological environment" (Sanders 1968:90, emphasis in original). The ecological diversity and conditions of Central Mexico were optimal, from his perspective, for the development of intensive, irrigation agriculture. They also underwrote the growth of inter-regional commerce and the development of city-states, each of which was composed of a principal market town and its dependent villages. The market towns were the foci of the sociopolitical systems and economic specialization. The city-states were not only the stable political groupings of the area, but they were also the largest level of sociopolitical organization that could be linked directly with ecological factors (Sanders 1962:41). They were "the outcome of the natural population growth of a few rural communities situated in exceptionally favorable segments of the landscape" (Sanders 1968:100). They continually confronted poor transport and overpopulation, both of which were chronic problems in Central Mexico (Sanders 1962:41). In 1968, Sanders (1968:106) summed up his conclusions in the following way:

> In the history of Mesoamerican civilizations, two basic interactive patterns between environment and culture were intimately related to its growth. One was the evolution of irrigation agriculture in the arid highlands and of a social system involving supra-community monarchial states, developed as a response to the problem of excavation and maintenance of canal and dike systems and policing of water distribution. The other pattern was community economic specialization and regional markets that tended to integrate communities into larger socio-economic groupings. This, I have called "Economic System Symbiosis." The sharply contrasting microgeographic patterns characteristic of the natural environment of Mesoamerica tended to intensify symbiotic relationships.[7]

Following Leslie White, Sanders and Barbara Price (1968:9) suggested that "the nonmaterial aspects of culture have evolved as adaptations to technological revolutions. . . . Technological change as a basic causal factor is, we feel, significant only where such change results in a *substantial increase in the numbers and densities of human beings, or in the markedly increased efficiency of the individual human producer*" (emphasis in original). Sanders and Price quickly developed arguments relating population growth to the rise of civilization. In the process, they introduced various neo-Malthusian concerns as well as notions of scarcity and competition derived from neoclassical economics. They indicated that "[p]opulation growth may be considered as a primary process in the cause-and-effect network, with competition and cooperation as derivative processes. Civilizations by definition are large social systems characterized by intense social stratification and economic specialization" (Sanders and Price 1968:74). In their perspective, the most stable civilizations in Central Mexico and Mesopotamia were those with populations of 12,000 to 30,000 persons who were concentrated in relatively small areas and who possessed reasonably efficient systems of communication and transportation. In other words, they exhibited relatively high population densities. Sanders and Price (1968:83) maintained that there was "a close correlation between population density and complexity of social structure." They contended that the major theoretical problem, from their viewpoint, was to determine "the minimal and maximal population densities for each of Service's [1962/1971] various levels of socioeconomic integration" (Sanders and Price 1968:75).

Sanders and Price (1968:84, 94–7) proceeded to argue that the organizational stresses found in a society increased as its numbers grew larger and its density increased. These stresses stimulated the development of more effective means of social control. Population growth provoked competition for scarce resources, resulting in the elaboration of new systems of resource distribution and allocation. It also promoted cooperative projects that improved productivity or reduced or eliminated overpopulation; these included more efficient utilization of the land, economic specialization, political control of surplus food produced outside the region, migration, warfare, and various checks on population growth such as infanticide or birth control.

Paul Baker and Sanders (1972:162–3) presented an alternative gloss on the demographic models discussed above: The evolution of large-scale political systems may reflect the nature of population growth over short periods of time. They suggested further that

[f]or societies organized on a tribal level, a tribal size of up to 5000–6000 people is conceivable, but a doubling of population to 10,000–12,000 would require a chiefdom type of social organization in order to maintain a stable society. This means that chiefdoms would evolve from tribes within a single century. Although chiefdoms of 24,000 (doubling of the 12,000) can exist, their stability is extremely low and when their size doubles to 48,000 they can usually exist only for a generation or two. This means that the state level of social organization can evolve within a period of only two centuries from the chiefdom level, and the process of political evolution from a tribe to a state could occur during a period of two or three centuries.

In spite of a considerable amount of ethnographic evidence to the contrary, the relationship they posited between population growth and political development has remained influential.

Sanders (1972) and Price (1971) subsequently expanded their views on the importance of irrigation agriculture as a motor that underwrote population growth and the rise of states. Sanders (1972:153) wrote:

One of the more interesting aspects of Mesoamerican history is the close relationship between the appearance of large urban centers like Teotihuacán, Cholula, Tenochtitlán, and Monte Albán and hydraulic agriculture. The interrelationships between hydraulic agriculture and the emergence of these large urban centers and of the huge political systems that they governed can only be outlined very briefly here. Hydraulic agriculture provides first of all a new dimension of power – control of water as well as control of land. The maintenance of an irrigation system also requires coordinated organization of labor in a way that other agricultural systems do not. Furthermore, irrigated land is universally private land because of the heavy investment of capital labor (that is, dikes, canals, and dams), and this stimulates class distinctions based on land ownership. Irrigated land also is permanently cropped land, and the demographic capacity of permanently cropped land of this type is considerably greater than any other system of farming. This permits greater regional population density and the establishment of larger agrarian communities. Communities of this type with continued population growth and pressure may easily evolve into urban centers.

In the late 1960s, sociocultural anthropologist Robert Carneiro added important dimensions to the arguments relating population growth to the rise of civilization. Building on Herbert Spencer's observations, Carneiro (1967b:239) argued that societies do not necessarily become more complex merely by growing larger; rather, he contended, "if a society does increase significantly in size, and if at the same time it remains unified and integrated, it must elaborate its organization" in order to deal with the internal stresses created by population growth. This typically meant an increase in structure that underwrote new forms of cohesion and gave rise to successively more differentiated forms of society.

Carneiro (1970:733) proposed an ecological theory of state origins, also rooted in Spencer's Social Darwinist arguments, that explained how intensive warfare could lead to the rise of state-based societies – i.e. autonomous political units composed of many communities and having centralized governments with the power to tax, draft labor, and issue and enforce laws. In this view, the pressures created by population growth in a naturally or socially circumscribed area, such as one of the river valleys that cross the coastal desert of Peru, ultimately put strains on the available resources and lead to warfare *within* the area. Carneiro (1978:207) described the process in the following way: "As population density in such [circumscribed] areas increased and arable land came into short supply, competition over land ensued. This competition took the form of war, and those villagers vanquished in war, being unable to flee as they might have done in areas of uncircumscribed land, had to remain in place and be subjugated by the victors."

By the mid-1970s, some new archaeologists were critical of the economic exchange and neo-Malthusian theories of state formation proposed by Sanders, Price, and Carneiro. Wright and Johnson (1975:267), for example, defined a state as

> a society with specialized administrative activities. By "administrative" we mean "control," thus including what is commonly termed "politics" under administration. In states . . . decision-making activities are differentiated or specialized in two ways. First, there is a hierarchy of control in which the highest level involves making decisions about other, lower-order decisions rather than about any particular condition or movement of material goods or people. Any society with three or more levels of decision-making hierarchy must necessarily involve such specialization because the lowest or first-order decision-making will be directly involved in productive and transfer activities and second-order decision-making will be coordinating these and correcting their material errors. However, third-order decision-making will be concerned with coordinating and correcting these corrections. Second, the effectiveness of such a hierarchy of control is facilitated by the complementary specialization of information processing activities into observing, summarizing, message-carrying, data-storing, and actual decision-making. This both enables the efficient handling of masses of information and decisions moving through a control hierarchy with three or more levels, and undercuts the independence of subordinates.

For Wright and Johnson, the existence of such control hierarchies was manifest in the settlement hierarchies of a region like Mesopotamia. In chiefdom-level societies, site-size was distributed trimodally. The inhabitants of the more numerous, small sites engaged directly in subsistence production; those in the settlement with the largest area and presumably population occupied the highest level in the decision-making and control hierarchy.

Wright (1977a, 1977b, 1978) subsequently used the idiom of systems theory to elaborate a perspective on the origins of the state. In this view, chiefdoms and states could be viewed simultaneously as societies with specialized decision-making apparatuses and as sociocultural systems with differentiated, internally specialized decision-making subsystems that regulated the flows of information among other subsystems and with other systems (Wright 1978:56). He also noted that chiefdoms did not automatically evolve into states, and that it was necessary to isolate the conditions that destroyed or transformed the chiefly mechanisms of regulation and generated new stately forms of regulation (Wright 1977b:385).

Wright and Johnson pointed out that empirical evidence from Southwestern Iran did not fit the hypotheses outlined by Sanders, Price, and Carneiro. In Iran, population seemed to have actually declined before the appearance of the first states, and local, intra-regional trade seemed more important than inter-regional exchange. This led Wright and Johnson to reject single variable explanations of state formation. By themselves, they argued, neither exchange nor population growth was a "prime mover." They suggested instead that state formation was more likely a response to changes involving a number of variables. Such interactions may have been additive, in which case the capacity of the society's decision-makers to process information was exceeded. In other instances, there might have been "a required time order in which a set of variables must change" (Wright and Johnson 1975:285). In still other instances, the variables may have interacted with one another, producing positive feedback resulting in the reorganization and increased specialization of the decision-making hierarchy.

Other archaeologists, notably George Cowgill (1975), took a less sanguine view of Malthusian and neo-Malthusian perspectives on population growth itself. He challenged the idea that the natural tendency of sedentary populations was to increase in size. It was wrong, in his view, to assume uncritically that population growth promotes social differentiation. He further questioned whether "social or individual stress automatically generated effective demand" and underwrote social or political-economic change (Cowgill 1975:506–7). Cowgill (1975:515) phrased his ideas about the incentives and motivations for new kinds of behavior in the following way:

> I believe that one's notions about what is in the best interests of oneself, one's close kin or associations, institutions, or social categories or classes with which one closely identifies, are major determinants of politically and economically-relevant aspects of behavior. Furthermore, I think that if we understand the situational and institutional contexts in which individuals find themselves, their notions about their own self-interest become quite understandable, and perhaps even predictable. I certainly do not mean that all people are just alike, but I do suspect that when whole categories or classes of people (as opposed to occasional deviant individuals) behave in ways which at first seem peculiar or inexplicable, it is not because they have some drastically different ways of formulating their preferences which we have not fathomed, but because we have not understood how they perceive their situational and institutional positions and possibilities.

Thus, Cowgill's critique of the population growth theories had little in common with the new archaeologists' perspectives on the utility of demographic explanations. His argument did, however, resonate with Marxist perspectives on population and the historical specificity of the population regimes characteristic of different modes of production (Coontz 1957). The ways in which Cowgill and other archaeologists engaged Marx's legacy in the decades immediately following the Second World War will be discussed in the next section.

Dialogue: The Urban Revolution Revisted

Childe's works as well as those of Marx, Engels, and their successors were appreciated by anthropologists working in Mexico in the years following the Second World War. Pedro Armillas (1948, 1951), René Millon (1954, 1955), and Eric Wolf (1959), among others, engaged in a meaningful dialogue with Marxist social thought. Their publications struck resonant chords from the 1950s onward for a number of anglophone North American scholars – including Robert Adams (1955, 1956, 1960a, 1960b, 1965, 1966) and Bruce Trigger (1967, 1972), whose works also exhibited an engagement and dialogue with the legacies of Marx and Childe.

In an early publication, Robert Adams provided a nuanced interpretation of the developmental schemes described in the opening section of this chapter. He wrote that "for purposes of understanding historical development we can only proceed by isolating what we believe to be the basic patterns of political and socio-economic organization to some degree from their cultural and historical setting" (Adams 1955:6). Like Childe, he was less concerned with aesthetic and technical innovations than with their relationship to underlying political and socioeconomic relations. He also paid close attention to Durkheim's views about the role religion played during the early stages of the civilizational process.

Adams modified the terminology used by the Americanist archaeologists who had engaged social evolutionary thought. He restricted the term "Formative Era" to those societies that lacked full-time craft specialization and "substantial concentrations of wealth under either secular or religious auspices (as reflected in tomb furniture and 'monumentality' of architecture)" (Adams 1955:7). The regional networks of agricultural villages during the Formative Era were integrated "by individuals whose authority devolved from their positions as religious spokesmen. . . . For a time, it seems probable that the religious elite played an increasingly important role in the administration of group activities as communities grew larger and more complex" (Adams 1956:228). The Formative Era ended when "the changed needs of the communities transformed earlier part-time cult specialists into a theocratic class serving as a kind of organizing authority" (Adams 1956: 231).

Adams saw the subsequent "Florescent Era" largely in terms of temple dominance and processes of social differentiation that were promoted by the temples themselves: "Technical advance in the Florescent Era seems to have become more rapid as social stratification, advancing in step with the 'urban' revolution as a whole, made effective new demands and sanctioned the devotion of increasing numbers of specialists to their fulfillment" (Adams 1955:10). He pointed to the contradictions that emerged during this era of temple dominance and related them ultimately to processes of class and state formation. The authority of temple establishment was based on the kind of mechanical group solidarity that was characteristic of Formative villages, which Adams viewed as homogeneous. However, the social differentiation promoted by the temples eroded that form of social solidarity without effectively putting another form in its place. Moreover,

> the increasing wealth of the temples offered vastly greater inducements to military activity than had existed previously. . . .
>
> Under the influence of all these forces the effective integration of communities . . . required an increasingly authoritarian, militaristic, and centralized character that was also fundamentally in opposition to the traditional activities of the temple. The priestly hierarchies . . . only survived as corporate entities still responsible for an important share of the secular affairs of the groups under their charge where they were able to adopt to same autocratic outlook as their rising secular competitors. . . .
>
> To some extent, the competition for control that seems to have ensued may consciously have been directed toward the expansion of royal wealth and authority at the expense of the temples. (Adams 1956:229)

Warfare, conquest, looting, slavery, and class distinctions, in addition to large-scale private ownership of land, were characteristics of the secular-territorial societies that developed as the contradictions remained unresolved.

In 1960, Adams explicitly rejected Steward's evolutionary explanations of causal processes. In his view, Steward had created a false dichotomy when he equated an evolutionary methodology with generalizing and an historical methodology with particularizing. Moreover, Steward's cross-cultural methodology did not pay sufficient attention to the sequential and functional particulars of what happened in given regions, and it relied too much on comparison of independent sequences to establish causal relationships. In Adams's (1960c:160) view, "A frequent defect in the very general statements of historical cause-and-effect relationships that are derived from an exclusively comparative method is that they tend to rest on unilinear sequences of abstractions having little relation to real historical entities or processes." Adams was not arguing that cross-cultural comparisons should be neglected. In fact, he concluded that they "highlight differences in explanatory syntheses prepared for different areas, not only in order to formulate broad generalizations applying, for example, to all early civilizations, but also to assist in the re-examination and refinement of the more detailed causal processes assumed to operate on a particular historical scene" (Adams 1960c:160).

After working out what actually happened in two regions, Adams concluded that two particularly defective abstractions in the studies of the rise of civilization were those concerned with population pressure, on the one hand, and the administrative requirements of large-scale irrigation management, on the other. He called instead for an examination of the formation of the "coercive state," for "an emphasis on rapidly developing, *emergent* institutions. In the context of early civilizations, urbanism, class stratification, kingship, trade and markets, craft specialization, and militaristic expansion comprise the essentials of this emergent configuration" (Adams 1960c:164–5, emphasis in original).

Adams recognized that state-based societies were qualitatively different from ones organized by kin-communal social relations. This perspective contrasted with those of Fried (1967) and Service (1962/1971), who viewed the differences largely as quantitative. Adams also recognized the pivotal, historically contingent role played by the contradictions resulting from class and state formation, the dissolution of kin-communal relations, the emergence of exploitation and coercive social relations, and resistance to those processes and to the exactions of the ruling classes. At the same time, he pointed out that the coercive state also underwrote the extension of redistributive institutions, improvements in subsistence technology, and the elaboration of occupational specialization. For Adams (1966:12), "the transformation at the core of the Urban Revolution lay in the realm of social organization. . . . [It] seems to have been primarily changes in social institutions that precipitated changes in technology, subsistence, and other aspects of the wider cultural realm, rather than vice versa."

In *The Evolution of Urban Society*, Adams (1966) pointed to three major transformations in the development of Mesopotamian society. The first involved changes in food-producing activities, the products of which were collected, exchanged, and redistributed by temple communities. The moral authority of the temple communities allowed them to persuade farmers and herders to intensify production and produce surplus crops and animals. These surpluses underwrote population growth, occupational specialization, and the formation of wealth differentials based on differential access that farmers had to water. The second transformation involved the shift from kin-organized to class-stratified society. Families who had access to water and high-quality agricultural land or who controlled the distribution of foodstuffs and craft goods constituted themselves as a ruling class who continued to use the institutions and practices of the temple to extract surplus goods and labor from their neighbors and kin. The third transformation involved the transfer of power from the temple communities to the state itself.

Seven years earlier, Eric Wolf (1959:19–20) had also described the development of precapitalist, state-based societies in Mesoamerica in terms of the consolidation of exploitative social relations:

A society which can divert some of its members from the food quest into full-time specialization can at the same time free skills and knowledge from the narrow confines of the individual household and speed their development in a multitude of crafts and occupations. Inevitably, in the development of human societies, such a growth of economic surplus and diversification of labor are accompanied by still a third phenomenon: the rise of the full-time political specialist, to co-ordinate the increased efforts of an increasingly diversified population and to arbitrate the disputes of newly formed interest groups. Inevitably, also, such political specialization constitutes a turning point in the lives of most societies; for the functions of co-ordination and arbitration spell power, and power is translatable into special liens on goods and services. Perhaps . . . there is no inherent reason why such services should be rewarded more heavily than those of other skilled specialists. Yet, inevitably, where political specialists have assumed the task of concentrating and reallocating the surplus to other members of their society, they have concentrated both wealth and the power that goes with wealth in their own hands and for their own purposes.

The primitive farming communities of Mesoamerica successfully resisted efforts at class and state formation until the first millennium B.C. By then, in Wolf's view (1959:20, 69), the crops they produced more than met subsistence needs, and the surpluses they produced were employed to support craft specialists and to provide them with the raw materials they needed. These surpluses were also used to support religious specialists who possessed special esoteric knowledge and lived apart from their neighbors. These religious specialists possessed power over the members of their communities. They organized their communities and extracted labor and tribute from their members. Wolf (1959:79) wrote:

> Such rule has been called theocratic; under it the power to rule and the power of religion are one. Ultimately, the social order is but an aspect of the universal order. If the gods work to keep men in their place, and men labor to keep the gods in their heaven, the balance of society is maintained.
>
> All early states were based on the combination of supernatural terror and secular power.

Wolf proceeded to point out that theocratic states contained fundamental contradictions. While the priests succeeded in bringing together peoples with divergent interests, they created conditions for dissent and disagreement based on the divergent interests of these groups. In such circumstances, the priests not only advised the various groups but also handed down decisions and executed decisions to resolve the conflicts. This sowed

> the inevitable seeds of internal dissension and the possibility of revolt, and with these dissensions it created – again inevitably – the need for that form of warfare between rulers and ruled which we call the state. Finally, the flames of revolt and the violence of repression left the old gods impotent and brought to power the gods of war and human sacrifice. (Wolf 1959:106)

The exploitative social relations that developed between town and countryside constituted the second contradiction in theocratic society. The towns grew wealthy, because the peasants toiled in the hinterlands. Exploitation bred envy; it fueled the peasants' desires to keep the surpluses for their own use; it fanned the possibility for revolt. Wolf (1959:108) proceeded to elaborate a theory of revolution, arguing that "[r]evolt occurs not when men's faces are ground into dust; rather, it explodes during a period of rising hope, at the point of sudden realization that only the traditional controls of the social order stand between men and the achievement of still greater hopes." In his view, rebel groups appeared in the countryside and on the periphery where the controls of the religion and state were weakest.

Although Adams and Wolf did not use the term "mode of production," their efforts to unite underlying political-economic processes and social relations and to explain how they developed in particular historical circumstances were reminiscent of the way that Marx deployed the theoretical construct. Moreover, it was reminiscent of the procedure he used to discuss the development of capitalism in *Capital*.

In the chapters that follow, we will examine how archaeologists drew upon the diverse explanations of the rise of civilization discussed above. We will pay particular attention to the impact that structural Marxism had for them and for sociocultural anthropologists concerned with the historical development of human societies under different circumstances.

-4-

Theoretical Ferment and Dialogue, 1975–1990

Various social theoretical currents crafted after the Second World War permeated archaeological thought with increasing frequency from the mid-1970s onward. Currents and legacies discussed in the previous chapter persisted, confronted, or merged with new readings of Spencer, Durkheim, Malthus, and Marx.[1] The diversity of approaches to state formation was chronicled, for example, in collections edited by Henri Claessen and his associates as well as in review articles written by Robert Carneiro and Christine Gailey, among others (Carneiro 1987; Claessen and Skalník 1978, 1981; Claessen, van de Velde, and Smith 1985; Gailey 1985).

Processual archaeology became hegemonic in the United States during the 1970s. This was part of a shift in the discipline's center of gravity from the academy to the private sector; its perspectives, protocols, and procedures were then codified in various regulations that were written to implement cultural resource management legislation enacted by the federal government between 1966 and 1974. As the processual archaeologists increasingly became technicians and state functionaries concerned with methodological issues, instrumental rationality, and value-neutrality, they sought standardized concepts and procedures that could be applied uniformly in diverse circumstances.

At the same time, other archaeologists with different theoretical perspectives challenged the neopositivist underpinnings of processual archaeology. Some rooted their critiques in the arguments of structuralism or symbolic anthropology. Others built on one or another strand of Marxist social thought, many of which were decanted of their political implications. Some echoed the efforts of French anthropologists to examine the relevance of Marx's writings for anthropology or to merge structuralism with Marxism. Others commented on the weaknesses of their contemporaries' efforts.[2]

What were the contours of the critiques, both internal and external, that crystallized from 1975 onward? What were the terrains of the debates that occurred between archaeologists with different perspectives? How did archaeologists articulate their viewpoints with earlier and ongoing commentaries and critiques? Let us examine these questions in terms of theoretical arguments and critiques that appeared after 1975; let us also consider the backtalk, crosstalk, silences, and dialogues that ensued.

An Explicitly Marxist Archaeology: Critiques and Debates

In 1975, Phillip Kohl and Antonio Gilman organized a pathbreaking symposium that dealt with the relationships between Marxism and archaeology; it was the first session on Marxism and archaeology ever held at an annual meeting of the American Anthropological Association. A year later, Matthew Spriggs (1984) organized a second symposium concerned with Marxist perspectives in archaeology, and Carole Crumley (1976) commented critically on the use of central place theory to conceptualize and discuss processes of state formation.

In their view, the processualists' search for universal laws of human behavior did not account for the variation seen in the historical development of particular cultures. Like their predecessors, the processualists separated the study of process from the study of history. Their functionalism, which gave equal weight to all of the subsystems of a culture, ultimately forced them to rely on human needs or propensities in order to explain change. The processualists' models of social change gave descriptive and analytical priority to the synchronic rather than diachronic aspects of society. Their emphasis on the ecological and economic realms of society paid too little attention to social relations and what particular ancient peoples thought about the world they lived in. More particularly, the processualists paid insufficient attention to the historical specificity of the state-level societies they studied or to the fact that these societies had diverse settlement systems.

The processualists' discussions gave the illusion that more was known about the historical development of particular societies than was actually the case, especially in regions where relatively little research had been carried out. Further, their explanations, which were clad in the language of science, did not adequately recognize how the hegemonic cultures of the United States or Great Britain, for instance, shaped the theory and practice of archaeology or affected archaeologists' reconstructions of ancient societies and cultures (Leone 1982; Patterson 1986a, 1986b; Trigger 1998:30–4; Wilk 1985).

Those archaeologists who drew inspiration from Marxist social thought made the following claims: (1) there is a structural discontinuity between non-state and state-based societies; (2) class-stratified, state-based societies are expressions of exploitation; (3) the division of labor, including gender and kin relations, is transformed during episodes of state formation; (4) class and state formation occur rapidly; (5) class and state formation produce uneven social development; and (6) it is essential to examine the internal dynamics and contradictions of societies undergoing class and state formative processes (e.g. Gailey and Patterson 1987, 1988; Zagarell 1986a, 1986b).

A good place to begin our discussion of the explicitly Marxist perspectives in archaeology that appeared in the mid-1970s is with three papers: Crumley's (1976)

"Toward a Locational Definition of State Systems of Settlement," Kohl's (1975) "The Archeology of Trade," and Gilman's (1976) "Bronze Age Dynamics in Southeast Spain."

Crumley was concerned with the relation between state-level sociopolitical organizations and their systems of settlement. She pointed out that the state-based societies studied by archaeologists involved diverse settlement systems. Some states sustained cities whose residents engaged in diverse activities – manufacturing, trade, administration, religion, and so forth; in other state-based societies, such activities were dispersed across the countryside rather than consolidated in one or more densely populated settlements. In some state-level societies, there were small populations whose members resided in the countryside and engaged in subsistence activities; other state-based societies lacked rural populations. In other words, there were both urban and non-urban state-based societies.

Crumley (1976, 1979) was critical of the ways that processual archaeologists used central place theory to discuss state formation; in her view, the explanatory power of central place theory was limited by its underlying premises: a closed or bounded capitalist economy engaged in retail marketing across an unbounded, featureless plain.[3] Implicit in her work was a criticism of those processual archaeologists – most notably Greg Johnson and Henry Wright (Johnson 1972; Wright 1977a, 1977b, 1978; Wright and Johnson 1975) – whose work was discussed in the previous chapter. Wright and Johnson postulated a relationship between sociopolitical complexity and settlement hierarchies composed of sites with different sizes and populations: Settlement hierarchies with three tiers were indicative of chiefdoms; those with four tiers were hallmarks of state-based societies.

In Crumley's view, besides the limitations imposed by the underlying premises of central place theory, it was also difficult to generalize from economic activity to decision-making or even to discuss settlement hierarchies when there was so little available information about the functional relations of the populations residing at the various sites that composed the alleged settlement hierarchies. Critical of the idea that hierarchy existed everywhere, Crumley (1979, 1987) introduced the term *heterarchy* to describe the relation between structure and process manifested in the changing settlement systems of the state-level societies in Burgundy, where settlement hierarchies were absent for most of the last 2500 years, and central place theory could be used to explain only limited spatial and temporal portions of the archaeological record (Crumley and Marquardt 1987).

Kohl's (1975) tack was a different one. He was dissatisfied with the way that processual archaeologists, especially Renfrew, had dealt with the issue of exchange. As you will recall, Renfrew (1969) argued that trade played a central role in the development of Aegean civilization. He conceptualized society in terms of five subsystems, two of which were technology and exchange. Kohl pointed out that Renfrew's model removed trade from the socioeconomic contexts in which it occurred and separated exchange from the economic relations in which the objects exchanged were produced and used. Following arguments in Marx's (1857–8/ 1973) *Grundrisse*, Kohl indicated that the production, exchange, and consumption of articles were merely different moments of the relations of production, and that it was essential to examine the conditions imposed by social class structures and by the differential access that the various social classes had to the means of production.

Gilman (1976) was also critical of the determinant role that Renfrew assigned to trade. He argued that processual arguments which saw trade as an external trigger for the emergence and development of Bronze Age civilization in areas like southeast Spain overlooked internal changes – the adoption of irrigation, plow agriculture, and Mediterranean polyculture (vine and olive cultivation), and offshore fishing. Such productive activities laid the foundations for the creation of surplus social goods that were subsequently appropriated by an emergent warrior elite in the region who made use of metal objects that could be traded. Gilman (1976:317) also pointed out that "the evolution toward social stratification took place in the southeast faster than in areas of Spain where intensification of farming had less dramatic effects and [where the people] were able to maintain the traditional social order." The observation that the processes of class formation produce uneven development in an area was important; it contrasted markedly with the claims of processual archaeologists, like Renfrew (1986), who would assert that class and state formation produce homogeneous political-economic landscapes composed of clusters of polities at the same level of sociopolitical development.

Kohl (1978) and Gilman (1981) soon elaborated their views in *Current Anthropology* articles that included the supportive and critical comments of colleagues as well as the authors' responses to those remarks. Kohl reiterated his earlier point that it was essential to consider trade and production as aspects of a complex set of social relations of production that were developing differently in different parts of southwest Asia during the third millennium B.C. He pointed out that, while trade linked the regional social formations into a network, the regional societies themselves were developing along different trajectories. He viewed this not in terms of a world system composed of a core and periphery but rather as a world economy with multiple cores; this world economy was not coterminous with a single political entity (Kohl 1987a, 1987b, 1989).

Gilman (1981) criticized the functionalist accounts of the processual archaeologists, which focused on the supposedly beneficial services provided by ruling classes rather than on exploitation. He reiterated his earlier argument that there was a connection between changes in the forces of production and in property relations – that is, in the social relations of production – which underwrote social stratification in southeast Spain. He explored the implications of this observation in a subsequent article that addressed the question of whether Marxist analyses could shed light on the pre-class societies traditionally studied by archaeologists. He focused his attention on the Upper Palaeolithic cultures of Europe, which were marked by technological innovations and the appearance of style, and which processual archaeologists, notably Binford, saw as "the technological and social manifestation of the biological achievement of a full capacity for culture" (Gilman 1984:119). Gilman (1984:122) argued instead that the Upper Palaeolithic revolution involved "a critical change in the balance of social security, a change brought about by the development of the forces of production," and that this change underwrote a narrowing of a group's alliances and relations with other groups. In his view, "the changes in social organization arise from a shift in group interests ultimately caused, but not determined, by more effective technologies" (Gilman 1984:123).

One of Gilman's (1984:123–4) goals in the later article was to revitalize "the basically correct notion of primitive communism."[4] The most distinctive features of primitive communism – what others have called the kin-ordered or kin-communal mode of production – are (1) collective ownership of the primary means of production, and (2) the absence of a social division of labor, in which the members of one group permanently appropriate the social product or labor of the direct producers. In other words, social relations are not exploitative; the members of one group do not extort goods or labor from other groups throughout the entire developmental cycle. There is no exploitation in societies manifesting the primitive communist mode of production because of the unity of the production process and the direct participation of all adults in the production, distribution, circulation, and consumption of goods. This means that each individual is dependent on the group as a whole. It also implies that there are no structural differences between producers and non-producers. Such a distinction exists only from the perspective of a given individual who is too young, too old, or not a participant in a particular labor process. The distinction disappears when the focus is extended beyond a particular individual and a single labor process. It becomes inverted from one labor process to another, as a direct producer in one instance becomes a consumer in the next.

Elsewhere, in a 1983 paper critical of system-theory approaches to the origins of the state, I argued that one of the premises of Marxist theory is that the emergence of the state is closely linked with the process of class formation and with the progressive autonomy of politics (Patterson 1983a).[5] The common thread of human society is life in the community, where the opposition between the private and the public is non-existent or very poorly developed. This thread is broken, however, with the appearance of social classes – that is, when people begin to pursue individual or individual-class interests in the context of the continuing public institutions of the communal society. These institutions and the communal society itself are transformed in the process, as the structures of the old mode of production are displaced by those of the new. This focuses attention on the dual character of the relations of production and how they are transformed. It compels us, on the one hand, to consider how the society was organized for the production, circulation, distribution, and consumption of goods. It forces us, on the other, to examine how the organization in which the production of goods, knowledge, and human beings took place was itself reproduced. It also focuses attention on the contradictions that existed within the relations of production and how these were resolved with the dissolution of the communal formation and the emergence of civil society.

In the classless societies manifesting the primitive communal mode of production, the social categories that regulate the relations of production are non-economic, and the true nature of the economic is obscured; the emergent class structure consists of a hierarchy of social categories that cannot be reduced directly to economic class relations. This hierarchy of non-economic social categories disguises both the real economic class relations and the real contradictions that emerge from them. In such a situation, the economic class relations appear different from their real nature, while the hierarchical social categories of the class structure appear as "natural" relations.

The formation of the class structure is, in the last analysis, based on the economic order of the society – the unequal accumulation of surplus product by the various social categories that make up the hierarchy. The formation of the class structure is the condition for the formation of economic class relations to the extent that this process determines the place of the different social categories in the production process and that it determines the reorganization of the labor processes to incorporate exploitation and extortion by one or more of these categories. The reorganization of the labor processes, which involves the progressive differentiation of the activities of these categories, provides the conditions for the further development of the contradictions based on the appearance of exploitation and extortion.

The constitution of the state is connected with the conditions for the constitution of the class structure and for the reproduction of the dominant class as real economic class relations appear. Consequently, the state that emerges in the context of the non-state/state transition must be at least partly organized on the basis of the social categories of the class structure. The state appears "fragile" in the sense that its legitimacy and power rest on the control of ideological symbols. It is dependent, its structure unstable, for it exists simultaneously within and above society. It does not stabilize the class structure or prevent the formation of real economic class relations.

The agencies of the state subsume the administration of justice, the conduct of war and diplomacy, and other activities that were previously carried out by the community. They do this in the interest of the state and of the society as a whole. This, however, is the basic contradiction of civil society. The state is simultaneously the representative of the class in whose interests it was organized and the mediator of the oppositions between individuals of that class and among the opposing classes of the society as a whole. The autonomy of politics and of the state is the product of modern times. The state stands above society only when the economic class relations of appropriation have become dominant. This involves the ideological objectification of individual human beings; they cease to exist as real people and appear as formal entities – legal or civil personalities – in the eyes of the state.

In the early 1980s, I began depicting the dissolution of primitive communal societies in the Andes and the consolidation of class-stratified, state-based societies in their place (Patterson 1983b, 1991:12–41). In this perspective, the development of food-producing economies based on agriculture was less important than the appearance of class stratification, exploitative social relations, and state institutions and practices that struggled to reproduce the new social order. The state-based societies that emerged toward the end of the first millennium B.C. were marked by the relatively sudden appearance of a suite of new features in the archaeological record; these included fortified hilltop settlements, headless burials, individuals interred with "trophy heads," weapons, individuals with skull fractures or dart points embedded in vital areas, abrupt changes in settlement pattern, burials with different arrays and quantities of grave goods, and regionally distinct, skillfully made pottery styles with largely non-overlapping spatial distributions.

In her investigations of the transition to food-producing economies, British archaeologist Barbara Bender was concerned with the internal dynamics of communal societies manifesting the primitive communal mode of production. She focused not on the linkages between the environment and technology but rather on "the articulation between the relations of production, that is, the relations by which a society reproduces itself as a social and economic unit, and the forces of production – the resources, techniques, work-units that constitute the productive capacity" (Bender 1981:150). The level of the productive forces, from her perspective, determined only what could not happen rather than what could occur. This is because the productive forces are ultimately dominated by the social relations of production. Bender (1978, 1981, 1985a, 1985b, 1990) stressed the importance of examining the social milieu and the social relations of production that shaped and constrained the development of the productive forces. Shifts in the social relations characteristic of groups and in their alliances with others provided the milieu for changes in the productive forces, the intensification of production, and the emergence of socially differentiated societies.

Bender (1985a:52) also noted that Marxist analyses in British archaeology were developing along quite different lines from those in the United States. While both drew inspiration from the earlier work of V. Gordon Childe, some of the British were following the efforts of French anthropologists, like Maurice Godelier, and attempting to wed Marx's theory with structuralism.[6] Jonathan Friedman and Mike Rowlands's (1977) "Notes Toward an Epigenetic Model of the Evolution of 'Civilisation'" in their *The Evolution of Social Systems* was perhaps the classic example of this approach (cf. Gledhill 1981).

Friedman and Rowlands provided a complex model for the evolution of early civilizations that superficially resembled the one Steward developed thirty years earlier. It appeared unilinear because they examined only one trajectory of development that emanated from a fixed set of conditions, and it placed the dynamic for development in structures rather than in people making their own history under conditions not of their own choosing. The model was derived from Friedman's (1975) earlier study of the oscillations of political systems in highland Burma from tribal systems to Asiatic states. It was concerned with the emergence of new structures of domination. In Friedman and Rowlands's view, tribal systems generated short-term cyclical processes reflected in the growth and decay of chiefdoms and long-term, cumulative, irreversible effects – intersystemic contradictions – that, when combined with inter-societal interaction and ecological variation, culminated in combined, interdependent and uneven processes of social evolution and collapse (Gledhill 1981:17, 20).

Friedman and Rowlands also argued that those civilizations which appeared outside the areas where pristine states emerged followed different trajectories of development. Thus, it was necessary to model evolutionary processes in terms of units that are larger than the sociopolitical units often studied by archaeologists. In a phrase, they incorporated a world systems or core–periphery perspective in their model; furthermore, they implied that the rise of states involved processes of uneven development. In their view, the transition from a tribal system to an Asiatic state involved a conical clan breaking out from the cyclical processes of growth, expansion, and collapse. They explained the transition in terms of the social and economic effects that objects had when they were exchanged and integrated into the society. This was accomplished when a local segment of a conical clan asserted control over the prestige-good economy and transformed this into a higher social status. This fueled tendencies for further internal differentiation in the society and for further expansion through the exchange of these prestige items. This in turn fueled further increases in the production of goods for exchange and the elaboration of a regionally based division of labor in which the core states produced goods and the peripheral areas provided raw materials. In the process, arable land appeared as a commodity, which further consolidated the dominance of a wealth-based class which had the capacity to accumulate the means of production; this shifted the state apparatus to a more superstructural position (Gledhill 1981:23–4).

Using data from Mesoamerica, the American Southwest, and the Near East, John Gledhill analyzed exchange and the developments it stimulated in peripheral areas as well as the internal dynamics of archaic states (Gledhill 1978, 1984;

Gledhill and Larsen 1982). Making use of a core–periphery model, he suggested that trade relations with Mesoamerica had an impact on social development in the Southwest:

> Entry into the Mexican network implied a response to a specialised pattern of demand, which could not be generated locally on the same scale. Long-distance trade was linked to a local process of political hierarchisation, those at the top of the hierarchy promoting specialised production for export in return for prestige goods. . . . The Southwest was peripheral geographically as well as structurally, and it is clear that specialised and dependent marginal components of a world system dominated by distant centres are extremely vulnerable. A trade-lined process of socio-political development can take that development beyond a level which can be sustained if areal linkages are disrupted. Through their effects on socio-political structures, such recessions will create social stress, and magnify any stress conditions which have been induced in the course of development. (Gledhill 1978:268)

Gledhill (1984; Gledhill and Larsen 1982) then turned his attention to archaic states and Marx's undeveloped concept of the asiatic mode of production, which had already been used by some Mesoamericanists in their descriptions and analyses of the Aztec state. He pointed to the contradictions that existed within the dominant class of the Aztec society, contradictions that were promoted by the expansion of the Aztec state. Here the state was not an agency that mediated between the particular interests of different fractions of the dominant class, since "political centricity is itself constantly threatened in imperial systems, and conflict and competition at the top of the social hierarchy underpin change at the politico-administrative and socioeconomic levels" (Gledhill 1984:141). In a phrase, discrepancies appeared between the interests of the ruler and those of the dominant class. Aztec society witnessed "the emergence of specific organs of class struggles, such as court cliques," as well as the appearance of private domains (Gledhill 1984:141).

In 1986, Christine Gailey and I prepared two papers on class and state formation (Gailey and Patterson 1987, 1988). In the earlier paper, we argued that the rise of civilization – i.e. class and state formation – entailed what Stanley Diamond (1974:1) had characterized as "conquest abroad and repression at home." It involved exploitation – the emergence of class-based patterns of production, distribution, consumption, and cultural practices. It was a process that created border peoples, whose relations of production were altered by virtue of tributary or exchange relations with their state-based neighbors. Since some states were more successful than others in specifying the labor and goods they demanded from subordinated classes and communities, and since some enveloped peoples were more successful in their resistance to those exactions, state formation tended to produce heterogeneous mosaics of societies rather than polities with the same sociopolitical structure. We also argued that states were, and still are, destructive of kin-ordered communities in their midst. Ethnocide and genocide were, and are, aspects of class and state formation. Class and state formation were also episodes when ethnogenesis, the creation of new cultural forms, occurred (Gailey and Patterson 1988).

Gailey and I further argued that class and state formation can be understood as the articulation of diverse communal and tributary modes of production. While strong tributary states specified what tribute they desired, weak tributary states were unable to demand in a consistent manner what labor or goods would be exacted from the subject communities, because the kin communities retained control over either their members or the goods they produced. Diverse trajectories of development were discerned as kin-ordered communities were enmeshed in tributary or exchange relations or succeeded in breaking away from them (Gailey and Patterson 1988).

In the other paper, we reasserted Marx's view that class structures are a manifestation of exploitative social relations, and that what distinguishes one social formation from another is the way in which surplus goods and labor are extracted from its members. It also is apparent that class formation affects men and women differentially. We further argued that the interests of the emergent state structures in these early civilizations are not necessarily the same as those of different fractions of the dominant class. Expansionary states, like the Inca Empire, emerge because of efforts to deflect internal dissent, to compensate for disruptions in state-sponsored or state-controlled production and consumption, or to consolidate tributary relations over neighboring communities and polities. The dialectic of resistance and efforts to dominate provide a rich medium for ethnogenesis – the creation of new cultural forms and practices, as well as for the development of merchants and trade in frontier regions (Gailey and Patterson 1987).

One implication of our work was that class and state formation occur rapidly, often within a few years or, at most, a generation or two. They are not gradual processes as chiefdoms slowly evolve into states. Other questions that emerged from this work, which Gailey (1987a) and I (Patterson 1983a, 1983b, 1985) explored independently elsewhere, include: What are chiefdoms, and under what circumstances are these hierarchically organized, kin-ordered communities transformed into states?

Independently Gailey and I were also examining the creation of culture in kin-communal and state-based societies (Gailey 1987b; Patterson 1985, 1988/1998). Gailey (1987b:35) described state formation as "a tense and contingent way of reproducing class relations. The extraction of tribute or labor service is oppressive to those who provide the goods or services, because not to do so involves the threat of forfeiting use-rights, continuance of a way of life, or life itself." She noted that state-based societies often made use of dominant ideologies that disguised class relations and exploitation. These ideologies typically used the "natural" categories of kinship, gender, rank, and community to structure the social relations of production and reproduction. They drew on the symbols and rituals of the dominant classes and sometimes on those of the subordinated groups. The effect was that state ideologies were not readily embraced by subordinated peoples and classes. While the dominant classes and the state presented these renditions as culture, these ideologies and practices often meant something different to the subject peoples. In Gailey's (1987b:35–6) view,

> culture in state-based societies is not continuously created on a consensual basis; it is an arena of conflict. Where there is no open rebellion, there may be accommodation, an appearance of quietude. This does not mean that culture is thereby shared. If it were, there would be no need for the civil authorities or other nonproducing classes to sponsor a litany of ritual occasions, spectacles, or other forms of public indoctrination.

While Gailey focused on how dominant classes attempted to reshape the cultures of subordinated groups, on the formation of gender hierarchies during state formation, and on the process of ethnogenesis, where those subject communities forged new understandings and sensibilities because of their shared class position, I was concerned with how creation of culture was an ongoing, continuous process in pre-class societies.[7] To do so, it was necessary to strip away the class-linked features inherent in the concept of ethnogenesis – most notably ownership or control over the means of production and hegemonic relations that were based on force, power, and domination. I suggested that culture was continually created along lines that followed the non-exploitative divisions of labor that exist in primitive communal societies. This linked the creation of culture with practical activity; it linked those individuals in a community who were engaged in the same forms of social production and reproduction. In these communities, society was the backdrop against which the drama of the individual's life unfolded. While this drama was revealed in ritual and buttressed by tradition, culture was continually created to explain the content of new scenes and the actions of new actors. While social relations may have changed slowly, the rate at which culture changed was not necessarily the same, because it constantly invested new facts and events with meaning and provided a continually revised account of how social relations are lived and experienced in a particular society at a given moment in history (Patterson 1988/1998).

Writers employing Marxist theoretical frameworks were concerned with other topics besides the dissolution of kin-communal societies, the emergence of states, and distinction between the creation of culture in kin-based communities and the invention of dominant ideologies by states. In a series of studies of the social relations that prevailed at different moments in the history of Teotihuacán, René

Millon (1976, 1981, 1988, 1992) reminded us that cities and states were not always the same and that states do fall apart as their inhabitants struggle to make their own history.

Crosstalk: Cultural Materialism and Processual Archaeology

By the late 1960s, the writings of William Sanders and his associates already showed the influence of Marvin Harris's theory of cultural materialism (Price 1982). Harris coined the phrase "cultural materialism" to describe a theory of societal structure and formation. In this view, every society was composed of an infrastructure, a structure, and a superstructure. The infrastructure was constituted by a mode of production and a mode of reproduction. The former involved "the technology and the practices employed for expanding or limiting basic subsistence production . . . given the restrictions and opportunities provided by a specific technology interacting with a specific habitat. . . . [The latter involved] the technology and practices employed for expanding, limiting, and maintaining population size" (Harris 1979:52). For Harris, the organization of production and reproduction by kinship, age and gender roles, and the division of labor constituted the structure of the society. The superstructure was constituted by the conscious and unconscious goals, rules, beliefs, and values held by the members of the society.

According to Harris (1979:66), changes in the infrastructure – especially those that occurred in the mode of reproduction – explained changes in the mode of production. These infrastructural changes, in turn, affected both the structural and superstructural levels of the society. In sum, population growth underwrote changes in the subsistence technology and practices of a society as it articulated with the ecological habitats occupied and used by its members.

Harris (1979:141–64) and Barbara Price (1982:715–18) claimed that cultural materialism built on and improved Marx's social thought by linking it with Darwin's evolutionary theory. Two of the problems with Marx's method, in their view, were his commitment to dialectical analysis and the lack of attention he paid to demography. Harris's arguments, but not those of Price, were repeatedly criticized by sociocultural anthropologists whose work was informed in different ways by Marx's method and theory. Eleanor Leacock (1972:61–6) launched a withering attack on Harris's "double-talk" about dialectics. Don Nonini (1985) criticized Harris's neo-Malthusian determinism, the distinction he drew between emic and etic analysis, and his base–superstructure model of society; he suggested that "cultural materialism may be best viewed as a form of *capitalist* materialism" (Nonini 1985:7, emphasis in original). Jonathan Friedman (1974), meanwhile, was critical of Harris's techno-environmental determinism.

Sanders and his associates, with the exception of Price, did not make much of Harris's claims about the relationship between cultural materialism and Marxist social thought (Logan and Sanders 1976; Sanders and Nichols 1988; Sanders, Parsons, and Santley 1979; Sanders and Webster 1978). They viewed cultural materialism instead as a special case of Darwinian evolutionary theory.

Sanders reiterated his earlier beliefs about the interrelationship of population pressure, environmental conditions, and sociocultural evolution:". . . population pressure is the primary cause of increasingly complex social and political patterns. However, rising demographic stress can result in such increased complexity *only* if the society's environment and technology are capable of supporting the increase in population" (Logan and Sanders 1976:32, emphasis added).[8] In this view, the rates of population growth were constant; consequently, the carrying capacity of the environments found in different regions acted "as a limiting factor in terms of how far evolutionary trajectories go, since there is a correlation between social complexity and population size" (Sanders and Webster 1978:298). For Sanders and his associates, this explained the uneven sociopolitical development found in areas like Mesoamerica. States arose autochthonously through coercion in regions like the Valley of Mexico or Oaxaca, while chiefdoms were the most complex political forms – i.e. levels of sociocultural integration – that emerged in the low-risk, high-diversity types of environments found in regions like highland Guatemala. Barbara Price (1977) coined the term "cluster interaction" to emphasize the connections that existed among societies with different levels of sociocultural integration in different parts of Mesoamerica.

Archaeologists critical of the work of Sanders and his colleagues have focused on various aspects of the theoretical framework they used to discuss sociocultural development both in the Valley of Mexico and in Oaxaca. For example, George Cowgill (1988:54) suggested that their strongly materialist approach was incomplete because it did not adequately consider the important role played by ideational factors. Similarly, Kent Flannery (1988:58) noted that "the key to urban civilization lies not in man–land relations but in man–man relations." Elizabeth Brumfiel (1976) argued that a change in social complexity – i.e. state formation – was the motor for population growth in the Valley of Mexico during the Terminal Formative Period; in Marxist terms, the population regime and dynamics were transformed by the appearance of a new mode of production based on the extraction of labor or goods from the direct-producing class. Charles Spencer (1988) remarked that Sanders and his associates did not adequately explain which patterns of archaeological evidence demonstrated the formation or presence of state-based societies. Marcus Winter (1988) noted that erosion not only buried archaeological sites, making population estimates notoriously unreliable, especially for early periods; it also changed over time the spatial distribution of productive agricultural soils. Neither Sanders and his associates nor many of their critics who worked in

the Oaxaca Valley have taken adequate account of the importance of geomorpho-
logical changes induced by human occupation of the area.[9] In a phrase, the modern
spatial distribution of soil types is not the same as the ones that existed at different
times in the past.

In the late 1970s, processual archaeologists – notably Kent Flannery, Colin
Renfrew, Henry Wright, and their associates – took a different tack from the one
pursued by Sanders and the cultural materialists. The former began to examine the
specificity of the processes of class and state formation that unfolded in particular
regions. They focused on the interplay of what they perceived to be general
sociocultural evolutionary processes and the historical contingency of changing
social relations in those particular societies.

In *The Cloud People*, Flannery (1983) invoked the idea of "divergent evolution" to portray and explain the different pathways followed by the Zapotec, who
resided in the Valley of Oaxaca, and the Mixtec, who adapted to the small, high-
elevation valleys located to the north.[10] Building on the distinction that Sahlins and
Service drew between "specific evolution" (the developmental pathway followed
by a particular culture as it changed through time) and "general evolution" (the
appearance of successively higher levels of sociopolitical integration), Flannery
and his colleagues examined a situation in the Valley of Oaxaca and its environs
that involved both specific and general evolution. They focused their attention on
different developmental pathways followed by the two societies – one culminating
in a highly centralized state, the other in a series of territories ruled by local lords.
They were less concerned with whether a given society was a tribe or chiefdom
than with the gradual appearance of particular sociopolitical institutions.

Flannery and Joyce Marcus (1983a:79–80) reiterated the former's earlier
definition of the state, which is worth quoting at length:

> The state is a type of very strong, usually highly centralized government, with a
> professional ruling class, largely divorced from the bonds of kinship which characterize
> simpler societies. It is highly stratified and extremely diversified internally, with
> residential patterns often based on occupational specialization rather than blood or affinal
> relationship. The state attempts to maintain a monopoly of force, and is characterized by
> true law; almost any crime may be considered a crime against the state, in which case
> punishment is meted out by the state according to codified procedures, rather than being
> the responsibility of the offended party or his kin, as in simpler societies. While indi-
> vidual citizens must forego [*sic*] violence, the state can wage war; it can also draft
> soldiers, levy taxes, and exact tribute.
>
> States have a powerful economic structure; they are characterized by both reciprocal
> and redistributive exchange, and often by markets as well. The economy is largely
> controlled by an elite (usually hereditary) with preferential access to strategic goods and
> services; this elite constitutes the usual stratum from which high officers are recruited.
> (Flannery 1972:403–4)

They then posed a series of questions. The first was: *"When did a highly central-ized government with a professional ruling class first appear?"* (Flannery and Marcus 1983a:80, emphasis in original). Following Sanders's (1974:109) earlier argument that, while chiefs can recruit considerable amounts of labor for public construction, "they cannot amass such levels of manpower for the construction of residences for themselves," they concluded that the appearance of monumental palaces with both residential and public spaces marked the appearance of a ruling class. Such structures were beyond the capabilities of an extended family and required corvée labor for their construction; they also suggested that such struc-tures as well as the differences between elite and commoner burials represented the gradual withering after 500 B.C. and eventual separation around 200 B.C. of kin ties between the nobility and their commoner relatives (Flannery and Marcus 1983a: 80–1).

Flannery and Marcus adopted Richard Blanton's (1976, 1983) argument that Monte Albán was founded on unoccupied land, and that it marked the appearance of a confederation between previously autonomous chiefdoms in different branches of the valley. In their view, it

> was the first administrative center of valley-wide significance, considerably extending
> the authority of such as elite. . . . While it is doubtful that *political* ties to their respective
> regions ever vanished completely, 300 years of prestigious intermarriage at Monte Albán
> might eventually have converted them into a class-endogamous stratum of professional
> rulers by severing their *kin* ties to the commoners of those regions. (Flannery and Marcus
> 1983a:81, emphasis in original)

Continuing this line of argument, they suggested that "the occupants of Monte Albán . . . [were] aggressors against a whole range of weaker neighbors outside the valley, preferably in regions where a different range of products could be pro-duced" (Flannery and Marcus 1983a:81).

Flannery and Marcus's (1983a:82) second question was: *"When do the 'public buildings, works, and services' of the state appear, including 'public works of a religious nature' with full-time specialists maintaining a state religion?"* (emphasis in original). Their answer was around 200 B.C. with the appearance of public buildings that had a stereotyped ground-plan shared by sixteenth-century Zapotec temples. They suggested that the appearance of such buildings at Monte Albán coincided with the appearance of a priesthood associated with a state religious cult whose members took over activities that were performed earlier by individuals, families, or sodalities. In other words, the state cult was one potential site for the extraction of goods and services from the direct producers of the valley.

Their third question was concerned with the appearance of a four-tiered admini-strative hierarchy in the valley. After pointing to the "ambiguity of the relationship between a site-size hierarchy and an administrative hierarchy," Flannery and Marcus (1983a:82) concluded that it emerged in the Oaxaca Valley with the rise of the Monte Albán state around 200 B.C. They also discerned secondary and tertiary centers with public architecture and small, fourth-tier settlements that lacked large-scale architecture – all of which were contemporary with the primary center.

Their fourth question dealt with the prerogatives of state-based societies: waging war, drafting soldiers, levying taxes, and exacting tribute. Following David Webster's (1975) argument, Flannery and Marcus (1983a:82–3) suggested that the Zapotec rulers waged war against neighboring communities whose residents were not kin and, further, that they extracted tribute from them after 200 B.C.

Flannery and Marcus (1983a:83) also noted that state-based societies appeared in the Mixteca at roughly the same time as or slightly later than the Monte Albán state. However, they had a different form from the Zapotec state in Oaxaca (Flannery and Marcus 1983b:xix). Their colleague Ronald Spores (1983:123) portrayed these polities as analogs of the sixteenth-century Mixtec kingdoms that existed in the area. He indicated that the early Mixtec polities probably consisted of ruling families whose members resided in settlements that were much smaller than Monte Albán. They exercised control over land, water, and resources. They also established and maintained marriage networks that were socially and economically significant and arranged appropriate marriages with the members of other ruling families in the area.

Marcus (1983:357), seemingly equating state formation with the development of small urban centers in the Mixteca, argued that they "lagged a few centuries behind the Valley of Oaxaca, and such early centers were clearly influenced by their Zapotec counterparts." She proceeded to argue that all of the centers were in contact with each other and, consequently, that developments in the two regions were interdependent. Patricia Plunket (1983, quoted by Byland and Pohl 1994:53) suggested that chiefdoms in some parts of the Mixteca might have become enmeshed in the web of the Monte Albán state through elite marriage exchange, while others were conquered. This implies, in my view, that the rules of succession to the various thrones in Oaxaca and Mixteca were probably ambiguous; it may account for the appearance at a later time of Mixtec polities in the Zapotec homeland.

Richard Blanton and Gary Feinman (1984) attempted to deal with the apparent inability of the divergent evolutionary model to deal with the connections that existed between sociocultural traditions that followed different pathways of development. They adopted Immanuel Wallerstein's (1974) idea of a world system and Jane Schneider's (1977) notion of a precapitalist world economy. In their perspective, the precapitalist world economy of Mesoamerica was held together by exchange, where the elites of different regions exchanged luxury goods in order to accumulate and maintain power within their homelands through the redistribution of the status goods they possessed and acquired from different lands. While exchange relations perpetuated linkages between peoples living in different regions, they did not account for "the growth of [the] powerful core states" or for the fact that some polities reoriented their economic priorities "toward production and exchange in the world-system arena," which affected areas far beyond those they had subordinated through military force (Blanton and Feinman 1984:678).

Colin Renfrew retained his sociocultural evolutionist perspective during the 1970s and 1980s but began to elaborate various elements of his scheme. In the mid-1970s, he argued that "the whole part of the development toward urban and civilized living" lies between two organizational levels: the egalitarian tribe and the civilization-state (Renfrew 1974:71). In his view, the great merit of neo-evolutionists in the 1960s was the examination of those intermediate-level societies, called chiefdoms, that exhibited degrees of social integration and features usually lacking in tribal societies. After listing the features that were frequently seen in chiefdoms – such as social ranking, greater population density, chiefly redistribution of produce, greater productivity, clearly defined borders, larger residential groups, priesthoods, elaboration of rituals for social purposes, centers that coordinated socioeconomic and religious activities, organization and deployment of public labor, some craft specialization, reduction of internal strife, pervasive inequality, distinctive dress for those of high status, and "no true government to back up decisions by legalized force" – Renfrew (1974:73) pointed out that there was considerable diversity in the kinds of societies bearing this classification chiefdoms. He then drew an interesting distinction between two types of chiefdoms, both of which were found in Europe during the third millennium B.C.

Renfrew (1974:74) correctly asserted that this was not an exercise in social typology but rather that it was

> an attempt to distinguish different groups of features which appear to be structurally related in some of these societies. . . . At one extreme lie societies where personal wealth in terms of valuable possessions is not impressively documented, but where the solidarity of the social unit was expressed most effectively in communal or group activities. And at the other are societies where a marked disparity in personal possessions and other material indications of prestige appears to document a salient personal ranking, yet often without evidence of large communal meetings or activities.

The first type he termed *group-oriented chiefdoms*; the second he called *individualizing chiefdoms*, because the role of the individual seemed to loom so much larger.[11] Let us look at each type in more detail.

Renfrew based his description of the group-oriented chiefdoms on ethnographic examples from Polynesia. He characterized them in the following manner: (1) the technologies were relatively low-level or undeveloped and had only limited craft specialization; (2) the chiefs redistributed foodstuffs and other gifts at regularly scheduled feasts and public gatherings; (3) the chiefs mobilized large labor forces to construct impressive public works; and (4) the chiefs remained relatively faceless and anonymous. Furthermore, since many of the group-oriented chiefdoms were found in areas with limited ecological diversity, he argued that chief's role "as the focus for the redistribution of produce from ecologically diverse microenvironments . . . was sometimes fulfilled only to a limited extent" (Renfrew 1974:75).

Renfrew (1974:76) contrasted this social type with a range of non-civilized societies that "impress us with their 'barbaric' splendor." He portrayed the individualizing chiefdoms in the following terms: (1) it was possible to distinguish individual leaders either by the number, richness, or symbolic value of their possessions or by the scale and prominence of their residences; (2) technology, often metallurgy, was highly developed; (3) public monuments, other than those associated with the chief, were either fortified or absent; and (4) redistribution was continuous rather than periodic. As you will recall, the appearance of palaces and public buildings signaled the rise of the state for Flannery and Marcus. Renfrew (1974:76) realized that "in discussing these [individualizing] societies it is sometimes difficult to draw a clear boundary between chiefdom and state."

At this point, Renfrew (1974:84) revisited the distinction Durkheim drew between mechanical and organic solidarity. While he eschewed reviving all aspects of *The Division of Labor in Society*, he thought that one of Durkheim's observations did apply to the distinction between group-oriented and individualizing chiefdoms. He quoted this passage at length:

> The first [mechanical solidarity] can be strong only if the ideas and tendencies common to all the members of a society are greater in number and intensity than those which pertain personally to each member. . . . But what makes our personality is how much of our own individual qualities we have, what distinguishes us from others. This solidarity can grow only in inverse ratio to personality. There are in each of us, as we have said, two consciences: one which is common to our group in its entirety, which is consequently not ourself, but society living and acting within us; the other, on the contrary, represents that in us which is personal and distinct, that which makes us an individual. . . . There are here two contrary forces, one centripedal, the other centrifugal. . . . If we have a lively desire to think and act for ourselves, we cannot be strongly inclined to think and act as others do. If our ideal is to present a singular and personal appearance, we do not want to resemble everybody else. Moreover, at the moment when this solidarity exercises its force, our personality vanishes, as our definition permits us to say, for we are no longer ourselves but the collective life. (Durkheim 1893/1964:129–30)

While he saw Durkheim's remarks as illuminating, Renfrew (1974:84) wrote that

> the equation between organic solidarity and individualizing chiefdom is not altogether an acceptable one.

The point is valid, however, that in the desire for rich and prestigious objects, which is the most evident feature of such princely burials, a measure of competition and personal aggrandisement seems to have overcome what one may term the *egalitarian ethos* common in many band societies and some tribal ones. . . . [T]hese supposedly universal human attributes in fact first make their appearance in the archaeological record in what we have called individualizing chiefdoms. . . . Why do competition and competitive display become so striking a feature in certain kinds of tribal and chiefdom society? (emphasis in original)

Renfrew (1974:85) attempted to provide an answer to the question. He argued that the development of technology was not independent but rather was embedded in the relationship "between purely material and productive considerations (such as metal technology) and social and symbolic ones (notably prestige and conspicuous consumption) which lie at the root of sustained growth and culture change in most early societies." He noted that this relationship raised additional problems. The production of new products did not necessarily lead to increased demand. It did, however, when the new production was linked to prestige and competition which implied "the potential equivalence between material goods and personal prestige" (Renfrew 1974:85). In his view, the linkage of prestige with status implied that there was also some degree of social mobility in individualizing chiefdoms. Unstated, I believe, was Renfrew's belief that the quest for prestige and whatever conspicuous consumption it might entail resided not in the realms of the social or the cultural but rather in the personalities and motivations of those individuals or groups that sought to optimize gratification.[12]

During this period, Renfrew restated his earlier views on the importance of exchange and redistribution as motors that underpinned the development of class-stratified, state-based societies. For example, he wrote with approval that

Flannery [1968b] . . . offered a model for the growth of state society among the Olmecs by proposing that the status of those chiefs who controlled access to exotic goods obtained from outside by means of exchange was so positively and progressively enhanced by doing so that their power and authority consistently increased, leading to the emergence of a social organization of very marked centrality. This is a process that can be recognized as significant in the formation of other hierarchical societies also. (Renfrew 1979a:34)

While Renfrew acknowledged that the intensification of production – viewed broadly as both the production of a greater range of goods and foodstuffs and increased productivity – was indeed a motor of change, he nevertheless focused his attention more on the dynamic roles played by exchange and redistribution. He discerned two broad types of exchange: contact between societies at different levels of economic development, and *peer polity interaction* or exchange between societies with approximately the same level of the same complexity.[13] The former permitted the elites of ranked societies to acquire a range of sophisticated prestige goods from their socially more complex trading partners and to consolidate their social positions by redistributing them to their kin and neighbors (Renfrew 1982a:6). The latter was concerned with the exchanges between developed chief-doms or early states that existed beside or in close proximity to one another in the same geographical region. It entailed the transmission of those features held in common by the cluster of polities; peer polity interaction was accomplished by various means – warfare, competitive emulation, the adoption of symbolic systems, the spread of innovations through imitation, as well as increased flows of information and exchange goods, to name a few mechanisms (Renfrew 1986).

In his work on Melos, Renfrew discerned a succession of three modes of organizational structure on the island: non-state, independent state, and subordinate regional unit within a larger state or empire. The intensification of agricultural production was "crucial to the transition from the acephelous society of mode I to the state society of mode II" (Renfrew 1982b:271). Agricultural intensification also involved increased population density, increased per capita input of labor, and increased efficiency as a result of technological innovation. While the emergent state-based polity was politically autonomous, its citizens participated in a wider economic system. Renfrew (1982b:264) noted that the processes of state formation – both the emergence of the independent polity and its subsequent incorporation as a province in the larger political entity – affected all aspects of life. He described the effects in the following manner:

> The resulting production beyond subsistence was ultimately used to support [besides the agricultural workers] an administrative elite and the craft specialists resident at the primary centre (which for much of later bronze age times under mode II seems to have been the only settlement). These administrative and craft specialists may well have been involved in agriculture, but there can be little doubt that they benefited from the PBS [i.e. production beyond subsistence], and from the results of exchanges with other polities which it facilitated. (Renfrew 1982b:284)

Earlier, Renfrew (1982b:270) had characterized the structure of the earliest independent state as

> a centralised organisation, with two kinds of specialists in addition to the agricultural workers. The first are the craft specialists who produce goods either for trade or for exchange with subsistence goods. The second are the leaders, spiritual and temporal, who often do not produce material goods, but regulate the society. With the latter must be included any coercive armed forces, whether for internal use to maintain allegiance, or for external use in defence.

Renfrew pointed out that the earliest state-based society on the island of Melos lacked the kind of settlement hierarchy thought by Wright and others to be characteristic of early states. He attributed this to the small size of the island and of other Greek states, which had populations ranging from 1,500 to 10,000. Since the elites could manage their affairs on a face-to-face basis, there was, in his view, "only limited need, in terms of the information carried, for a highly complex decision-making organisation" (Renfrew 1982b:281–2). He described Melos and contemporary states found elsewhere in the Aegean area as an example of the emergence of an *Early State Module* pattern – autonomous polities roughly similar in size with populations numbering about ten thousand and territories that radiated twenty to thirty kilometers from the seats of power (Renfrew 1975:14; 1982b:282). It was this pattern that underpinned peer polity interaction.

More than most of his processual colleagues, Renfrew recognized the fragility of states. When the central administrative organizations, class structures, and centralized economies of early states collapsed, they were replaced by societies with lower levels of sociopolitical organization – i.e. non-states. In Renfrew's (1979b:482–4) view, the collapse of imperial states generally took around a century, but the process was frequently more rapid when central imperial authority was withdrawn in provincial areas. As specialization increased, the various segments of the population often became increasingly interdependent, and options for further development narrowed. This was potentially an ominous sign, for "stability (in the sense of peace and prosperity) is assured only by continued growth. Zero growth does not for . . . [some societies] represent a stable state, and negative growth can accelerate to distintigration [*sic*]" (Renfrew 1979b:489). Renfrew (1978, 1979b) drew an analogy between the collapse of early states and the cusp catastrophe models described by mathematicians concerned with the branch of topology known as catastrophe theory. In his view, early states were composed of a number of variables, and, when the value of one of these (e.g. charismatic authority) changed suddenly (i.e. over a century or so), it affected other variables and frequently precipitated changes in them, leading to a collapse (i.e. rapid transformation) of the system as a whole. Renfrew believed that the cusp catastrophe model appropriately described the sudden transition from a state to a non-state society. Thus, for him, state formation was a two-way street: states emerged (anastrophe, in his terms) and states fell apart.

Both the cultural materialists and the processual archaeologists adopted the kind of liberal social theory elaborated by Herbert Spencer and Émile Durkheim. Kent Flannery (e.g. 1972) and Colin Renfrew (e.g. 1974) have acknowledged this debt in their writings. Both Flannery (e.g. 1986) and Renfrew (e.g. 1978, 1979b) have also relied on models and metaphors drawn from ecology, biology, and mathematics to explain sociocultural phenomena. This is not remarkable, since it is also part of the legacy left by Spencer and Durkheim. Spencer, as you will recall, was concerned with developing a theory that accounted for the evolution of everything from human society to the cosmos. His was a unified theory of science, analogous to the views advocated by Rudolf Carnap and the other logical positivists who launched the *International Encyclopedia of Unified Science* after the Second World War. Durkheim's project of establishing the epistemological foundations of sociology took cognizance of both the social and the psychological realms. As you saw earlier in this section, he attempted to deal with the interplay between the social and psychological and, in this instance, seemed to explain sociological phenomena in terms of psychological drives and motivations. In a phrase, the tendency to seek reductionist arguments in order to account for the social in terms of the psychological or the natural is an integral part of the legacy left by Spencer and Durkheim. It is also an integral part of the processual archaeology that developed from the 1960s onward.

Arenas of Discussion: Chiefdoms and State Formation

If Elman Service (1962/1971, 1975) conceptualized the idea of chiefdoms, then Robert Carneiro (1981b, 1991) has been its leading advocate. If Colin Renfrew (1973) was among the first to use the idea to interpret the archaeological record, then archaeologists at the University of Michigan in the late 1970s explored the implications and limitations of the concept as they sought to hone and refine its utility. At issue for the processualists and the Marxists are (1) whether chiefdoms are a necessary stage or evolutionary type in the formation of state-based societies; (2) whether some of the societies identified as chiefdoms – such as Renfrew's "individualizing chiefdoms" discussed earlier in the chapter – might in fact already be state-based civilizations; and (3) what mechanisms are involved in the transformation of kin-based tribal communities into chiefdoms and chiefdoms into class-stratified, state-based societies. Another set of issues involves how societies develop and states form: Are the processes of societal change slow, gradual, and continuous, or are they discontinuous and potentially rapid?

Service (1962/1971:134), as you will recall, described chiefdoms as "*redistributive societies* with a permanent central agency of coordination" (emphasis in the original). They appeared among relatively populous sedentary communities in response to the development of continued rather than sporadic economic specialization in environmentally diverse regions. This economic specialization involved either or both the pooling of individual skills in large-scale cooperative production projects, and the specialization that existed at the level of residential units located in different ecological habitats. "Most chiefdoms," Service wrote(1962/1971:136), "seem to have arisen where important regional exchange and a consequent increase in local specialization came about because ecological differentiation was combined with considerable sedentariness."

The chiefly level of the societies, the permanent central agencies of coordination, evolved as an efficient means to distribute goods among the various economically specialized local communities. The chiefs coordinated the efforts of the
society; they organized activities and coordinated the redistribution of surplus
goods. The authority of the chiefs rested neither on their powers of persuasion nor
on their abilities to coerce, but rather on the legitimacy of the social hierarchy,
which was acknowledged by both the chiefly and non-chiefly strata of the society.
Their authority and independence in political decision-making grew over time,
especially when hierarchies of charismatic leadership were transformed into
institutionalized, permanent positions. Thus, this hereditary authority was a form
of institutionalized power that buttressed institutionalized inequality. The chiefs
increasingly resorted to religious and ideological means to gain the consent of their
non-chiefly neighbors (Service 1975:293–4).

Service argued that chiefdoms followed two distinct developmental pathways.
One was the formation of *archaic civilizations*. This "'road to civilization' was the
developmental career of a few bureaucracies, which under rather unusual [circum-
scribed] environmental conditions fulfilled themselves eventually in ruling what
must have been hundreds of former petty chiefdoms" (Service 1975:306); archaic
civilizations were not states in the sense that political organization was based on
coercion and physical force. The other developmental pathway involved the
appearance of *primitive states*, which resulted from contact between a chiefdom
and an already existing state (Service 1975:289, 302–4).

Carneiro took a different tack from Service. While the latter viewed economic
redistribution as the defining feature of chiefdoms, Carneiro saw warfare as the
mechanism that brought chiefdoms into existence. For Carneiro (1981b:67),
following Herbert Spencer, political development had been a continuous process
leading from autonomous villages through chiefdoms to states and finally empires.
In order to determine whether a particular society was a chiefdom or had already
passed the threshold of statehood, it was essential to differentiate chiefdoms from
states. He defined a chiefdom as *"an autonomous political unit composed of a
number of communities under the permanent control of a paramount chief"*
(Carneiro 1981b:45; 1991:168, emphasis in the originals). States were also composed of a number of communities, but what distinguished them from chiefdoms
was the fact that they had centralized governments *"with the power to draft men
for war or work, levy and collect taxes, and decree and enforce laws"* (Carneiro
1981b:69; 1991:168, emphasis in the originals). The powers to draft, tax, and
enforce laws were the most diagnostic features of states. The authority of chiefs,
in Carneiro's (1991:178–81) view, rested not on their redistribution of surplus but
rather on the success of their military campaigns; this enhanced their political
power as well as their economic circumstances.

Carneiro provided an alternative to Renfrew's distinction between group-oriented and individualizing chiefdoms and to a distinction that several archaeologists (e.g. Steponaitis 1978) drew between simple chiefdoms with one administrative tier and complex chiefdoms which had two or three decision-making levels (Steponaitis 1978:420). He described three types of chiefdoms: (1) *minimal* chiefdoms, which met the minimal requirements of a chiefdom – i.e. a couple of villages under the control of a paramount chief; (2) *typical* chiefdoms; and (3) *maximal* chiefdoms, which were "large and complex enough to approach the threshold of the state" (Carneiro 1981b:47).

Warfare, from Carneiro's (1981b:63–71) perspective, was the motor driving the formation of both chiefdoms and states. Chiefdoms appeared when the formerly autonomous villages in an environmentally circumscribed region fell under the permanent sway of a paramount chief or a centralized government. Carneiro (1981b:71) also wrote that "most societies we would want to call chiefdoms rather than states show at least the rudiments of conscription, of taxation, and of law enforcement."[14] Carneiro (1991:185–6) was also concerned with why chiefdoms in some regions – like the Cauca Valley of Colombia – had not evolved into states; the reason, he argued, was that large chiefdoms

> built up slowly and painfully, [and] could and often did fragment into their component units. And if they did not lapse all the way back to autonomous villages, they regressed at least to the level of smaller and simpler chiefdoms. . . . The gains of decades, or even centuries, can be quickly undone, leaving the process of growth, amalgamation, and consolidation to begin all over again.

What Carneiro did not address was why these chiefdoms, like states, fragmented and fell apart. Nor did he address the kinds of internal sociocultural transformations that occurred in those once-autonomous villages as they fell under the sway of a paramount chief.

Timothy Earle (1977, 1978, 1987) and Henry Wright (1977a, 1977b, 1978, 1984, 1986), among others at the University of Michigan, were generally critical of the explanations of chiefdoms provided by Service and Carneiro, and began to refine and reformulate the concept in the late 1970s.[15] Earle (1977, 1978:167–96) argued that archaeological and ethnohistoric data from Hawaii did not support Service's contention about the importance of redistribution. He found that the chiefs' role in food distribution was not socially integrative since it occurred only infrequently during times of disaster. Chiefs exchanged status goods that they used to forge alliances. With regard to the development of complex chiefdoms in Hawaii, he wrote:

> Hawaiian irrigation and warfare were important aspects of the political economy for which expanded productive capacity was an essential goal. A positive feedback relation-

ship existed between competitive political organizations, environmental potential, and population. The commoner population was essential to the chiefs because the surplus production generated from the total economies was used to finance the political system. The articulation between subsistence production and political finance was critical: through the system of land tenure dominated by the chiefs, labor and obligatory offerings from the commoners were exchanged for land use rights. A significant effect of the expanding regional organization was an increased isolation of the local community socially and economically, and an increased dependency of the total population on the regional sociopolitical superstructure. (Earle 1978:192)

Earle's (e.g. 1987:279) perspective, like those of Service and Carneiro, was essentially a top-down management view of the role claimed by members of the chiefly strata. The chiefs, who were set off from the rest of the society, organized the activities of the regional population. Furthermore, they organized these activities and drew goods from the community to satisfy their own wants and desires rather than to meet some common good.

In the late 1970s, Henry Wright (1977a, 1977b, 1978) conceptualized chiefdoms in terms of systems and information theory. From this perspective, a chiefdom was

a cultural development whose centralized decision-making activity is differentiated from, though it ultimately regulates, decision-making regarding local production and local social process. . . . Lacking internal specialization, any delegation of decision-making prerogatives is a complete delegation, and the subordinate decision-maker would be capable of independent action. The dominant strategy of decision-making with regard to lower level organization is that there should be only two levels of actual decision-making hierarchy – local and central – and that local units should handle as many of their own operations as possible, each placing few demands on the central regulator and thus allowing it to control a larger number of local units given its limited capacity or span of control. (Wright 1977b:381)

Wright also viewed states through the lens of systems and information theory, seeing them as cultural developments with decision-making apparatuses that were both externally and internally differentiated with regard to the local processes they regulated. They involved three or four levels of decision-making, in which the dominant strategy was "to encourage as much hierarchy and segmentation as possible in order to create contexts of [Durkheimian] organic solidarity" (Wright 1978:383).

Wright (1977b:385) noted that one should not assume that "chiefdoms will develop inevitably into states; one must isolate the conditions which destroy or transform chiefly mechanisms of regulation and generate new ones." In his view, state formation involved more than the appearance of coercive mechanisms, since they differed from chiefdoms in a number of ways – e.g. regulatory pattern, dominant regulatory strategy, and hierarchical structure. Any study of state origins must, from his perspective, take into account changes in a whole series of sub-systems.

In the mid-1980s, Wright (1984:69) elaborated his argument, suggesting "that class-organized, socio-political organization flourished for centuries before actual state formation. Complex chiefdoms were not merely evolutionary curiosities, transformed immediately into states in the continental heartlands, persistent only on islands not large enough to sustain states." Focusing on complex rather than simple chiefdoms, he further argued "that continued competition for alliances and offices among local ranking groups would weld such groups into a region-wide chiefly or noble class" (Wright 1984:69). Wright was also concerned with the process of state formation. He indicated that state formation was not merely a consequence of an increase in scale, but rather that complex chiefdoms underwent a crisis which affected the patterns of competition within and between polities. In the process, chiefs expanded their ritual and political control first over production, then over warfare, and finally over aspects of societal life (Wright 1984:49). These changes were coincident with the appearance of three- to four-level central hier-archies, rapid population growth, and increased conflict, raiding, and warfare (Wright 1986:358).

The Michigan archaeologists had a top-down, generally positive view of chiefly and state bureaucracies.[16] These managers integrated society and ensured that it functioned smoothly. As a result, they did not adequately consider the dependence of chiefly and ruling strata on the direct producers from the commoner layers of society. What would have happened to the chiefs of complex chiefdoms or the rulers of early states if they had denied the commoners access to land and other means of production? The answer might be that there would have been no surplus to finance the political system.

Jonathan Haas (1981, 1982) was critical of the "integration perspective" adopted by the Michigan archaeologists. He advocated instead what he called a "conflict position." Following Morton Fried (1960, 1967), he saw the state as a coercive mechanism that resolved internal class conflict in a stratified society. For Haas, social class structures were rooted in the economy and represented differential access to the total social product and labor of the society. Unlike the advocates of the integration perspective, Haas, like Carneiro (1970) and my work with Gailey (Gailey and Patterson 1987, 1988), viewed the state as a repressive apparatus and state formation as a process that involved repression at home and conquest abroad.

Nevertheless, implicit in Haas's argument is an idea shared with Wright: namely, that socioeconomic class structures existed before the emergence of state institu-tions and practices. For Marxist writers the issues here are (1) how long did these economic class structures exist before the appearance of the state, and (2) were the social hierarchies found in chiefdoms the same as the economic classes found in states? For processualists, the appearance of the state apparatus involved decades if not centuries; for Marxists, the development of state institutions and practices occurred rapidly in a matter of months or a few years.

Scholars inspired by various strands of Marxist social thought took different tacks regarding the origins of inequality. Some questioned the fundamental premises of the sociocultural evolutionists. For example, William Marquardt (1987) challenged the long-held view that an agricultural economy was a necessary prerequisite for the development of social complexity and the state. He pointed out that the Calusa, a foraging society in South Florida in the sixteenth century, had noble and commoner social strata, and that the paramount chief/ruler collected tribute from the territorial districts under his control. The authority of the paramount ruler was enforced by a military elite whose members did not engage in direct production. In a phrase, the Calusa was a tributary state.

In different ways, Barbara Bender (1990), Bruce Trigger (1990), and James Zeidler (1987) pointed out that some societies manifesting a primitive communal or kin-based mode of production had foraging economies, while other societies manifesting the same mode of production had subsistence economies based on agricultural production. Furthermore, they observed that the social relations found in these kin-communal societies ranged from relatively egalitarian (the Iroquois) to hierarchical (the Northwest Coast). In other words, they did not see chiefdoms as some kind of middle-range society that was intermediate between tribal societies and states.

Trigger, Bender, and Zeidler also focused on the internal dynamics of these societies and on the mechanisms of resistance that impeded or prevented assertions of exploitative social relations. As Trigger (1990:145) noted, the powerful, well-integrated mechanisms that defended equality in kin-communal societies had to be eliminated if hierarchical organizations were to develop. Thus, he pointed indirectly to the dialectic of state formation. On the one hand, state formation entailed the crystallization of hierarchical structures marked by exploitative social relations and resistance to the imposition of those structures. On the other hand, it involved the distortion and dissolution of those institutions and practices that were the foundation of equitable, non-exploitative social relations. Furthermore, Trigger and Bender challenged the sociocultural evolutionists and the French structural Marxists who argued that (1) all social change in kin-ordered societies was a result of conflicts among interest groups; and (2) all societies, including the kin-ordered ones, were to some extent class societies in which age and gender groupings in a sense constituted "classes in themselves" (Trigger 1990:120).

Other archaeologists – notably Antonio Gilman (1991) and Kristian Kristiansen (1991) – focused their attention on trajectories of social development in Europe. Gilman (1991:146–7) observed that one difficulty with the integration model of the Michigan archaeologists was that it did not tell us why the elites inherited privilege.

He stressed the importance of exploitative social relations in the process of state formation. Exploitation, as you will recall, occurred when the members of one class relied on the efforts of the members of the direct producing classes for their livelihood; the most distinctive feature of a society was the manner in which surplus was extracted from the direct producers. Gilman (1991:149–58) argued that surplus extraction in the Mediterranean world of Classical Antiquity involved labor services and rent from the more or less unfree laboring classes, and various indirect taxes and services from the free classes.[17] In his view, a stratified society emerged in southeastern Spain when an incipient ruling class began to extract rent from agricultural producers. This coincided with the appearance of intensified subsistence agriculture based on irrigation, the exploitation of animals for secondary products – like cheese and hides – and the cultivation of olives and vines. Rents underwrote the appearance of luxury goods.

Gilman (1991:158) discussed the appearance of class-stratified societies in terms of Engels's discussion of "military democracies" or the germanic mode of production rather than chiefdoms. Engels (1884/1972:205) had earlier described military democracies in the following way:

> A military leader who had made himself a name gathered around a band of young men eager for booty whom he pledged to personal loyalty, giving the same pledge to them. The leader provided their keep, gave them gifts, and organized them on a hierarchic basis: a bodyguard and standing troop for smaller expeditions, and a regular corps of officers for operations on a larger scale. Weak as these retinues must have been and as we in fact find them to be later . . . they were nevertheless the beginnings of the decay of the old freedom of the people and showed themselves to be such during and after the migrations. For in the first place they favored the rise of monarchic power. In the second place, . . . they could only be kept together by continual wars and plundering expeditions. Plunder became an end in itself. If the leader of the retinue found nothing to do in the neighborhood, he set out with his men to other peoples where there was war and the prospect of booty.

Gilman also remarked that, while the societies of southeastern Spain and the Aegean were relatively similar about 2000 B.C., they followed different development pathways during the second millennium B.C. After describing interpretations which stressed the role of exchange of luxury goods for the elites in the eastern Mediterranean, he wrote that "once the Minoan/Mycenaean wealth exchange bubble burst, the unintegrated 'Germanic' side of the political economy would once again become the basis of stratification" (Gilman 1991:167).

After indicating that the term "chiefdom" glossed a wide range of societies, Kristiansen (1991:17) suggested that it was only one variant of the social types that existed between tribal societies and states. Following Friedman and Rowlands's (1977) idea that the particular developmental trajectory followed by a given society is determined by its initial condition, he outlined two pathways of state formation. Both were rooted in societal types that existed between chiefdoms and state-based societies. The initial condition of both trajectories was a stratified society with strong economic divisions, emphasis on territorial rather than kin relations, and no bureaucracy. The initial condition of one pathway was Renfrew's individualizing chiefdom; its end-product was the "Germanic" military democracy, in which the chieftains and kings set themselves apart from the agrarian substrate from which they extracted tribute. The initial condition of the second pathway was Renfrew's group-oriented chiefdom; its end-product was the "Asiatic" state described by Friedman and Rowlands (1977:216–22), in which there were tribute relations between local nobles and commoners and between local chiefs and the paramount ruler; the tribute was in staple goods or labor time rather luxury items.

By contrast, Elizabeth Brumfiel (1983), drawing on Aztec society as a case, focused attention on the internal political dynamics and strategies that underwrote state formation. She viewed the state as a powerful, permanently instituted system of political administration that was buttressed by the use of force. She too argued that trajectories of development were shaped by initial conditions (Brumfiel 1983:262–3). States, in her view, arose from political rather than purely economic conflicts or population growth. She pointed out that social conflict in Aztec society had both political and economic bases in political systems where leadership was instituted in weak but permanent offices – like those that prevailed in the Valley of Mexico before the formation of the Aztec state. She argued that the decline of the Toltec state created a political vacuum in the Valley of Mexico that was filled by a host of unstable, mutually hostile polities. These resembled chiefdoms in two ways: (1) they had simple administrative structures with two to three levels; and (2) they were politically unstable. Paramount chiefs distributed wealth to counter threats of revolt and diverted resources for conspicuous display.

The intensification of civil war, invasion, and shifting alliances between these polities underwrote fundamental structural changes that led to the formation of the Aztec state. The first step in the process involved the collapse of the existing prestate structures. It involved Aztec militaristic expansion and undermining local resistance as local nobles competed with each other for patronage. The second step involved a series of organizational reforms that ensured the continuation of the political status quo; in Brumfiel's (1983:274) words, these reforms "did little to enhance the efficient flow of information to and the decision-making capability of the state." The third step in the process entailed the consolidation of power through large-scale public works projects in the Valley and ceaseless military activity on its margins to acquire new sources of tribute in luxury goods, raw materials, and foodstuffs. The final step involved gradual development of a state bureaucracy.

Brumfiel (1980, 1987a, 1987b, 1998) pursued this analysis of Aztec state formation in the context of a wider study that focused on the development of inter-regional markets, consumption, and elite and commoner production in the Valley of Mexico and its environs. She argued that regional polities, like Huexotla, participated more extensively in market exchange following the Aztec consolidation of political power in the basin because of increased demand for rural foodstuffs and urban control of imperial tribute goods (Brumfiel 1980). Observing that there was an impressive array of elite goods in the Valley, she turned her attention to political factionalism and argued that "intra-class competition and political factionalism provide[d] an important dynamic for social change. . . . [In her view] the essence of factionalism is the absence of any functional differences between competing groups that would enable them to be identified archaeologically. However, the very absence of functional differences . . . means that unity has to be created by symbolic means, often through elaborate consumption rituals" (Brumfiel 1987a:683). As a result, "once the wealthy Aztec state imposed its evaluation of persons and events upon regional elites, the scale and elaboration of their household rituals declined" (Brumfiel 1987a:683). In a phrase, public rituals and consumption sponsored by the state were substituted for the earlier household rituals of the local elites. Moreover, the production of elite goods by independent specialists for the market flourished, although the distribution of these ritual items was controlled by the Aztec state. This was an effective political tool even in the absence of state control over their production (Brumfiel 1987b).

If the issues of state formation and the virtues of particular theoretical frameworks promoted crosstalk and backtalk, then discussions concerned with chiefdoms, the transformation of intermediate societies into states, and the nature of these intermediate societies promoted some genuine dialogue in the 1980s. Processualists, cultural materialists, and Marxists presented their views and then wrestled with the ideas of archaeologists whose theoretical underpinnings were different from their own. In the next chapter, we will examine how these conversations played out in the 1990s.

–5–

Convergence and Dialogue after 1990

At least a dozen books and edited volumes concerned with the rise of civilization (the formation of states) appeared after 1990. Some – such as Gary Feinman and Joyce Marcus's (1998) *Archaic States* or my *The Inca Empire* (Patterson 1991) – can be viewed in many respects as restatements of perspectives that were forged and refined from the 1970s to the late 1980s.[1] Others – such as Deborah Nichols and Thomas Charlton's (1997) *The Archaeology of City-States*, Elizabeth Brumfiel and John Fox's (1994) *Factional Competition and Political Development in the New World*, or Gil Stein's (1999) *Rethinking World-Systems* – broke new ground or represented important developments of or departures from earlier studies.

Archaeologists dealt with the explicitly Marxist analyses of the preceding decades in different ways after 1990. Some built on the analyses, extending them into new areas, most notably in historical archaeology, which they reconceptualized as the archaeology of capitalism and its expansion across the globe (e.g. Paynter 1988). Others, both Marxists and processualists, honed the theoretical frameworks they employed as they sought to clarify the internal dynamics of class and state formation. Still others came to grips with the issues they raised and sought to accommodate them in terms of theoretical frameworks they used. A few continued to downplay or disregard altogether the impact and implications of the Marxist analyses. In sum, the decade of the 1990s witnessed an interesting convergence in discussions about the rise of states that were built on different theoretical foundations.

In this chapter, let us consider the impact that the Marxist analyses had. How did archaeologists deal with their legacy after 1990? How did Marxist scholars extend these analyses, and what aspects of their work did the archaeologists find useful? How did archaeologists incorporate features of those analyses with their own ongoing commentaries on state formation? What were the consequences of juxtaposing or articulating Marxist analyses with other theoretical frameworks? Let us examine these questions in terms of the silences, backtalk, crosstalk, and dialogues that ensued after 1990.

Discussion and Critique I: Historic Specificity, Politics, and State Structures

Since the Marxist archaeologists sought to reunite the study of social process with the study of history, historical archaeology became a stronghold for this approach in the 1990s. Mark Leone (1995), Randall McGuire and Robert Paynter (1991), and Charles Orser (1996), among others, believed that their object of inquiry was the historical development of capitalism – a subject on which Marx had a great many original observations, most of which are still relevant today. They shared a belief that the only way to understand particular social arrangements or institutions was to understand how they developed historically. They viewed the members of society as active agents who worked within culturally imposed constraints to provide for the material conditions of life rather than adapting passively to the world around them. They did not seek universally valid explanations of change and development, but rather sought to understand the conditions that set the stage for the appearance of capitalism and its subsequent different pathways of development in various parts of the world. Their method was simultaneously particularist and comparative. They used insights gained from detailed examinations of one case to shed light on other similar processes of development elsewhere.

In the 1990s, some processual archaeologists began to address issues raised a decade earlier by Marxist-inspired studies of class and state formation. Authors who wrote about the evolution of civilization in the 1970s now discussed the process of state formation (e.g. Flannery 1999). Some recognized "the importance of such 'Marxian' factors as political competition, class struggle, and power seeking" (Spencer 1990:5) or wrote about the "goods and labor [that] were extracted from rural producers, probably to support rural elites" (Wright 1998:196). Others suggested that state formation involved ethnogenesis and indicated that the rulers of stratified archaic states "expected individual citizens to forego [*sic*] violence, while the state could wage war, conscript soldiers, levy taxes, and exact tribute" (Marcus and Flannery 1996:26, 171). These authors now recognized that episodes of state formation were often quite rapid, that states collapsed, and that, in many instances, the processes of state formation were nipped in the bud (Flannery 1999; Marcus and Flannery 1996:156; Spencer 1990:14, 19). They also relied more heavily than before on the particularities of specific episodes of class and state formation – in Uruk or Oaxaca, for example – in drawing their conclusions about the processes involved.

Some processual archaeologists rejected the gradualism implied in their earlier models of sociocultural evolution by adopting the viewpoint of the theory of punctuated equilibria, which they borrowed from evolutionary biology. This theory implied that class and state formation "occurs at moments of rapid evolution between periods of stability of slow evolution" (Marcus and Flannery 1996:156;

cf. Spencer 1990). Flannery (1999) examined political processes – like chiefly cycling, biased transmission, and territorial expansion – that he believed were integral features in particular episodes of state formation – such as the ones that occurred in Natal, the Gold Coast, Hunza, Hawaii, or Madagascar. He viewed these as akin to the processes of promotion and linearization he described in the early 1970s in "The Cultural Evolution of Civilizations" (Flannery 1972). Nevertheless, for many processual archaeologists, state formation still involved continually increasing social differentiation; now in the 1990s, however, they viewed it as occurring in sudden spurts rather than gradually. In my view, the difficulty with this approach is that it still does not deal adequately with the dialectics of the class and state formative processes that were generated as the members of one group attempted to exploit those of other groups and the latter resisted or ameliorated those exactions.[2]

Elizabeth Brumfiel (1992) was also critical of the ecosystems approach adopted by the processual archaeologists. Because of its focus on abstract behavior, she argued that this approach (1) made invisible the activities of particular groups of actors defined in terms of gender, class, and faction whose members controlled resources and power; (2) underestimated the difficulties of systemic change; and (3) overestimated the importance of external as opposed to internal causes of change. She advocated instead defining rather than assuming gender roles in order to reconstruct the gendered workloads of a society. She pointed out that the emergence of elites – i.e. non-producing ruling classes – did not leave the producing classes unchanged, but rather the responses of the direct producers were integral to the processes of class formation and had important shaping effects on the emergent class structures. She indicated that successful rulers typically manipulated both resources (wealth) and social relations; they forged alliances by redistributing wealth to the members of some factions and not to those of others.

In the early 1990s, Brumfiel was already buttressing these recommendations with empirical information drawn from Aztec society. She pointed out that women played an important role in defining the limits and the changing circumstances created by the formation of the Aztec state. Their expanded household production and role in population reproduction and growth underwrote the development of labor-intensive *chinampa* (raised-field) agriculture and allowed the Aztec state to field large armies. The cloth they wove circulated far beyond the household through the market and tribute systems controlled by the state (Brumfiel 1991a).

Brumfiel (1991b) examined what she called the interaction of trade and tribute in the Aztec state. Like others, she argued that the residents of Tenochtitlán, the capital city of the Aztec empire, were mainly elite administrators, warriors, priests, craft specialists dealing in elite goods, and urban service workers as well as a few craft specialists who produced utilitarian goods (Brumfiel 1980:466; 1991b:178). She pointed out that, when the Aztecs conquered Xaltocan in the late fourteenth century, the latter was transformed from a tribute-receiving capital to a tribute-paying provincial town under the control of a military governor sent by the Aztec ruler in Tenochtitlán. The local market in Xaltocan declined as the goods that were formerly exchanged there now found their way indirectly to the central market in the Aztec capital. The Aztec ruler put some of the tribute goods received by the state into the market; the attraction of the central market for the inhabitants of the imperial city as well as for those of the Valley of Mexico was the variety of nonlocal products that were available. Thus, the exchanges that took place between the ruling elite and the commoners were based on tribute, redistribution, and commercial activity. Again, Brumfiel went to great lengths to point out that the nature of the tribute–trade interactions in the Aztec state was shaped by both the elite and producing classes.

Elsewhere, Brumfiel (1991c) examined changes that occurred in class structures as formerly independent towns like Huexotla, Xaltocan, and Xico were enmeshed in tributary relations with the Aztec state. In pre-Aztec times, lords controlled both *chinampa* and non-*chinampa* agricultural lands; the land was worked by commoners who were organized into corporate groups (*calpulli*) that distributed plots to individuals, oversaw the collection of tribute, and arranged personal service for the lords. After the Aztec conquest, some of the agricultural lands were held as private estates by nobles who resided in Tenochtitlán; these lands were worked by commoners who were detached from allegiances and obligations to their former communities. While the two classes of commoners had slightly different consumption patterns, their standards of living were generally similar. What distinguished the classes of direct producers was whether tribute was paid to local rulers or to non-resident Aztec lords.

Brumfiel (1998) soon turned her attention to the organization of craft production. She had already pointed out that craft production was organized differently in rural communities and in the imperial city. The urban specialists, both men and women, tended to work full-time at their crafts and were often organized into *calpulli*; those who produced above and beyond the tribute demands of the state sold their surplus goods in the market to the noble, warrior, and priestly residents of the city. By contrast, the rural specialists tended to be food producers who worked part-time at their crafts. Since the rural communities were small, there were only a few specialists in each village; they produced a different array of goods from their urban counterparts; and they were typically not organized into corporate groups. Like their urban counterparts, they too sold goods in the market; however, it was a different market, and their customers were usually not members of the nobility.

Brumfiel (1994a) wrote perceptively about factional competition, which she viewed as conflicts within classes and conflicts between groups formed by cross-class alliances. As a result, she viewed factional competition as a complement to class struggle. In her view, factional competition interacted with class struggle to shape not only the course of political development but also the emergent contours and limitations of exploitation. She pointed out that ruling classes frequently incorporated the leaders of factions into the state bureaucracy and strove to make their interests coincide with those of the ruling class and the state apparatus its members controlled. This, of course, transformed the structure of the ruling class and often diminished the ability of the state to maintain existing levels of exploitation.

Brumfiel then developed her argument about factional competition by examining the way in which ethnicity was manipulated in the Aztec state. She pointed out that

> ethnicity seems to have provided no fixed alignments for factional competition. Rather ethnicity was a tool, fashioned to the needs of political actors as defined by the existing political structure. In late prehispanic Mexico, when the most important political unit was the petty kingdom, ethnicity defined relationships within and between such communities. With the emergence of larger states, ethnicity began to operate at the regional level. It appears, then, that ethnicity is itself shaped by political development; its value as a political resource to build factions and to engage in political action is a function of the size and complexity of the existing political structure. Ethnic-based political factions that cut across class lines to mobilize entire regions for political action probably emerged only as the products of larger states. (Brumfiel 1994b:102)

In a phrase, the Aztec state simultaneously encouraged the formation of ethnic groups to further its goals and discouraged their development by promoting the superiority of its own civic culture. Thus, ethnicity emerged at the regional level of the state partly by intent and partly independent of the state. It was a product of Aztec rule, resistance to Aztec rule, and recognition of commoners who found themselves in the same structural position vis-à-vis the state.

Brumfiel was also critical of the structural Marxist approach elaborated earlier by Friedman and Rowlands (1977), which was cited with approval by a number of processual archaeologists during the 1990s (e.g. Flannery 1999). She suggested that the weakness of their structural Marxist "epigenetic" model of political development was that it saw political change as a consequence of structural incompatibilities within and between the economic base and the social and ideological superstructure; power was not constructed by individuals but fell to particular groups because of the shared cultural rules. Thus, "in the initial phases of political complexity and social inequality, the conferring of subordinate status occurs with the consent of the subordinate groups, with superordinate status falling to those who control the imaginary means of social reproduction through religious ritual" (Brumfiel 1994a:13). The problems with this approach, in her view, were that it postulated (1) "consensus within the body politic prior to the emergence of class and class struggle," and (2) a "strict behavioral determinism" like the functionalism of the ecosystems approach (Brumfiel 1994a:13).

Structural Marxist analyses appealed to the processual archaeologists because of their emphases on superstructural elements – like ideology and religion – and on prestige-goods exchange as the motor of political development. Superstructural elements – like religion, morality, and law – and the importance of exchange relations were, of course, central features of Durkheim's historical functionalism.

Tom Saunders's (1990) critique of structural Marxist approaches in archaeology took a slightly different tack from Brumfiel's. He pointed out that Friedman and Rowlands emphasized the dynamic role played by superstructural elements in the evolution of precapitalist societies. In his view, their epigenetic model was essentially functionalist. By separating the forces and relations of production, they reduced the economy to the level of technology and saw it as a limiting condition, "marking the boundaries beyond which a social formation cannot go" (Saunders 1990:73). Furthermore, Saunders (1990:73) argued, they fetishized "the sphere of circulation, conceiving it as a dominant autonomous instance with its own dynamic" that was distinct from the relations of production and the way in which goods and labor were extracted from the producing classes by those who controlled the means of production. Like Brumfiel (1994a:8), Saunders pointed out that his critique of structural Marxism did not extend to other strands of Marxist social thought that were being engaged by archaeologists in the 1970s and 1980s.

In the early 1990s, Norman Yoffee (1993) extended his earlier critique (Yoffee 1979:26) of the neoevolutionist, socioeconomic growth model employed by many processual archaeologists, focusing his attention on the concept of the chiefdom as a non-egalitarian social type that must precede state-based societies and yet was not quite a state itself. Implicitly, he was also criticizing Friedman and Rowlands's (1977) epigenetic model of political development, which also involved a teleological unfolding of a sequence of social types. Yoffee (1993:69) pointed out that

the most important necessary and jointly sufficient condition that separates states from non-states is the emergence of certain socioeconomic and governmental roles that are emancipated from real or fictive kinship; that is, the basis of relations between the occupants of governmental offices and those who are governed is not ascription. The social corporation of such governmental roles includes the quality of paramount and enforceable authority, and more than ephemeral stability. It is further asserted that the process by which states develop depends on the cumulative accretion of power available to incumbents of prospective governmental roles.

His proposal for studying the rise of states involved Weberian analyses of the varieties of power that existed in particular societies – e.g. the Uruk period societies of Mesopotamia or Teotihuacán.

About the same time, John Baines and Yoffee (1998, 2000) undertook a comparative study of state formation in Egypt and Mesopotamia, focusing on the interrelations of such Weberian analytical categories as power, the maintenance of social order, legitimacy, and wealth; they also examined the development of "high" or elite culture in the two areas. In the process, they pointed out that "inequality, such as existed in both [Egyptian and Mesopotamian] civilizations, created a large surplus for a small elite – the ruling group of high official in Old Kingdom Egypt numbered perhaps 500 people" (Baines and Yoffee 1998:232).

As I pointed out in another context, Weber's (e.g. 1894/1989, 1923/1981:337–50) analyses of class and state formation and power relations were not completely antithetical to the dialectical inquiries of Marx and Engels; instead they were informed by and built on certain features of Marx's method and theoretical analyses (Patterson 1999a:29–55). Yoffee's (1995) reliance on Igor M. Diakonov's (e.g. 1969) and Mario Liverani's (e.g. 1988) dialectical, Marxist analyses of socio-economic relations in the Early Dynastic city-states of Mesopotamia underscored the compatibility of certain features of Weber's and Marx's discussions of class and state formative dynamics in that region and, by extension, other parts of the world as well.

Yoffee, of course, was not the only archaeologist who made use of Weber's insights on early states and the processes of class and state formation. Bruce Trigger (1993a, 1993b), George Cowgill (e.g. 1992), Mogens T. Larsen (e.g. 1987), and René Millon (e.g. 1976, 1981), among a significant number of others, have often engaged in simultaneous dialogues with the theoretical legacies of both Weber and Marx.

Trigger (1993a), for example, situated ancient Egypt in the context of a comparative study of other early civilizations. His analysis broke with the tradition of earlier comparative studies – such as those of Robert McC. Adams (1966) or Paul Wheatley (1971) – which focused mainly on "ecology, trade, and sociopolitical organization, while treating art, religion, and values as epiphenomenal and hence of little real interest, [and] . . . tended to treat all early civilizations as developing along similar lines" (Trigger 1993a:3). He advocated instead paying attention to the differences as well as the similarities that existed in the developmental trajectories of the various early civilizations. He drew a distinction between two types of early civilizations: city-state systems and territorial states.

Trigger (1993a:8–9) suggested that those early civilizations based on city-state systems

> took the form of a network of adjacent states whose elites tended to compete with one another, often militarily, to control territory, trade routes, and other resources while at the same time sharing common status symbols and making alliances with each other, often through intermarriage among their ruling families. Each city state had a relatively small territory . . . [and] might have a number of smaller centers as well as numerous farming villages and hamlets. . . . These cities also supported craft production, which sought to

satisfy the demands not only of the urban elite but of society as a whole. The development of craft specialization and of commercial exchanges between town and countryside, as well as between neighboring urban centers, encouraged the growth of public markets.

Civilizations composed of city-state systems included Sumer, the Aztecs and their neighbors in the Valley of Mexico, and the Classic Period Maya.

Territorial states – like those of ancient Egypt, China during the Shang and Western Chou periods, and the Incas – were characterized as having

> a hierarchy of administrative centers at the local, provincial, and national levels . . . [with] small populations. . . . This was because these centers were inhabited almost exclusively by the ruling class and by the administrators, craft specialists, and retainers who served them. Because of the security provided by the state, farmers tended to live in dispersed homesteads and villages. . . . In territorial states a clearly demarcated two-tiered economy developed, with distinct rural and urban sectors. Farmers manufactured their own tools and household possessions on a part-time basis during periods of each year when they were not fully occupied with agricultural labor. Usually they utilized only locally-available raw materials and exchanged goods at local markets. Elite craftsmen . . . were employed by the state, either in provincial centers or at the national capital, to manufacture luxury goods for the king and the upper classes, often from raw materials that were imported specifically for that purpose. Unlike the city state, the only significant economic link between rural and urban centers . . . tended to be the payment of rents and taxes in the performance of corvées by peasants. The transfer of food surpluses from the countryside to urban centers took place principally in terms of appropriative rather than commercial mechanisms. Insofar as markets existed, they were usually small and served the local rural population and the urban poor.
>
> Because of their large size, territorial states required large bureaucracies to ensure the collection of taxes that could be used to support state activities. Peasant communities, while becoming internally more hierarchical within the context of the state, tended to preserve more of their prestate culture than survived in city states, where large numbers of farmers came to reside in or near urban centers. Production was less specialized than it was in city states, full-time specialists fewer, and the quality of goods available to farmers poorer. (Trigger 1993a:10–11)

The socioeconomic and class structures as well as the forms of political organization of the two types of state systems were distinctive. Trigger (1993a:14) suggested that the differences might be explained in terms of the "varying costs of decision-making and political control in different kinds of societies." He further pointed out that both types occurred in widely separated areas of the Old and New Worlds and at various times in history.

Trigger (1993b) noted that many archaeologists concerned with early civilizations accepted the idea that state-churches were important institutions of social control.[3] Drawing on data from Egypt and Mesopotamia as well as on theoretical perspectives derived from those of Marx and Engels, he sought to discern the role that religion played in them. His was a dialectical analysis that revealed the contradictory roles played by religious cults in early civilizations:

> . . . religious ideologies preserve class societies not only by reinforcing the rightfulness of social hierarchies but also by preserving the exploited from experiencing the most damaging psychological ravages of despair and self-contempt. Religion must provide such individuals with acceptable explanations for their social inferiority and convince them that, in spite of their sufferings, they live in a social and supernatural order that is fundamentally just and benevolent. To do this effectively, however, religious institutions must curb at least the worst abuses that can arise from exploitation in an inegalitarian society. Religion had a dual function in sanctioning the power of the central government while at the same time asserting the rights of subordinate regional, ethnic, and occupational groupings and providing an apparently nonpolitical focus for their opposition to state domination. (Trigger 1993b:104)

In other words, religious institutions and the state operated in different fields and involved different administrative hierarchies. The cults simultaneously supported the activities of the state and strove to ameliorate the worst of its excesses.

While some processualists – e.g. David Wilson (1997) – did not find Trigger's distinction between city-state systems particularly useful, this was not so for many of their colleagues who wrote papers for Nichols and Charlton's (1997) *The Archaeology of City-States* did.[4] For example, Yoffee (1997) pointed out that, in many of the city-states described in this volume, political offices were not in fact divorced from kinship, and Anne Pyburn (1997) suggested that there was no absolute dichotomy between kin-based and non-kin-based societies. What city-states offered were "new arenas of competition among the leaders of socially differentiated and stratified co-resident groups" (Yoffee 1997:262). They were different from the arenas of competition that arose in Trigger's territorial states.

On a different tack, Glenn Schwartz and Steven Falconer (1994:1) pointed to the "urbanocentric" bias of many studies concerned with class and state formation and the rise of civilization. They noted that these studies simultaneously treated cities as if they were the most heterogeneous and efficient managerial nodes of a complex society, and rural communities as if they were the lowest, least diverse components of the larger settlement system. Schwartz and Falconer correctly pointed out that the social strata found in the urban centers often relied on agricultural production in the countryside; they and others noted that city-dwellers occasionally but not always engaged in subsistence production. They further observed that the self-interested strategies adopted by the urban classes must have prompted compensatory strategies in the rural communities at the other end of the social hierarchy. In other words, there was a dialectical relation between town and countryside. This implied, as Philip Kohl (1981:109) and others had noted earlier, that early civilizations were not coherently adaptive wholes, but rather that they were structured and historically determined totalities whose parts were "linked to each other in a constantly shifting and changing, dynamic set of interrelations and reciprocal determinations" (Mészáros 1991:537). In sum, they were unities of interacting contradictions.

As Schwartz and Falconer correctly suggested, the place to locate and understand the rural–urban dialectic in early civilizations was not in their urban capitals but rather in their rural communities. They stressed the importance not only of understanding the processes of rural class formation but also of not adopting uncritically the models used to explain the creation of peasantries and rural class structures in twentieth-century capitalist societies. In different contexts, Michael Smith (1994) and Wendy Ashmore, Jason Yeager, and Cynthia Robin (in press), among others, have begun to examine social differentiation and the formation of rural class structures and how they articulate with general class structures of those precapitalist, tributary states.

Robert McC. Adams (2001) surveyed the current state of studies concerned with early states. He lamented the lack of comparative studies of "pristine" civilizations and the fact that many humanistically inclined archaeologists have continued to view each of them as a unique cultural achievement rather than as a constituent of a social type that shared important, underlying features with others members of the same type. He further lamented that many archaeologists trained in the social sciences still viewed "early states deriving from antecedent chiefdoms." In his view, the rise of civilization – i.e. state formation – was, in fact, a context-dependent, emergent quality as well as "the primary engine behind a larger, dependent set of changes" (Adams 2001:346). Finally, Adams indicated that theoretically informed, synthetic and cross-cultural approaches to understanding the processes of state formation have received less attention than archaeological methods; they have not, in his view, kept pace with technical innovations concerned with data recovery.

Adams (2001:352) also viewed early states as totalities, arguing that they were "evolving systems . . . [that] cannot be understood by isolating their components and additively assembling sets of the interactions between small numbers of these components," and that they involve "the emergence of new wholes that are different from the sums of their parts." He suggested that these new totalities were "risky, transitory constructs" in which permanently ranked, hierarchical structures alternated episodically "with various forms of institutional rivalry or heterarchy" (Adams 2001:354). If early states came and went, he argued, then capital cities – like Teotihuacán – may have had more enduring ritual and symbolic roles that persisted through shifts of internal and external authority.

In Adams's (2001:354–5) view, craft specialization and technological complexity were emergent qualities of early state societies. Eschewing the distinction between part- and full-time specialists, he found Brumfiel and Earle's (1987:5) characterization of independent and attached specialists more useful: Independent specialists worked for themselves or their communities, whereas attached specialists, separated from their natal communities, toiled for the state or its ruling classes. From Adams's (2001:355) perspective,

> [t]echnology was in general a key sphere of increasing complexity. Internal stratification and growing stress on an external projection of authority and prestige clearly led to an increasing differentiation between mundane and ritual or luxury articles. The production of luxuries, in turn, directed an increasing component of external trade toward the procurement of precious or exotic substances. That led to more pronounced gradations in skill, responsibility, and status among producers.

Adams correctly pointed out that there was internal differentiation among craft specialists in many early states. Implicit in his argument was the idea that craft specialists attached to the ruling classes and the state produced luxury goods, while the independent specialists in the villages produced subsistence goods that they exchanged with their kin and neighbors. Also implicit perhaps was the idea that the rates of technological innovation were higher among the attached specialists. This hypothesis focuses attention on the loci of technological innovation in early states.

Here, I think Adams broke with Childe's perspective that the class structure of tributary states inhibited technological innovation. That is, traditions of continual technological innovation were not characteristic of early state societies whose motors and internal logics were based on the appropriation of labor power and goods from direct producers. From this point of view, the organization as well as the knowledge required to produce the foodstuffs and other goods that were appropriated by the ruling classes and the state were those of the direct producers, regardless of whether they lived in farming villages, towns, or capital cities. Under the conditions of exploitation, there was no economic incentive for either the ruling classes or the direct producers to adopt innovations that would increase productivity either by improving efficiency or by reducing investments of labor time; however, there were potential reasons why independent peasants or artisans producing for the market might want to adopt labor- or time-saving innovations.

In sum, the critiques of structural Marxist and evolutionist arguments about the rise of states were that neither paid sufficient attention to the specificity of the processes of class and state formation in particular instances. Moreover, Adams and other writers sensed either the absence or the relatively undeveloped nature of comparative, cross-cultural approaches in studies concerned with the rise of civilization. What they required was the development of ways to consider simultaneously the historical specificity of particular instances of state formation and the underlying processes and structures that manifested more generally. This has led to considerations of the motors driving state class and state formative processes and to Trigger's attempt to identify different trajectories of state development that culminated, in his view, in city-state systems and territorial states. Brumfiel, Schwartz, and Falconer showed how important it was to consider what happened in the rural communities and towns located outside capital cities, since these were the sites where both exploitative social relations and processes of social differentiation and rural class formation occurred. They also showed the linkages between the political and economic realms of tributary states, whose rulers relied on non-economic means of extracting labor and goods from subject populations.

Discussion and Critique II: Heterarchy and Transformation

The issue of the structural antecedents of early states remained an important focus of discussion in the 1990s. Many processual archaeologists continued to adhere to the notion that class and state formation meant increasing social complexity – that is, tribes evolved into chiefdoms, and some chiefdoms, at least, evolved into states. However, a number of them rejected the idea that chiefdoms represented a single stage of development and argued instead that significant distinctions existed among the societies assigned to this social type. Not only were there differences between simple and complex chiefdoms – i.e. those with one level of hierarchy as opposed to those with two levels of hierarchy – but a second perspective distinguished chiefs who redistributed from those who "acted to mobilize their own power by collecting tribute rather than to benefit the society as a whole" (Feinman and Neitzel 1984:44).

For Marxists, these typologies described two quite distinct kinds of society. On the one hand, there was the simple chieftainship in which the chief was the collector and dispenser of goods and the organizer of the communal projects by means of which commoners announced and reproduced their membership in the community. While the members of such societies were ambiguously ranked and may even have belonged to hereditary estates, the societies themselves were not class-stratified and, hence, lacked exploitative social relations. They manifested some variant of the communal mode of production. On the other hand, there was the advanced or complex chieftainship in which the chief and the hereditary nobility had the power to exact tribute. They controlled the means of production and had differential or exclusive access to some of the goods and services of the direct producers. In contrast, they were class-stratified, and the chiefs quickly attempted to elaborate institutions and practices that would ensure the social reproduction of exploitative social relations and social inequality. They were tributary states which manifested the tributary mode of production, and which attempted to resolve the contradictions posed by an exploitative class structure and the resistance of subordinated classes and subject populations.

Societies manifesting variants of the primitive communal mode of production, as a number of scholars drawing on diverse strands of Marxist thought observed, accommodated a great deal of organization variability (e.g. Kristiansen 1991:17; Saitta 1988). For example, together and separately, Gailey and I (Gailey 1987a; Gailey and Patterson 1988; Patterson 1988/1998) had argued that the germanic and lineage modes of production were variants of the primitive communal mode of production that emerged because of their connections with tributary states, and that some chieftaincies also manifested kin-communal rather than tributary social relations of production. Like Trigger (1990:143–5; 1993c:179) and many socio-cultural anthropologists, we were acutely aware that the social relations of primitive communal societies were structured differently from those found in either tributary or capitalist states, and, further, that the kinds of interpersonal relations and behaviors valued in those societies were also different from the alienated, exploitative, and competitive relations found in capitalist societies today. In sum, the social relations and valued behaviors of non-class communities differed from those of class-based societies. Implications of this perspective were that human nature was historically contingent, that it differed from one society to another, and that it refracted in some way the modes of production that were manifested in each.

Drawing on structural Marxist as well as other lines of argumentation, Dean Saitta (1994a, 1994b, 1997, 2001; McGuire and Saitta 1996) advocated an alternative perspective on the nature of social relations in primitive communal societies.[5] He was concerned specifically with the social organization of prehistoric Pueblo societies of the American Southwest: Were their social relations egalitarian or organized hierarchically? How did they affect the economic processes involved in the production and appropriation of surplus? He pointed out that surplus appropriation was different in societies governed by communal, tributary, and capitalist social relations. He also noted that a given society might manifest one or more modes of production, and defined class "as an individual's position in a *relationship* of surplus flow" (Saitta 1994b:25, emphasis in original).

Saitta then distinguished two kinds of surplus flows – i.e. class processes that existed in different combinations in all societies. *Fundamental* class processes involved the production and appropriation of surplus labor. *Subsumed* class processes involved "the distribution of surplus labor *by* the appropriators *to* specific individuals who provide the political, economic, and cultural conditions that allow a particular fundamental class process to exist" (Saitta 1994b:25, emphasis in original). These class processes were influenced by a number of non-class processes and power relations. From his perspective, all societies were to some extent class societies. In the Puebloan societies of the Southwest, while the fundamental class processes were collective – i.e. producers and appropriators belonged to the same class – the subsumed class processes and positions were not collective because of extended divisions of labor in which some individuals or groups specialized in particular productive activities and exerted some control – i.e. power, in Saitta's terms – over who had access to the products of their labor. Such subsumed class positions included political functionaries, ritual and craft specialists, and warriors. With regard to Puebloan social organization, Saitta viewed it in terms of a number of historically contingent forms of organization ranging from relatively communal at one extreme to institutionalized social ranking without the erosion of collective appropriation at the other. For McGuire and Saitta (e.g. 1996:197, 202), prehistoric Puebloan society was both egalitarian and hierarchical.

Trigger (1993c:179), among others, was critical of the uniformitarian perspective of human behavior advocated by the French structural Marxists – and Saitta by extension – who "maintain[ed] that in preclass societies, interest groups (consisting of young versus old, men versus women, or members of rival clans) struggle in the same way as classes do in more advanced societies." Moreover, I am not certain how much Saitta's conceptual framework, including his notion of "class as an individual's position in a relationship of surplus flow," actually tells us about the process of producing, appropriating, and distributing the products of surplus labor; I believe his focus on the "individual" is too limiting. I also believe that Saitta does not pay sufficient attention to the ambiguities, potential and real, that are inherent in such roles. Sometimes a gift is just a gift; sometimes it is part of generalized exchange and carries with it expectations of future returns; occasionally the process breaks down, and the gift is not a gift at all but becomes an exaction or extortion instead. Nevertheless, Saitta does focus attention on the activities and motivations of those individuals whose culturally recognized social positions may mandate that they do not participate fully in direct production, that they may appropriate labor and goods under certain conditions, or that they must redistribute most or all of what they received from the community's direct producers.

According to Susan McIntosh (1999:4), African data challenged notions widely held by processual archaeologists that view "complexity as differentiation by political hierarchization and provide[d] an instructive counterpoint to formulations that locate power centrally in individuals and focus analysis primarily on the economic strategies used by these individuals to maintain and expand operational power." Following Robert Paynter (1999:369), she viewed complexity as *"the degree of internal differentiation (horizontal as well as vertical) and the intricacy of relations within a system"* (McIntosh 1999:11, emphasis in original). She noted that the organizational structures of some African societies moved fluidly back and forth between lineage, village headship, regional chieftaincy, and kingship, and that, in these and other African societies, power was not consolidated exclusively in readily distinguished political realms. In fact, power was often counterpoised between a king and other associations such as secret societies, cults, or lineage heads – in societies that Aidan Southall (1998, 1991, 1999) had described as *segmentary states.* In segmentary states, the king's influence often had a different geographical distribution from the power wielded by secret societies or cults. This led McIntosh to reconsider how archaeologists have conceptualized power as rational, secular, and something possessed by individuals. She pointed out that this derived from Max Weber's (1922/1947:152) definition of power as "the probability that one actor within a social relationship will be in a position to carry out his own will despite resistance." In Weber's view, rationality was what distinguished power from authority, the legitimacy of which was accepted without reflection. For McIntosh, this perspective was too narrow to account for the distribution of power in segmentary states. She preferred instead to view power as

> *the capacity for effective action.* . . . [and noted that] power, in order to be translated into authority, requires a cosmology – an understanding of the forces that effect outcomes in the world and the knowledge to influence them – and cosmologies cannot be created by force or coercion. The mobilization of appropriate specialist knowledge and ritual power is a key element in the capacity for effective action in many African societies. (McIntosh 1999:17, emphasis in original)

McIntosh's alternative to the Weberian notion of power focused on the importance of power strategies that were based on collective action and that were not exclusively economic in nature. She noted that Blanton, Feinman, Kowelewski, and Peregrine (1996) had elaborated an idea of power that elucidated the interactions and contradictions between two individual versus group-oriented patterns of political action. At the same, DeMarrais, Castillo, and Earle (1996) pointed out that ideology was an important source of social power, especially when it could be materialized and controlled by a dominant group.

Carole Crumley (1987, 1995, 2001) took a different tack in addressing the antecedents of class-stratified, state-based societies. She criticized the idea of complexity, pointing out that writers concerned with the origins of the state focused mainly on the hierarchical structures, patterns of inequality, and power relations that emerged during the process. She advocated instead focusing on the dialectics of state formation and on the existing structures – such as coalitions, federations, or democracies – that were counterpoised to the consolidation of state power (Crumley 2001:32). She used the term *heterarchy* to refer to such structures. She defined heterarchy

> as the relation of elements to one another when they are unranked or when they possess the potential for being ranked in a number of different ways. For example, power can be counterpoised rather than ranked. Thus, three cities might be of the same size but draw their importance from different realms: one hosts a military base, one is a manufacturing center, and the third is home to a great university. Similarly, a spiritual leader might have an international reputation but be without influence in the local business community. The

relative importance of these community and individual power bases changes in response to the context of the inquiry and to changing (and frequently conflicting) values that result in the continual reranking of priorities. (Crumley 1995:3)

Her concern with both the dialectics of state formation and heterarchical structures was important. It provided some archaeologists with a conceptual apparatus and language for describing how power shifts occurred during state formative processes as well as a way for understanding the conditions in which various distributions and configurations of power relations might be stable or unstable (Crumley 1995:4). Some began to see heterarchy in the historical background of states (e.g. White 1995:104).

In the mid-1990s, Robert Ehrenreich, Crumley, and Janet Levy (1995) edited a collection of essays concerned with heterarchy and the analysis of complex societies. In her commentary on the volume, Elizabeth Brumfiel (1995:125) noted that "the concept of heterarchy provides new perspectives on the nuts-and-bolts foundations of archaeology: settlement pattern data, resource procurement, artifact type distributions, design elements, and burial lots. It also stimulates critical review of such basic concepts as craft specialization, the function of central places, the structures of tribes and chiefdoms, and the definition of social complexity."

Brumfiel proceeded to point out that the contributors to the volume interpreted heterarchy to include a number of different structures: an array of independent, homogeneous networks; membership of elements in many different unranked interactions systems with participation in each determined by the needs of each element; membership of elements in many different systems of ranking where the same element occupies a different position in the various systems; two or more functionally discrete unranked systems that interact as equals; and two or more distinct hierarchies that interact as equals. "Why," she asked, "has heterarchy been interpreted in so many ways?" Her answer was that "the concept of *hierarchy* includes a number of implicit assumptions: that ranking is present, that ranking is permanent, and that the ranking of elements according to different criteria will coincide" (Brumfiel 1995:124). The diversity of interpretations was a consequence of the fact that the authors challenged each of the implicit assumptions about hierarchy.

This led Brumfiel to suggest, correctly I believe, that some widely held assumptions about precapitalist economies are probably wrong. She also raised questions about the linkages between political economy and ideology: Can they operate independently? Can ideology be the basis for social hierarchy when the political economy is heterarchical? Here she challenged those structural Marxists who argued that control of ideology was the primary source of power available in the early stages of the rise of inequality. Since the concept had been applied to and probably represented a number of different types, Brumfiel (1995:128) concluded that "we probably should not use heterarchy to replace the tribes-chiefdoms-states terminology with which we are familiar; instead, we should use heterarchy to look at these constructs differently."

Robert Carneiro (1998:22–5) continued to view chiefdoms as a useful concept; however, he revised his earlier arguments about the formation of chiefdoms. As you will recall from the preceding chapters, he had contended that chiefdoms appeared in environmentally circumscribed areas when the members of one village conquered their neighboring communities but extracted neither tribute nor labor from their residents. He now focused on the activities and motivations of powerful war leaders or big men in tribal societies.[6] He argued that chiefdoms emerged (1) when war chiefs or big men from one village conquered neighboring communities and extended their temporary, war-time powers, and (2) the residents of the subordinated communities were unable to flee because of environmental circumscription. He noted that the desirable qualities of a war chief differed from those of a village chief in peace-time. The former incited his neighbors and led them into battle, while the latter maintained order and promoted harmony. Many chiefdoms devolved into tribal communities, especially in areas like large parts of Amazonia, where environmental circumscription was not always present; the subject communities merely moved away into uninhabited or sparsely settled regions. Chiefdoms became stable when hereditary succession to the office of the paramount chief was institutionalized; this meant that the chief was succeeded by his son in patrilineal societies or by his sister's son in matrilineal ones. Heredity was also the vehicle for the formation of a ruling class; class formation occurred when the war chief's close supporters from the early campaigns were able to transmit their special status as warriors to their own descendants. Elsa Redmond (1998), among others, developed a similar argument.

John Clark and Michael Blake (1994) proposed an alternative scenario. They contended that the appearance of early sedentary villages on the Pacific coast of southern Mexico was linked to social differentiation among previously egalitarian and largely self-sufficient households during the early second millennium B.C. Both resulted when big men emerged under conditions of increased exchange, especially of exotic goods. Big men manipulated social relations to create personal followings, to gain control over the production of others, and to siphon off goods to enhance their own prestige and that of their followers. They redistributed the exotic goods they obtained at village feasts, supported part-time craft specialists around their households, and buried their dead with different arrays and quantities of goods.

I proposed an alternative scenario to those developed by Carneiro, on the one hand, and Clark and Blake, on the other; it sought to account for the rise of civilization in coastal Peru (Patterson 1999b). I argued that the appearance of sedentary villages on or near the coast was linked with the development of net fishing, food-preservation techniques, and the construction of storage facilities. Parts of these communities resided in permanent fishing villages, while the remainder of their members foraged or resided in small, inland farming hamlets. The appearance of sedentary village life may have set the stage for population growth. It marked the appearance, in some localities, of a new spatially organized, technical division of labor involving the economically specialized settlements. The men and women residing in coastal villages fished and harvested marine resources, while their counterparts in inland hamlets farmed. The two types of community were linked together by exchange. The construction of storage facilities and platform mounds signaled the appearance of new relations of production that operated at the level of the community rather than at the household level. Men and women from the households constituting the community built or remodeled public buildings where periodic community-level gatherings were held. Participation in these community-level activities constituted the conditions both for membership in the community and for the reproduction of the community. These essentially egalitarian communities were destroyed toward the end of the first millennium B.C., when community-level appropriations of labor ceased and were replaced with a social class structure based on exploitative social relations and individual or class-based appropriations of goods or labor; this shift was marked by burials with significantly different arrays and quantities of grave goods (Burger 1992:28–42, 60–75).

Comparison of the three arguments is intriguing. The first two claimed that the shift from one form of the communal mode of production involved the appearance of war chiefs and big men, who drew followers who were not kin and who perhaps lacked the kind of authority that derived from participation in the traditional or customary production relations in the community;[7] consequently, their positions were inherently unstable, because they were always faced with the possibility that their followers would align themselves with other, competing leaders or big men and that they would be unable to re-create the conditions that sustained their support – i.e. the public redistribution of goods or booty seized during raiding. The third pathway emphasized that socioeconomic development was a manifestation of the elaboration of community-level relations of production – i.e. of those systems of customary rights and obligations moored in kin and neighborly relations. The three interpretations agree that the societies involved manifested variants of the communal mode of production; however, they also imply that the societies involved manifested different forms of the communal mode of production.

The dialogue that appeared in the 1990s began to unpack the implications of concepts – such as tribes, chiefdoms, complexity, and power – and to focus on diversity. Both Marxists and non-Marxists alike viewed tribes and chiefdoms as analytical concepts that concealed a variety of social relations that were portrayed variously as relatively egalitarian, estate-ordered, heterarchical, situationally variable, complex, and temporarily or even permanently hierarchical. Furthermore, the organizational forms of these societies were seen by some as dependent on the kinds of relations their members had with nearby state-based societies. In addition, the developmental pathways leading from tribal or kin-organized community to state-based society were viewed increasingly as historically contingent two-way streets. The hierarchical social organizations crystallized into nascent proto-states often fell apart. Participants in the dialogue also began to examine the dialectic of control. They distinguished power from authority. They moved away from the idea that state formation involved the concentration and centralization of power exclusively in the political realm, noting that there were often multiple centers and alternative forms of power and authority in early tributary-state societies (Feinman 1995; Haas 2001). They further noted that there was dialectical struggle between groups that possessed different forms of power and occupied different positions in the power structure.

The participants in the dialogue developed a comparative method that was dialectical at times. They began with notions of general processes and strategies and then turned to specific cases to clarify and elaborate their understanding of them before returning to the broader questions with more textured appreciations of the processes and strategies involved in class and state formation. Some continued to employ the familiar tribe–chiefdom–state succession (e.g. Carneiro 1998). Others continued to use this evolutionary succession even as they focused their analyses of the diversity of tribes or chiefdoms (e.g. Earle 1997). A few did not find the typology particularly useful and preferred instead to consider the diversity of forms embedded in kin-communal societies and to contrast them with the forms that emerged during episodes of class and state formation (e.g. Yoffee 1993). With different theoretical frameworks, they were beginning to ask new questions: How and under what circumstances were the kin-ordered social relations of simple chiefdoms transformed into class structures? Under what conditions did men and women begin to pursue individual or individual-class interests in the context of the continuing public institutions of the communal social formation? How were these public institutions simultaneously dissolved and transformed in the process? Under what conditions did individuals or groups succeed in imposing exploitative social relations on their kin and neighbors? Under what circumstances were such efforts blocked?

The dialogue also led to heightened concerns with the issues of action, agency, and practice – all of which, in one way or another, involve the interplay of actors, the arrangements of social relations they inhabit, and "their abilities to work on those conditions in the reproduction and transformation of their own identities and conditions of existence" (Barrett 2000:63). Action, agency, and practice had, of course, been important issues for Marx (1852/1978:103), who wrote in his *Eighteenth Brumaire* that "men [and women] make their own history . . . under circumstances directly encountered, given and transmitted from the past." They have been important issues for other social theorists as well. One consequence of these new concerns has been the increasingly frequent citation by archaeologists of works concerned with social theory – such as the neo-Weberian perspectives of Pierre Bourdieu's (1980/1990) *The Logic of Practice* and Anthony Giddens's (1984) *The Constitution of Society*, or the neo-Durkheimian views of Clifford Geertz's (1973) *The Interpretation of Culture*. In this regard, a second consequence has been a convergence in the perspectives and interests of some processual, Marxist, and post-processual archaeologists.[8]

Discussion and Critique III: Exchange, Influence, Diaspora, and World Systems

Perspectives on the interrelations of exchange and development took a new turn in the late 1960s (Patterson 1999a:113–36). The economic growth and modernization theories that dominated the period from the end of the Second World War to the mid-1960s portrayed development as directional, proceeding gradually through a fixed succession of stages, and culminating with the appearance of a modern, industrial capitalist society sympathetic to the West. However, social scientists from Latin America knew that convergence was not taking place as the growth theorists predicted; in fact, Third World societies were diverging and becoming increasingly dependent each year on the industrial capitalist countries. The issues for them were to explain in theoretical terms how this was taking place and to transform the conditions and relations that permitted it to occur. They began to explain it in terms of dependency and underdevelopment resulting from unequal exchange and their position on the periphery of a capitalist world system. Immanuel Wallerstein (1974), among others, consolidated this perspective in the mid- 1970s.[9]

Archaeologists were sensitive almost immediately to this shift and began to write about patterns of interactions between different regions and the differential effects they had on social, political-economic, and cultural development in those regions. If they mainly used the concepts of exchange, trade, or interregional interaction in the 1970s, they had adopted the those of center–periphery, core–periphery, world economy, and world system by the late 1980s. While Philip Kohl (1987a, 1987b) wrote about world economies as well as the use and abuse of world systems theory, Michael Rowlands, Mogens Larsen, and Kristian Kristiansen's (1987) *Centre and Periphery in the Ancient World*, Timothy Champion's (1989) *Centre and Periphery: Comparative Studies in Archaeology*, Peter Peregrine and Gary Feinman's (1996) *Pre-Columbian World Systems*, and Edward Schortman and Patricia Urban's (1992) *Resources, Power, and Interregional Interaction* reflected consolidations of and departures from earlier studies.

While archaeologists working in the Middle East, Mesoamerica, and the American Southwest were the first to use Wallerstein's world systems approach, Philip Kohl (1987b) was among the first to examine critically its theoretical underpinnings and applicability in the Middle East. He pointed out that Wallerstein distinguished between empires, which he thought had been a feature for the last five millennia, and the modern world system, which emerged in the sixteenth century. The former were characterized by political centralization, which Wallerstein thought was a primitive means of economic domination. The latter, Kohl (1987b:2) wrote, was

> distinguished by primarily economic as opposed to political, cultural, or presumably even ideological linkages among its constituent parts. Political diversity, primacy of the economic sphere, and control and development of a technology capable of supporting and expanding such a system are the critical variables . . . that distinguish the modern era from ancient and medieval times. The modern world system also is characterized by a highly complex global division of labor that results in major regional differences: some areas become exporters of primary resources, while others produce and successfully market industrial products. The exchange uniting different regions is not symmetrical but structurally weighted in favor of the politically more powerful and technologically advanced core states of the West. The exchange relations that develop are thus beneficial to the core areas and detrimental to the peripheries, which essentially are exploited or "underdeveloped" by these relations.

Kohl's aim was to examine the utility of the world systems concept for understanding the development of complex society in Western Asia during the fourth millennium B.C. In passing, he noted that Wallerstein had replaced the Marxist analytical category of mode of production with that of a world economy dominated by politics. This implied that "ancient world empires expanded by incorporating new territories and obtaining necessary resources through the coercive imposition of tribute and taxes. Goods flowed to the political center, and . . . were redistributed by the state according to is own specific rules of allocation" (Kohl 1987b:13).

Kohl (1987b:13–16) noted that trade between resource-poor southern Mesopotamia and resource-rich highland areas transformed the production activities of all of the societies that were involved in the exchange network, and, further, that it did not underwrite the emergence of an overarching political empire. He also noted that the cities of southern Mesopotamia had a competitive advantage in the exchange relations, because they obtained goods from a number of autonomous highland societies that were relatively isolated from one another and yet came to rely on the cities for textiles and possibly foodstuffs. This led Kohl to question the utility of Wallerstein's postulates that (1) world economies and political empires were commensurate, and (2) world economies would be transformed into political empires.

Kohl pointed out that there was a basic discontinuity between Wallerstein's modern world system – characterized by a developed core and an underdeveloped periphery – and that of Western Asia during the third and second millennia B.C. In the latter, there were multiple, independent core areas with transferable technologies that were linked together by fragile exchange systems that functioned sporadically for short periods before they fell apart and were replaced by new networks. He concluded that the world-systems model must be modified to account for the archaeological records of West and Central Asia.

Christopher Edens (1992) examined more closely the dynamics of the so-called "Mesopotamian world system" during the third and second millennia B.C. His major point was that, while trade was a basic economic dimension of the center–periphery relations that existed in the societies of Mesopotamia and the Arabian Gulf, political, military, and cultural forces had shaping effects on those societies that were at least as important as the economic ones. In his analysis, Edens followed Anthony Giddens's (1981, 1985) neo-Weberian argument about the distinction between class-divided and class societies, which stressed the importance of sociopolitical, authoritative sources of power rather than purely economic forces. In addition, he drew upon Arjun Appadurai's (1988:38) distinction between necessities and luxuries, the latter being "goods whose principal use is *rhetorical* and *social*, goods that are simply *incarnated signs*. The necessity to which *they* respond is fundamentally political" (emphasis in original). Edens pointed out that necessities were also politically constructed. He further added that "to the extent that center–periphery relations supply the physical and/or symbolic objects of consumption, the economic character of these relations is contained within their authoritative context. Relations of consumption indirectly mediate trade and its presumed economic consequences" (Edens 1992:122). Edens's views about the interplay of the social, political, cultural, and economic realms were not reductive. He was responding to weaknesses he perceived in world systems theory; at the same time, he was developing a theoretically informed, analytical framework focused on sociopolitical factors to account for the historical trajectories followed by societies in Western Asia.

Guillermo Algaze (1989, 1993a) took a different tack with regard to core–periphery relations in Southwestern Asia. He argued that the city-states of southern Mesopotamia were more developed than the highland societies on their peripheries with whom they established exchange relations during the later half of the fourth millennium B.C. Depending on the pre-existing conditions and structures of the peripheral societies, the city-states used different strategies to establish and maintain trade relations; these included colonies, urban enclaves, stations on major overland routes, and outposts in remote mountainous areas. He characterized this configuration as an "informal empire" that was based on unequal exchange and a hierarchically organized, international division of labor; however, he noted that this informal empire lacked a single political center. Like Kohl and Edens, Algaze also argued that sociohistorical development in Mesopotamia could only be understood in the context of inter-regional, cross-cultural exchange. He contended that the expansion of the Uruk city-states during the late fourth millennium B.C. was the first instance of the cycles of political centralization, expansion, and collapse that occurred episodically in Western Asia (e.g. Algaze 1989:574). He concluded that the indigenous societies on the periphery became stronger and more complex because of the exchange relations initiated by the southern Mesopotamian city-states; moreover, they became more independent as the core disintegrated during the third millennium B.C. Algaze (1993a:9–10) suggested viewing the dynamics of the expansion of Uruk societies in the following way:

> From the perspective of the core, those dynamics may be profitably visualized within a framework of cross-cultural interdependency, largely economic in nature, and competition between rival polities. From the perspective of the periphery, however, the expansion of Uruk societies can be conceptualized in terms of a continuum from more formal to more informal modes of imperial domination. . . . A more formal mode involved an actual process of colonization. . . . [In more distant areas with different subsistence economies], Uruk settlements appear only at strategic locations, principally at the juncture of the most important overland routes and waterways. The policy that can be inferred is one of "informal" economic control.

Not only were they writing about different periods, but it also appears that Edens and Algaze had different perspectives on the relative importance of purely economic factors as opposed to sociopolitical and cultural ones in the formation and maintenance of the West Asian world economy. Gil Stein (1990:66) added a third view, when he asserted:

> Clearly, interregional exchange with Syria, Anatolia, and Iran has often played an important role in Mesopotamian history, but it cannot be seen as more significant than endogenous factors in the maintenance and collapse of Mesopotamian complex societies. . . . One can argue quite plausibly that these internal dynamics [i.e. shifting ecological conditions, local warfare, problems of scale and control, and the pursuit of urban centers and their hinterlands] structured the organization of long-distance trade rather than vice versa.

Stein pointed to a second difficulty with Algaze's thought-provoking analysis: Wallerstein had failed to distinguish three important processes – "the *production* of surplus, the *appropriation* of surplus by a specific social group, and the *transformation* of surplus production into social capital, increasing productivity and creating more surplus" (Stein 1990:66, emphasis in original).

In different ways, Kohl, Edens, and Algaze affected commentaries on world systems theory from the mid-1990s onward. Kohl and Edens heralded a series of essays that sought to extend the applicability of world systems to precapitalist societies (e.g. Algaze 1993b; Hall and Chase-Dunn 1993, 1996), or to further develop critiques of its applicability to precapitalist exchange networks (e.g. McGuire 1996; Stein 1999). Algaze's works on the Uruk expansion which appeared at the beginning of the decade were precursors and stimuli to the advanced seminar held in 1998 at the School of American Research, the results of which appeared in Mitchell Rothman's (2001) *Uruk Mesopotamia and Its Neighbors: Cross-Cultural Interactions in the Era of State Formation.*

Thomas Hall and Christopher Chase-Dunn (1993, 1996), among others, described the features of world systems analysis and their implicit assumptions. They also pointed out that writers have used different theoretical frameworks to conceptualize world systems. What the various approaches shared was the idea that a system involved regularized interaction between societies. One distinguishing feature of the various positions was how the question of transition was conceptualized. Proponents of world systems analyses basing their arguments on geopolitical, cultural ecological, rational choice, or continual accumulationist theoretical perspectives believed there were no great transitions in history; those basing their arguments in Polanyian substantivism or various Marxist perspectives argued that there were significant transitions in human history (Hall and Chase-Dunn 1993: 126–8). Another set of differences between the various theoretical perspectives "cluster around the problems of how social labor is mobilized and how accumulation is accomplished. Thus, the Wallersteinian notion of an intersocietal division of labor in the production of basic goods and the idea of a core/periphery structure have broad utility. However, they cannot simply be imported wholesale into precapitalist settings. Rather Wallerstein's concepts must be modified" (Hall and Chase-Dunn 1996:12).

Hall and Chase-Dunn believed that Wallerstein's original formulation should be converted into a series of working hypotheses that required empirical investigation and validation. They also noted that Wallerstein's use of the concept of a mode of production made it difficult or impossible to examine the interaction of different modes of production within a system or between systems. Elsewhere, they expressed their belief that a world systems approach was applicable not only to capitalist systems but also to two other kinds of systems – one that was constituted by prestate societies, the other by precapitalist, tributary states. Furthermore, they argued that while some of these systems may have been hierarchically organized, others may have lacked the uneven development between core and periphery that many saw as characteristic of core–periphery structures.

Randall McGuire's (1996) approach to the applicability of world systems analysis was much less optimistic. He was critical of the focus on systemic aspects of the system rather than on relations that existed between the units that constituted the system itself. He wanted more specification of how the growth of the core created the periphery and underwrote the development of exploitative social relations and dependency. He also criticized the assumption implicit in some versions of world systems theory which viewed developments in the core as responsible for change in the periphery. McGuire further noted that while processes which occurred at different levels of the system were linked, they were not necessarily reducible to one another.

Building on the works of Algaze and others, Gil Stein's (1999) *Rethinking World-Systems* was perhaps the most extended analysis and critique of world systems explanations of precapitalist networks. Reiterating criticisms already noted above – e.g. the overemphasis of world systems analyses on long-distance trade and the dominance of the core over the periphery as primary motors of development – he observed:

> Core-controlled exchange networks of the world-system variety are just one in a range of possible economic and political relations between two different regions. The extent to which a core area can influence the development of other polities is mediated by such factors as transportation, economics, technological differences, the organization of production, and the balance of military power between the core and the periphery.
>
> In many cases, the polities on the periphery can set the terms of interregional interaction to their own advantage, even when dealing with a more powerful society in the core region. We cannot simply assume that every network of connections between societies forms a world-system. We need a more flexible perspective that *(a)* incorporates both the internal dynamics of political economy in the peripheral polity and the external dynamics of contact with neighboring societies into a model that allows for a range of different forms of interregional interaction, and *(b)* specifies the variables that shape the organization of interaction between societies at different levels of complexity. (Stein 1999:4)

With this in mind, Stein outlined two theoretical frameworks that provide alternatives to world systems analyses of inter-regional interaction. One he called the *distance-parity* model, the other the *trade-diaspora* model. On one hand, the distance-parity model suggested that the ability of the core to exercise political control over societies on the periphery diminished with distance; this led to parity or symmetry in the political and economic relations of the core societies with increasingly distant societies on their peripheries. In this view, inter-regional exchange networks were structured by the effects of distance on transportation costs (Stein 1999:62). The trade-diasporas, on the other hand, arose "in situations where culturally distinct groups engaged in exchange under conditions where communication and transportation are difficult, and where centralized state institutions are not effective in providing either physical or economic security to [the] participants" (Stein 1999:47).

Stein concluded that the world systems model had been too broadly defined and too uncritically applied to precapitalist inter-regional interactions. In his view, the underlying assumptions of core dominance, unequal exchange, and trade as the motor of development obscured what happened in precapitalist inter-regional networks. When these assumptions were discarded – as they were in the distance-parity and trade-diaspora models – a different picture emerged, one which Stein (1999:171–2) described accurately, I believe, as "messier, but truer to the fascinating range of interactional forms that we see in the historic and archaeological record."

From the mid-1980s onward, a number of historical archaeologists began to view their subject of inquiry as the archaeology of capitalism in its myriad dimensions. Wallerstein's world systems theory, which sought to account for the expansion and development of capitalism after 1500, was widely appreciated because of its apparent applicability. Robert Paynter (1985), for example, was one of the first to discuss the flow of surplus from frontier regions to the center, as he sought to develop an understanding of complex developments in the Connecticut River Valley of western Massachusetts. While his early work drew inspiration from Wallerstein, however, he quickly moved beyond world systems inter-regional exchange to focus on local historical developments in the region. This led him to consider a broader range of issues rarely touched on by many anthropological archaeologists concerned with state formation; these included the interplay of communities, power relations, class structures, gender, race, and the cult of whiteness in the region and how they articulated with wider structures in the society (Paynter 2000, 2001). While Paynter's dialectical analysis moved from the Connecticut Valley to the colonial state to the metropole and then back to the region, his theoretical framework began with the global, moved to the local, and then returned to the core areas of capitalist development and to other areas on the margins of the capitalist world. It also entailed peeling away the layers of meaning of concepts such as class, power, or race.

Charles Orser (e.g. 1994, 1996) was also an early advocate of a theoretically informed, global historical archaeology. Episodically from the late 1980s onward, he examined the structure of plantation slavery in the Antebellum South and its transformation into a system of capitalist tenant-farming after 1865 (Orser 1988, 1990, 1991, 1999). This led him to analyze, among other things, the processes of class formation and the class structures that developed on a Texas plantation that was worked by tenant-farmers and sharecroppers as well as by planter-owners after the Civil War. It also led him to consider how this class structure articulated with the institutions and practices of the state in the region. These were, of course, questions that were also being examined by anthropological archaeologists working in different contexts.

The route Orser took ultimately diverged slightly from the one followed by Paynter, even though they ended up roughly in the same place. Orser's (1996) definition of historical archaeology was more inclusive in that he viewed the field as "haunted" or "inhabited" not only by capitalism but also by colonialism, Eurocentrism, and modernity. Conceptualizing the discipline in this manner required that he look more closely at the underlying assumptions that shaped the practice of historical archaeology. The underlying premise guiding his examination of these concepts was that social change occurred not because of technology but rather because of the relations that were forged when people adopted particular technologies.

Claiming that historical archaeology was the archaeology of capitalism was not sufficient. It was necessary, in Orser's view, to understand what capitalism was in the past and is today. Furthermore, it was also necessary to understand the interconnections of capitalism with colonialism, Eurocentrism, and modernity. Briefly, Orser viewed capitalism as an economic system and distinguished two phases of capitalist development. During the earlier phase, which extended from the fifteenth to the early eighteenth century, merchants traveled to distant places to obtain new capital; during the later phase, industrialists built enormous factories and employed men, women, and children, often under deplorable working conditions, to produce commodities that were ultimately sold for profit in the market. This mode of production, based on the industrialists' ownership of the technology (means of production) as well as the goods produced by their employees, underwrote a class structure as well as a peculiarly economic form of surplus extraction – i.e. in return for wages, the workers took the raw materials and tools owned by the industrialists to produce goods that the latter sold for a profit. Orser (1996:76ff.) proceeded to point out that the break between precapitalist and capitalist modes of production was often easier to see outside of Europe, where industrial capitalism seemed to have had its historically contingent roots.

This led to a consideration of colonialism, which, from his point of view, was what happened when one group of people met those of another group and they entered into relationships with each other (Orser 1996:65). What was the nature of those interactions from the perspective of the members of each group as well as from the perspective of groups or classes in the countries from which the colonists came? What sentiments, emotions, and reactions did these encounters create? These and similar questions led Orser to consider issues such as the linkages between plantation slavery in the Antebellum South and the capitalist production of cotton textiles in Manchester during the late eighteenth century. It was possible to deal with this at different levels. One involved the purely economic relationships established by capitalism and colonialism. Another level involved the attitudes that emerged from these connections. Two of the attitudes that had profound shaping effects were Eurocentrism and modernity – the other two ideas that haunt historical archaeology.

Eurocentrism, which began to take form in the fifteenth century, was a complex set of beliefs and practices that reinforced the idea that Europe was somehow first or foremost, the world leader. Orser (1996:69) suggested that the term carried a variety of meanings which included an ideological rationale for the expansion of capitalism into the rest of the world. The ideology of racial superiority was this ideological rationale.

Modernity, he pointed out, involved the idea of novelty. It also involved the notion that Europe was modern or that its technology was superior to those of people residing in other parts of the world who continued to rely on traditional ways of producing the items they needed. Thus, the idea of modernity also drew a distinction between these "traditional" societies and those of Europe, whose industrial technologies relied on continuous innovations to ensure the continued flow of profits. Modernity emerged as Europeans and others began to see European countries as the most developed on earth. Thus, it also served to buttress racism and "us versus them" ideas associated with colonialism and Eurocentrism. Societies could become modern by jettisoning their traditional technologies and the social relations these engendered. As Orser and others know only too well, these ideas were intimately linked with the rise of Western civilization – that is, those episodes of class and formation that have occurred during the last five centuries (e.g. Patterson 1997a).

Since this volume has been concerned with ongoing dialogues about the rise of civilization – i.e. the formation of class and state structures – the ideas we hold about Western civilization and how they arose should be as important to anthropological archaeologists as ancient Mesopotamia or Peru. At one level, it is my hope that these dialogues, especially those that emerged in the 1990s, with their deep roots and rich connections to other disciplines, can be expanded in ways that further promote the exchange of ideas, constructive commentaries and critique, and non-acrimonious debate. To ensure that this happens, it is necessary to refine our understanding of the various theoretical frameworks we use, to spell out the significance of the explicit and implicit implications of each, and to develop a textured appreciation of how they are similar to and different from one another. In this way, we have a real opportunity to clarify our understanding of the rise of states and to pose theoretically informed questions or alternatives that can be used to shape future investigations of the issues involved.

At another level, these conversations require us to consider whose interests are served when we repeat claims that hierarchical social relations are inevitable or that oppressive social relations are the natural, immutable outcome of history. Such statements not only distort history, but they also trivialize the contributions of many communities and deny them any role in shaping their own lives or in making their own history. Recognizing the existence of societies that lacked social class and state structures as well as that of subordinated classes and communities, acknowledging the roles they have played in both historically contingent situations and human history at large, and understanding their views about everyday life challenges the validity of accounts that disregard their existence and deny them agency.

Notes

Chapter 1 Marx's Legacy

1. There are several biographies of Marx; David McLellan's (1973) *Karl Marx: His Life and Thought* is a good one.
2. Marx's (1840–1/1975) doctoral dissertation at the University of Berlin dealt with classical Greek philosophy, specifically the difference between the Democritean and Epicurean philosophy of nature.
3. Engels was Marx's editor, commentator, critic, popularizer, and source of inspiration. They engaged in intellectual discussions with one another for forty years, honing and refining ideas through their collaborative writings, their conversations, their correspondence, and their division of labor. My view is that Marx and Engels basically agreed with one another, that Engels was an intellectual force in his own right, and that their views, while perhaps not identical, are probably closer to a seamless whole than some writers believe (Hunley 1991). To sort them is beyond the scope of this book, and I will follow the prevailing pattern of referring to them as Marx's views even when it is clear that Engels contributed to their development and concisely stated them. That we talk and write today about "Marxian" or "Marxist" ideas and "Marxism" rather than "Engelsism" is a product of Marx and Engels's political opponents in the later half of the nineteenth century (Haupt 1982:266–7). They, rather than Marx or Engels, coined the terms and labeled the ideas; we have merely appropriated them.
4. Many authors discuss Marx's theory of society and history. I found the following writers especially helpful in preparing this section: W. Peter Archibald (1989), Norman Geras (1983), Paul Heyer (1982), George Márkus (1978), John McMurtry (1978), R. S. Neale (1985), Sean Sayers (1998), and Charles Woolfson (1982).
5. Like most of their contemporaries, Marx and Engels frequently used the term "man" in a generic sense, as they did in many of the passages cited below, to refer to both men and women; in other places, both of them used the terms "man" and "woman" in gender-specific ways (e.g. Marx 1844/1975b:294–6).
6. Marx's architectural metaphor has captivated writers since the 1880s (Larrain 1991). It is useful to keep in mind, however, that the German words translated as "foundation" and "superstructure" were apparently also slang terms used by

German-speaking railroad workers in the mid-nineteenth century to refer to "railroad tracks" and "rolling stock." If this was the case, then there was an alternative, more dynamic metaphor to the static one implied in the illusion to buildings. Marx and Engels first used the base–superstructure metaphor in *The German Ideology*, which they wrote in 1845–6, and both employed it at different times over the next fifty years. In spite of this, the model never occupied the same kind of central position in their thought as did other concepts – such as the labor theory of value.

7. It is important to point out at this juncture that not all societies have social divisions of labor and exploitative social relations. Descriptions of societies in which the forces of production are held communally by their members fill the pages of many ethnographic accounts (e.g. Leacock and Lee 1982). Marx and Engels were aware of such societies from their reading of classical authors and from the anthropological literature – e.g. Lewis H. Morgan's (1877/1963) *Ancient Society* – that appeared during the 1860s and 1870s. I will discuss their understanding of various types of communal societies – primitive communism as they called them – in more detail in a few pages. Suffice it to say that such societies existed in the past and still exist today against all odds on the margins or in the remote interiors of modern states.

8. Using some of the criteria elaborated by Marx, Eric Wolf (1982:73–100) discerned capitalist, tributary, and kin-ordered modes of production; the kin-ordered corresponded to Marx's primitive communism and the tributary to the ancient, feudal, and asiatic. Christine Gailey and Thomas Patterson (1988) argued that the various precapitalist modes of production exist in dialectical relationships with one another; they examined these relationships in contexts shaped by state formation and uneven development – i.e. the articulation of various forms of tributary states (feudal, ancient, asiatic) with diverse forms of primitive communism (e.g. kin-communal, germanic, slavonic).

9. My discussion of Marx's political-economic ecology in this section is informed by Paul Burkett (1998, 1999), John Bellamy Foster (2000), and Richard Levins and Richard Lewontin (1985). Ronald Meek (1953/1971) and Sydney Coontz (1957) stimulated my interest in Marx's views about population; Wally Seccombe (1992, 1993) added fuel.

Chapter 2 V. Gordon Childe and the Opening Dialogue

1. What made Childe a truly remarkable figure was that he succeeded in linking his towering intellectual achievements with his political activity. Both were informed by Marxist social thought and sought to address burning issues of the day – such as the rise of fascism in Europe in the 1930s. Because of the connec-

tions he forged between his academic and political endeavors, Childe ran afoul of conservative academics and governments in Australia, England, Scotland and the United States. His professional career suffered as well because of his politics and beliefs (Green 1981:1–57; Peace 1992). For example, he was denied university positions in Australia and was unable to obtain a visa in 1952 from the U.S. State Department to attend an international conference on the present and future state of anthropology. These were not the typical experiences of academics; however, these and similar experiences were familiar to academics of the Left – Franz Boas, Ruth Benedict, Gene Weltfish, Eleanor Leacock, Kathleen Gough, Richard Levins or Noam Chomsky, to name only a few – whose linkage of theory and practice manifested itself in their political activism.

Childe's career as an activist-scholar began at the University of Sydney, where he studied classics from 1911 to 1914 and reportedly read Marx, Engels, Hegel, and other philosophers. In the same period, he was also a regular, active participant in the Australian Workers' Educational Association, founded a few years earlier by the International Workers of the World (IWW). The IWW, or the Wobblies as it was called, was an anarcho-Marxist labor organization that advocated "One Big Union" instead of a number of smaller ones representing steamfitters, carpenters, and other skilled workers, each of which bargained on behalf of its members with the particular employer. Childe sailed for England in 1914 to continue his archaeological studies at Oxford University. He quickly joined the university's socialist Fabian Society and was a frequent visitor at the London offices of the society's Labour Research Department. In the late 1910s, the Labour Research Department became closely associated with the Communist Party. Like many socialists in Britain, Childe joined the No-Conscription Fellowship, which opposed the First World War and the conscription of working-class men for military service; while his British comrades in the Fellowship were imprisoned because of their beliefs, he evaded this fate because of his Australian citizenship. In 1917, he shared an apartment with Rajani Palme Dutt, who was a founding member of the British Communist Party and its leading theoretician. They discussed Marx and Engels's writings on a regular basis. Upon his return to Australia in 1917, Childe re-immersed himself in labor politics. The Labour Premier of New South Wales sent Childe to England as a research and publicity officer, where he began work on December 7, 1921. The Labour government in Australia was soon toppled by the Conservatives, who quickly terminated Childe's position. In June 1922, he suddenly found himself in England with no job, dismal prospects in Australia, and little money. For the next three years, he wrote, translated book manuscripts, and worked for the Labour Research Department to make ends meet. He finally got a full-time job in 1925, when he was appointed Librarian to the Royal Anthropological Institute (Gathercole 1989; Green 1981:1–57; Peace 1992:51–87).

Similar experiences are reported for other activist-scholars of the Left (e.g. Jorgensen 1993; Leacock 1993; Lee and Sacks 1993; Rai 1995).

In this light, the claims of Childe's archaeological colleagues who repeatedly sought to explain away his commitment to Marxist social thought do not make much sense. Some claimed that his commitment was not very deep, and that he merely advocated it to shock or annoy people. Others suggested that it was an eccentricity he adopted to disarm or amuse colleagues. Still others presumed there was a sharp dichotomy between his syntheses of archaeological data and his more political, popular writings such as *Man Makes Himself*. A few ignored Childe's Marxism altogether, while one of the more conservative members of the profession believed it crippled his work from the 1930s onward (Trigger 1980:14–16).

2. Jonathan Turner (1985), Robert Carneiro (1967a), and John Peel (1971) provide useful surveys of Spencer's career and social theory. While Marx and Engels were critical of Spencer's views, they rarely mentioned his work in their own writings. Spencer's name appears three times in the forty-nine volumes of the *Collected Works* of Marx and Engels published to date. Marx (1853/1979:161–2) quoted excerpts from Spencer's *Social Statics*, which appeared in 1851; fifteen years later, in a letter to Engels, he applauded Spencer's criticism of the economic analyses of the day but criticized him for his "pseudophilosophical or pseudoscientific" prose, which obscured meaning (Marx 1868/1988:38). Engels (1873–82/1987:536) mentioned his name in passing in *Dialectics of Nature*.

3. Turner (1985:95ff.) pointed out that Spencer's *Descriptive Sociology* constituted a third classification of social diversity. He used common categories to classify features of different groups in order to see which phenomena were habitually associated with one another, enabling him to make generalizations about the operation of society. The fifteen volumes in the series appeared between 1873 and 1934.

4. Steven Lukes (1977) provides a useful account of Durkheim's intellectual career; what follows is based on my earlier analysis of Durkheim's work (Patterson 1999a:38–46).

5. John Kautsky (1988), Gary Steenson (1978), and Michael Howard and John King (1989:65–105) provide helpful accounts of Kautsky's career and theory of evolutionary socialism.

6. This was a powerful claim. It influenced every U.S. presidential administration from Harry S. Truman to George Bush, the elder, whose senior officials and advisors were never really certain whether it was merely a claim or a frightening, preordained historical fact. In either case, it underpinned their responses, "containment" and the "domino theory," which they deployed to mobilize opinion and support for foreign policy objectives throughout the Cold War years.

7. Bruce Trigger (1980, 1982, 1984a, 1984b, 1986, 1987, 1989:254–63) outlines Childe's sociohistorical theory and discusses his many and varied contributions to archaeology. It would have been more difficult to write this section without his superb analyses.

8. See White (1943/1949, 1945a, 1945b, 1946, 1959). Carneiro (1981a) is the most useful discussion of White's career and sociocultural theory. Barrett (1989), Fluehr-Lobban (1986), and Peace (1993) provide additional insights.

Chapter 3 Disregard, Engagement, and Dialogue, 1945–1980

1. The late 1940s and early 1950s marked a highpoint in the anti-communist sentiment in the United States. Marxism as a theoretical perspective was conflated with membership in the Communist Party or affiliation with one or more progressive or Left political organizations (the FBI provided a multi-page list of such organizations in the United States). While some anthropologists did not cite Marx in their bibliographies, many more eschewed social evolutionary theory, believing that it might be confused with Marxist thought. Their fears were not unfounded, since some of their colleagues did in fact conflate the two perspectives. The latter implied or asserted that social evolutionism was merely the public mask of communism.

2. Willey and Phillips's reluctance to come to grips explicitly with social evolutionary thought was a manifestation of the times. The prevailing sentiments of the early to mid-1950s are described in the preceding note.

3. From the mid-1970s onward, the relations between such cases and developments in neighboring regions would, of course, have been described in the terms of "core–periphery" or "world systems" models.

4. Kent Flannery (1967) characterized the differences between historical and developmental interpretations in a widely cited and reprinted review of Willey's (1967) *An Introduction to American Archaeology*, vol. 1, *North and Middle America*. Flannery located the tension between the two modes of interpretation in the profession and portrayed Willey primarily as a culture historian; however, he did not adequately discuss the degree to which the tension was also an integral feature of the writings of the author whose work he reviewed.

5. Here, Willey acknowledged the pathbreaking work of Richard MacNeish in Mexico, both in the Sierra de Tamaulipas and the Tehuacán Valley. MacNeish (1978:46–7) had taken a seminar from Redfield at the University of Chicago in which he wrote a paper dealing with the theoretical contributions of Julian Steward and noted the relationships between Redfield's own folk–urban continuum and Durkheim's (1893/1964) discussion of societal development in *The Division of Labor in Society*. MacNeish added that Steward's ideas modified by

those of Leslie White and James Ford shaped his own theoretical perspective in the 1940s (Patterson 2000).

6. Flannery (1972:26) perceptively observed that different combinations and configurations of broad-spectrum foragers may have existed in Mesopotamia and Mesoamerica: "Only in Mesoamerica is there any evidence that 'the family', as such, was a basic unit of residence, food procurement, and storage as at 'microband' camps. In the Near East, the basic residential unit seems to have been an encamped band of flexible composition, crosscut by men's and women's work groups, not necessarily composed of siblings." He suggested that the difference might be attributable to greater emphasis on ungulate hunting in the Near East and to greater food scarcity in the late dry season in Mesoamerica.

7. This perspective echoed an argument made earlier by Karl Wittfogel (1955) about the relationship between hydraulic agriculture and the rise of states.

8. Spanish translations of Childe's books, beginning with *Man Makes Himself*, were published in Latin America from 1946 onward. In Mexico, José Luis Lorenzo studied with Childe at the Institute of Archaeology in 1953–4, and Julio Olivé Negrete's (1958) master's thesis used Childe's approach to organize archaeological information from Mesoamerica (Olivé Negrete 1987).

Chapter 4 Theoretical Ferment and Dialogue, 1975–1990

1. Elsewhere I have argued that the richness and diversity of social theory in the decades bracketed by the 1920s and the 1970s was a consequence of the general weakness of capitalism, socialist revolution, and various movements struggling for decolonization and political liberation in the wake of the Second World War (Patterson 1999a, 2001).

2. Postprocessual archaeology is an umbrella category used by its advocates to characterize the work of individuals with divergent views and commitments (Kohl 1993; Patterson 1989; Preucel 1995). It has roots both in the ferment of the period and in the inspiration, teaching, and writings of David Clarke. Clarke formulated his analytical archaeology at the same time that Lewis Binford and others conceived the early forms of processual archaeology. Both were critiques of traditional archaeology, but the programs they proposed had different theoretical roots and were ultimately incompatible with one another, in spite of attempts to subsume Clarke's agenda into that of processual archaeology (e.g. Earle and Preucel 1987). Several of Clarke's students and associates at Cambridge University – notably Ian Hodder, Glynn Isaac, and Christopher Tilley – were either critics of processual archaeology or proposed models that were criticized by processual archaeologists. Hodder and his associates were not the

only critics of processual archaeology. From 1970 onward, Bruce Trigger (1970, 1971, 1973, 1978) developed a highly original critique of processual archaeology; however, as he noted in the introduction to *Artifacts and Ideas: Essays in Archaeology*, his critique made little headway against the onslaught of the "new archaeology" (Trigger 2003). Trigger's comments were not necessarily rooted in Marxist social thought. They focused instead on the limitations he perceived in the theoretical foundations of processual archaeology: its oversimplification of the diversity of theoretical and practice approaches in archaeology in the 1950s, notably settlement pattern studies; its reductive equation of culture with behavior; its ecological determinism; and its avoidance of history.

In *Analytical Archaeology*, Clarke (1968) attempted to incorporate new developments in statistics, locational analysis, and systems theory into archaeological method and theory. His goal was to elaborate a set of theoretical constructs that dealt specifically with the entities studied by archaeologists. Like Binford, he was concerned with the distributional patterns found in the archaeological record and with the various natural and cultural processes that produced them. He sought models for these processes in economic anthropology and geography. This effort is most apparent in his "The Economic Context of Trade and Industry in Barbarian Europe till Roman Times," where, among other things, he pointed to the uneven social development of Europe during the Neolithic and Bronze Ages, raised questions about the self-sufficiency of its neolithic villages, and distinguished the production of commodities (i.e. goods to be exchanged) from production for use (Clarke 1969/1979:268, 287).

Clarke (1973/1979:85) also recognized that archaeological research was shaped and constrained by diverse factors; it was "related internally to its changing content and externally to the spirit of the times." The discipline of archaeology emerged in the context of various regional, national, linguistic, and educational environments. As a result, regional schools developed, and these regional schools had preferred bodies of theory and "forms of description, interpretation and explanation" (Clarke 1972/1979:28). Clarke proceeded to suggest that some schools had solved certain problems better than others, and that improved communications and the exchange of students were producing "internationally shared cross-school *approaches*" (emphasis in original).

3. Colin Renfrew and Eric Level (1979:145) also remarked that "sociopolitical organization is not the same as economic organization, and social space differs from the spatial ordering of markets and other spatial features of market economy." Elsewhere, Renfrew (1977:101–6) seemingly took the opposite tack, arguing that (1) the most distinctive feature of chiefdoms was the presence of a central place; (2) human spatial organization was modular and cellular; and (3) the highest order social unit may be identified by the scale and distribution

of central places. Joyce Marcus also conceptualized four-tiered site hierarchies in different terms from that of Wright and Johnson (1975). Her highest-order or primary sites "were not necessarily the largest sites in terms of surface area or number of major buildings" (Marcus 1976:24). These capitals were administrative centers that mentioned each others's emblem glyphs but not those of their affiliated, lower-order centers.

4. The idea of primitive communism underpinned a heated debate from the late 1980s onwards concerned with the historical development of the San social formation in South Africa. On the one hand, Eleanor Leacock, Richard Lee, and others "argued that foraging societies can only be understood as the product of a triple dynamic: first, the internal dynamic of communal foraging relations of production; second, the dynamics of their historical interactions with farmers, herders, and states; and third, the dynamic of articulation and incorporation within the modern world system" (Lee 1992/1998:180).On the other hand, Edwin Wilmsen (1989:3), who built on both world systems and poststructuralist perspectives, argued that the status of the San-speaking peoples as foragers on the edge of the South African political economy "is a function of their relegation to an underclass in the playing out of historical processes that began before the current millennium and culminated in the early decades of this [i.e. the twentieth] century. The isolation in which they are said to be found is a creation of our view of them, not of their history as they lived it." For Lee and others, primitive communism is a distinctive mode of production characterized by sharing and communal control of the means of production. For Wilmsen, primitive communism does not exist; he suggests that the psyches and social relations of San people are ultimately no different from those of other individuals involved in the modern world system. His perspective implies that oppression and inequality are natural features of all social relations rather than being constituted under particular, social and historical circumstances.

5. Archaeologists who employed the methodology of systems theory to study the processes of state formation never responded to the critiques of functionalist equilibrium models or the use of Weberian ideal types. Consequently, any critique of the "systems theory" approach must consider seriously these criticisms. It should contain the following elements: (1) the methodology does not adequately distinguish between social reality and the analytical categories devised to examine it; too often, the appearance of order is a product of the relations between the analytical concepts and has nothing to do with those "actually existing" in the real world; (2) the systems theory model contains a number of assumptions about human beings and social relations – e.g. utilitarian individualism, hierarchy, inequality, and equilibrium – that make it almost impossible to examine how these features developed since they are presumed to be characteristics of all societies; (3) the use of ideal types – like

tribes, chiefdoms, and states – and the concomitant discussions of the significance of their similarities and differences – which focus attention on the least
common denominators, building blocks, or functional prerequisites of social
structures – are abstractions within abstractions and ultimately confuse the
classification of variation with the explanation of development; (4) central to
the systems theory methodology is a functionalist theory of change which
views it as something that occurs automatically, gradually, and continuously
and that can be either internally self-generated and cumulative, on the one hand,
or externally imposed and intermittent, on the other; it separates people from
their history, which effectively prevents its advocates from dealing with the real
events and transformations of the historical record; and (5) the assumption that
the differentiated managerial mechanism or institution is essential for the
reproduction of society should be at least questioned if not challenged directly.

6. Marxist critiques of structural Marxism appeared in the late 1970s and early
   1980s (e.g. Appelbaum 1977; Benton 1984; Clarke 1980; DiTomaso 1982;
   Saunders 1990; Thompson 1978). The criticisms they leveled at this strand of
   Marxist social thought included the following: (1) its analytical method abandoned the dialectical, historical materialist perspective of Marx; (2) it preferred
   structure to action and reduced all social phenomena to the levels of structure
   or superstructure; (3) individuals were constituted as subjects by the requirements of different structural levels and were the bearers of those structures; (4)
   it focused on the systemic or structural features of society rather than on the
   ways in which people make their own histories; (5) it rendered social change
   untheorizable; (6) it did not conceptualize the relationships between structural
   determination and class struggle; (7) it left no room for oppositional subjectivi-
   ties and understandings; and (8) it emphasized the centrality of theory rather
   than dialectical connections of theory to practice and practice to theory.

   While the Marxist writers saw these as limitations, anthropologists steeped
   in the structural functionalism and evolutionism of Spencer and Durkheim saw
   them as strengths of the perspective in the 1990s.

7. Gailey's (1983, 1984, 1987a, 1988) analyses of the formation of gender hierarchies during state formative processes built on a Marxist tradition launched
   by Frederick Engels (1884/1972). This tradition was manifest in Stanley
   Diamond's (1951/1996) analysis of the Dahomey state. Eleanor Leacock
   (1972) elaborated Engels's perspective in her introduction to the International
   Publishers edition of *The Origin of the Family, Private Property and the State*,
   which appeared in 1972. Leacock's introduction provoked considerable discussion among feminist ethnohistorians and anthropologists, notably Karen Brodkin Sacks (1975, 1976, 1979/1982), Rayna Rapp (1977), Irene Silverblatt
   (1976, 1987, 1991), and Allen Zagarell (1986b). They focused on the transformation of gender relations during state formation. Their interests resonated

during the 1980s with those of the early feminist archaeologists – notably Janet Spector, Margaret Conkey, and Joan Gero – whose work was erected on a combination of liberal social theory and contemporary archaeological thought (Conkey and Spector 1984; Gero and Conkey 1991; Spector 1983); the work of the Marxists, which was diverse, was incorporated largely without comment into the dominant discourse of feminist archaeology from the late 1980s onward.

8. Sanders and his associates were not the only archaeologists using population arguments in the 1970s and 1980s. Mark Cohen and Gregory Johnson, among others, also used them. Cohen (1977, 1981) argued that the seemingly simultaneous adoption of agriculture in various parts of the world around 10,000 years ago was a consequence of population pressure. Human populations, in his view, had grown continuously, finally surpassing the optimum level or carrying capacity of the world's environments; this necessitated the "artificial augmentation of the food supply" (Cohen 1977:279–80).

   Johnson took a different tack, resuscitating the notion of social density and volume that Émile Durkheim (1893/1964:256–82) elaborated in his *The Division of Labor in Society*. Johnson (1982) argued that larger societies were more complex than smaller ones and that both population size and complexity were major variables in sociocultural evolution, and that the relationship between them was flexible. He suggested that an organizational threshold was surpassed when the social density of a group exceeded six individuals. This resulted in new layers of within-group organization as decision-making leadership roles appeared (Johnson 1982:393). Earlier, he had argued that these decision-makers facilitated not only the transfer of information within and between groups but also the coordination and integration of a large number of organizational units. Thus, the increase in complexity was, in his view, both horizontal (more units at the same level) and vertical or hierarchical as new organizational levels appeared (Johnson 1978).

9. Arthur Joyce and Raymond Mueller (1997) subsequently discerned four periods of landscape use in the Oaxaca Valley that were correlated with major shifts in land use and population size; they further argued that these variables were causally related. They concluded, for example, that the settlement of Monte Albán in the Late Formative Period underwrote a major episode of soil erosion that led to the "modification of stream channel dynamics, alluviation, and expansion of the agriculturally rich floodplain in the lower Río Verde Valley," which is fed by the rivers that drain the Oaxaca Valley (Joyce and Mueller 1997:75).

10. The School of American Research seminar on which *The Cloud People* is based took place in early October 1975. The publication appeared in 1983.

11. Terence d'Altroy and Timothy Earle (1985) subsequently elaborated Renfrew's distinction between group-oriented and individualizing chiefdoms; they described the differences in terms of staple finance and wealth finance.
12. American sociologist Talcott Parsons, perhaps the leading Durkheimian of the mid-twentieth century, developed a similar argument (e.g. Baldwin 1961; Parsons 1951:201–48; 1964; Parsons, Bales, Olds, Zedlitch, and Slater 1955).
13. As noted, Barbara Price (1977) had used the term "cluster interaction" to refer to what Renfrew and his associates called "peer polity interaction."
14. This view was also shared by cultural materialists like Marvin Harris (1979: 100), who had earlier written that "all the qualitative components of the state were already present to some degree among advanced chiefdoms. The asymmetric redistribution of harvest surplus already amounted to an incipient form of taxation."
15. Gary Feinman and Jill Neitzel (1984) provide a useful overview of the debates surrounding prestate societies.
16. Judging by citations, Roy Rappaport was an influential figure in the development of the systems theory or management perspective at the University of Michigan. Before beginning his career as an anthropologist, Rappaport had studied at Cornell University's famous school of hotel management and worked as "an innkeeper" (Hart and Kottak 1999:159).
17. Here Gilman follows Geoffrey de Ste Croix's (1981) *The Class Struggle in the Ancient Greek World.*

Chapter 5 Convergence and Dialogue after 1990

1. Feinman and Marcus's *Archaic States* was based on papers that were at a School of American Research seminar in November 1992. For example, Marcus's (1989, 1992, 1993) publications on cycles of expansion and fragmentation of early states date from the late 1980s and the early 1990s; her paper in the *Archaic States* volume seems an integral part of this larger project (Marcus 1998). By contrast, Marcus and Kent Flannery's (1996) *Zapotec Civilization* represents a new departure that focuses on the decision-making of self-interested, rational social actors who pursued what they wanted in the cultural and historical circumstances in which they found themselves. My *The Inca Empire: The Formation and Disintegration of a Pre-Capitalist State* (1991) or, for that matter, *Archaeology: The Historical Development of Civilizations* (1992) brings together research on the formation and dissolution of Andean states that I conducted between 1982 and 1990.
2. Several archaeologists have suggested that systems theory is, in fact, a dialectical approach. I would argue that it is, in fact, not dialectical. The systems

approach used by processual archaeologists assumes (1) the social system is composed of specialized, hierarchically arranged components that are linked together by feedback; (2) the relationships between the components are defined in terms of the flow of information that maintains or increases the stability and efficiency of the system as a whole; (3) it is the relationships between the components that change rather than the components themselves; and (4) the system exhibits purposive or goal-oriented behavior. By contrast, a relational dialectical approach assumes (1) contradictions involving oppositional forces of non-independent origin; (2) the combined and uneven development of contradictions; (3) distinctions between the primary and secondary characteristics of contradictions; (4) the interpenetration of these oppositional forces; and (5) the possibility of the appearance of emergent features (Bhaskar 1991; Lukács 1923/1971; Mao 1937/1975; Marquardt 1992).

3. Trigger (1993c:172) indicated that his paper on state-churches was actually written in 1981.
4. Wilson argued for a universal model of state formation – an updated version of the systems theory model – developed by Flannery, Wright, and Johnson – which paid attention to settlement patterns and site hierarchies.
5. Saitta acknowledged the similarities between his perspective and the structural Marxist perspective elaborated by Emmanuel Terray (1975). He also cited with approval the work of the William Roseberry (e.g. 1988), who at times was also a proponent of non-dialectical Marxist perspectives such as dependency theory, the articulation of modes of production, or world systems theory. This had other implications as well. For example, in the debate over foraging societies that raged in the late 1980s and early 1990s, proponents of non-dialectical Marxist perspectives tended to agree with Edwin Wilmsen, while their more dialectically inclined brothers and sisters sided with Richard Lee.
6. Robert Paynter and John W. Cole (1980), among others, have described the dynamics of big men.
7. Charles Spencer (1993:42–5) also distinguished between aspiring leaders who cultivated ties with non-kin and those who drew support from their kin and neighbors.
8. Bob Preucel (personal communication 2002) points out, correctly I believe, that Bourdieu and Giddens have engaged with and reworked Marx's notion of praxis. I would extend his view. Elsewhere, I have argued that Weber also engaged with and reworked Marx's theory and analytical method (Patterson 1999a:53–5). Others have made the same argument (e.g. Wright 1983). Archaeologists writing in the 1990s tended to cite Bourdieu and Giddens rather than examining their connections with the Marxist tradition. For example, the authors in Marcia-Anne Dobres and John Robb's (2000) *Agency and Archaeology* cite Bourdieu (1980/1990), Giddens, or even Foucault (1976/1994) rather

than Marx's (1852/1978) *Eighteeth Brumaire*, with whom they are engaged in a dialogue. They also cite Giddens's (1979) *Central Problems in Social Theory* and (1984) *The Constitution of Society* more frequently than his critique of historical materialism (Giddens 1981, 1985), where the linkages between neo-Weberian and Marxist social thought and their interplay are more apparent. This suggests that at least some authors in the Dobres and Robb volume are more comfortable with Giddens's or Bourdieu's appropriations of liberal social theory than they are with their engagement with Marxism. Eric Wright (1983: 34) observed that

> Giddens's position is not generally the polar opposite of Marxist positions. The actual structural typology of societies Giddens elaborates is much closer to conventional Marxist typologies than either is to typologies in "modernization" theory, for example. And on many specific topics, such as the analysis of the capitalist labour process, the developmental dynamics of capitalism or the structural contrast in forms of surplus extraction in capitalism and feudalism, Giddens's analysis hardly differs at all from most current Marxist formulations.
>
> What is less easily meshed with contemporary Marxism are Giddens's arguments of the duality of power rooted in the autonomous logic of control over allocative and authoritative resources. This leads Giddens to reject the possibility of any general theory of history, any general principles of historical development, in favour of more limited epochal theories of particular transitions. Most Marxists retain a commitment to constructing an overall theory of historical development, based in some version of historical materialism, within which the development of contradictions in class relations provides the central framework for analysis. Giddens not only rejects the substantive propositions of the project, he rejects the project itself.

Wright (1983:35) proceeds to point out that, for Giddens, class analysis was no longer "the core of general social theory." This was part of his appeal to archaeologists in the 1990s, who focused on issues of identity and under-theorized where in social totality differences of gender, race, or ethnicity were actually constituted and what their relationships were with class structures, which many Marxists see as constituted in the economic base.

Analogous statements could be made about the interrelations of liberalism and Marxism in Bourdieu's writings.

9. Underlying Wallerstein's account of the early stages of capitalist development in the sixteenth century was his textured appreciation of the "transition from feudalism to capitalism" debate that was waged in the pages of *Science and Society* in the late 1940s and early 1950s. The major figures in the debate were two Marxist economists: Maurice Dobb and Paul Sweezy. Dobb (1947) focused on the processes involved in the dissolution of the feudal mode of production, the consolidation of capitalist social relations of production in rural areas, and

the form in which goods or labor were extracted from the direct producers. By contrast, Sweezy (1952/1976) stressed the determinant role of exchange over production relations and sought to specify how long-distance trade engendered a system of production for the market. These were, respectively, Marx's revolutionary and conservative pathways of industrial capitalist development. The revolutionary path transformed production relations; the conservative route saw the merchant taking control of production and the feudal mode of production preserved (Patterson 1999a:34–5, 126–30).

Bibliography

Adams, Robert McC. 1955. Developmental Stages in Ancient Mesopotamia. In *Irrigation Civilizations: A Comparative Study*, by Julian H. Steward, Robert M. Adams, Donald Collier, Angel Palerm, Karl A. Wittfogel, and Ralph L. Beals. Pan American Union Social Science Monographs, no. 1, pp. 6–18. Washington, DC.

—— 1956. Some Hypotheses on the Development of Early Civilization. *American Antiquity*, vol. XXI, no. 3, pp. 227–32. Salt Lake City, UT.

—— 1960a. Factors Influencing the Rise of Civilization in the Alluvium: Illustrated by Mesopotamia. In *City Invincible: A Symposium on Urbanization and Cultural Development in the Ancient Near East Held at the Oriental Institute of the University of Chicago, December 4–7, 1958*, edited by Carl H. Kraeling and Robert M. Adams, pp. 24–45. Chicago, IL: The University of Chicago Press.

—— 1960b. Early Civilizations, Subsistence, and Environment. In *City Invincible: A Symposium on Urbanization and Cultural Development in the Ancient Near East Held at the Oriental Institute of the University of Chicago, December 4–7, 1958*, edited by Carl H. Kraeling and Robert M. Adams, pp. 269–96. Chicago, IL: The University of Chicago Press.

—— 1960c. The Evolutionary Process in Early Civilizations. In *Evolution after Darwin*, edited by Sol Tax, vol. 2, *The Evolution of Man*, pp. 153–68. Chicago, IL: The University of Chicago Press.

—— 1965. *Land behind Baghdad: A History of Settlement on the Diyala Plains*. Chicago, IL: The University of Chicago Press.

—— 1966. *The Evolution of Urban Society: Early Mesopotamia and Prehispanic Mesoamerica*. Chicago, IL: Aldine Publishing Company.

—— 1974. Anthropological Perspectives on Ancient Trade. *Current Anthropology*, vol. 15, no. 3, pp. 239–58. Chicago, IL.

—— 2001. Complexity in Archaic States. *Journal of Anthropological Archaeology*, vol. 20, no. 3, pp. 345–61. San Diego, CA.

Algaze, Guillermo 1989. The Uruk Expansion: Cross-Cultural Exchange in Early Mesopotamian Civilization. *Current Anthropology*, vol. 30, no. 5, pp. 571–608. Chicago, IL.

—— 1993a. *The Uruk World System: The Dynamics of Expansion of Early Mesopotamian Civilization*. Chicago, IL: The University of Chicago Press.

—— 1993b. Expansionary Dynamics of Some Early Pristine States. *American Anthropologist*, vol. 95, no. 2, pp. 304–33. Arlington, VA.

Appadurai, Arjun 1988. Introduction: Commodities and the Politics of Value. In *The Social Life of Things: Commodities in Cultural Perspective*, edited by Arjun Appadurai, pp. 3–63. Cambridge, UK: Cambridge University Press.

Appelbaum, Richard 1977. Born-Again Functionalism? A Reconsideration of Althusser's Structuralism. *The Insurgent Sociologist*, no. 9, pp. 18–33. Eugene, OR.

Archibald, W. Peter 1989. *Marx and the Missing Link: "Human Nature"*. Atlantic Highlands, NJ: Humanities Press International.

Armillas, Pedro 1948. A Sequence of Cultural Development in Meso-America. In *A Reppraisal of Peruvian Archaeology*, assembled by Wendell C. Bennett. Memoirs of the Society for American Archaeology, no. 4, pp. 105–12. Salt Lake City UT.

—— 1951. Tecnología, formaciones socio-económicas y religión en Mesoamérica. In *Selected Papers of the XXIX Congress of Americanists*, edited by Sol Tax, vol. 1, *The Civilizations of Ancient America*, pp. 19–30. Chicago, IL: The University of Chicago Press.

Ashmore, Wendy, Jason Yeager, and Cynthia Robin in press. Commoner Sense: Late and Terminal Classic Social Strategies in the Xunantunich Area. In *The Terminal Classic in the Maya Lowlands: Collapse, Transition, and Transformation*, edited by Don S. Rice, Prudence M. Rice, and Arthur Demarest. To be published by Westview Press, Boulder, CO.

Baines, John and Norman Yoffee 1998. Order, Legitimacy, and Wealth in Ancient Egypt and Mesopotamia. In *Archaic States*, edited by Gary M. Feinman and Joyce Marcus, pp. 199–260. Santa Fe, NM: SAR Press.

—— 2000. Order, Legitimacy, and Wealth: Setting the Terms. In *Order, Legitimacy, and Wealth in Ancient States*, edited by Janet Richards and Mary van Buren, pp. 13–17. Cambridge, UK: Cambridge University Press.

Baker, Paul T. and William T. Sanders 1972. Demographic Studies in Anthropology. *Annual Review of Anthropology*, vol. 1, pp. 151–78. Palo Alto, CA.

Baldwin, Alfred L. 1961. The Parsonian Theory of Personality. In *The Social Theories of Talcott Parsons: A Critical Examination*, edited by Max Black, pp. 153–90. Carbondale, IL: Southern Illinois University Press.

Barrett, John 2000. A Thesis on Agency. In *Agency in Archaeology*, edited by Marcia-Anne Dobres and John Robb, pp. 61–8. London, UK: Routledge.

Barrett, Richard A. 1989. The Paradoxical Anthropology of Leslie White. *American Anthropologist*, vol. 91, no. 4, pp. 986–99. Washington, DC.

Beardsley, Richard K., Preston Holder, Alex D. Krieger, Betty J. Meggers, John B. Rinaldo, and Paul Kutsche 1957. Functional and Evolutionary Implications of Community Patterning. In *Seminars in Archaeology: 1955*, edited by Robert T.

Wauchope. Memoirs of the Society for American Archaeology, no. 11, pp. 129–57. Salt Lake City, UT.

Bender, Barbara 1978. Gatherer-Hunter to Farmer: A Social Perspective. *World Archaeology*, vol. 10, no. 2, pp. 204–22. London, UK.

—— 1981. Gatherer-Hunter Intensification. In *Economic Archaeology: Towards an Integration of Ecological and Social Approaches*, edited by Alison Sheridan and Geoff Bailey. BAR International Series 96, pp. 149–47. Oxford, UK.

——1985a. Emergent Tribal Formations in the American Midcontinent. *American Antiquity*, vol. 50, no. 1, pp. 52–62. Washington, DC.

——1985b. Prehistoric Developments in the American Midcontinent and in Brittany, Northwest France. In *Prehistoric Hunter-Gatherers: The Emergence of Cultural Complexity*, edited by T. Douglas Price and James A. Brown, pp. 21–57. New York: Academic Press.

—— 1990. The Dynamics of Nonhierarchical Societies. In *The Evolution of Political Systems: Sociopolitics in Small-Scale Sedentary Societies*, edited by Steadman Upham, pp. 247–63. Cambridge, UK: Cambridge University Press.

Bennett, Wendell C., editor 1948. A Reappraisal of Peruvian Archeology. *Memoirs of the Society for American Anthropology*, no. 4. Salt Lake City, UT.

Benton, Ted 1977. *Philosophical Foundations of the Three Sociologies*. London, UK: Routledge and Kegan Paul.

—— 1984. *The Rise and Fall of Structural Marxism: Althusser and his Influence*. New York: St. Martin's Press.

Bhaskar, Roy 1991. Dialectics. In *A Dictonary of Marxist Thought*, edited by Tom Bottomore, Laurence Harris, V. G. Kiernan, and Ralph Miliband, pp. 143–50. Oxford, UK: Blackwell Publishers.

Binford, Lewis R.1962/1972. Archaeology as Anthropology. In *An Archaeological Perspective*, by Lewis R. Binford, pp. 20–32. New York: Seminar Press.

—— 1965/1972. Archaeological Systematics and the Study of Culture Process. In *An Archaeological Perspective*, by Lewis R. Binford, pp. 195–207. New York: Seminar Press.

—— 1968/1972. Post-Pleistocene Adaptations. In *An Archaeological Perspective*, by Lewis R. Binford, pp. 421–49. New York: Seminar Press.

—— 1972. Comments on Evolution. In *An Archaeological Perspective*, by Lewis R. Binford, pp. 104–13. New York: Seminar Press.

—— 1977. General Introduction. In *For Theory Building in Archaeology: Essays on Faunal Remains, Aquatic Resources, Spatial Analysis, and Systemic Modeling*, edited by Lewis R. Binford, pp. 1–10. New York: Academic Press.

—— 1978. *Nunamuit Ethnoarchaeology*. New York: Academic Press.

Blanton, Richard E. 1976. Anthropological Studies of Cities. *Annual Review of Anthropology* vol. 5, pp. 249–64. Palo Alto, CA.

—— 1983. The Founding of Monte Albán. In *The Cloud People: Divergent Evolution of the Zapotec and Mixtec Civilizations*, edited by Kent V. Flannery and Joyce Marcus, pp. 83–7. San Diego, CA: Academic Press.

Blanton, Richard E. and Gary M. Feinman 1984. The Mesoamerican World System. *American Anthropologist*, vol. 86, no 3, pp. 673–82. Washington, DC.

Blanton, Richard E., Gary M. Feinman, Stephen A. Kowelewski, and Peter N. Peregrine 1996. A Dual-Processual Theory for the Evolution of Mesoamerican Civilization. *Current Anthropology*, vol. 37, no. 1, pp. 1–14. Chicago, IL.

Bottomore, Tom 1981. A Marxist Consideration of Durkheim. *Social Forces*, vol. 59, no. 4, pp. 902–17. Chapel Hill, NC.

Bourdieu, Pierre 1980/1990. *The Logic of Practice*. Stanford, CA: Stanford University Press.

Braidwood, Robert J. 1952. *The Near East and the Foundations of Civilization: An Essay in Appraisal of the General Evidence*. Eugene, OR: Oregon State System of Higher Education.

—— 1960a. Prelude to Civilization. In *City Invincible: A Symposium on Urbanization and Cultural Development in the Ancient Near East Held at the Oriental Institute of the University of Chicago, December 4–7, 1958*, edited by Carl H. Kraeling and Robert McC. Adams, pp. 297–314. Chicago, IL: The University of Chicago Press.

—— 1960b. Levels in Prehistory: A Model for the Consideration of Evidence. In *Evolution After Darwin*, edited by Sol Tax, vol. 2, *The Evolution of Man*, pp. 143–52. Chicago, IL: The University of Chicago Press.

Brenner, Robert 1986. The Social Basis of Economic Development. In *Analytical Marxism*, edited by John Roemer, pp. 23–53. Cambridge, UK: Cambridge University Press.

Brumfiel, Elizabeth M. 1976. Regional Growth in the Eastern Valley of Mexico: A Test of the "Population Pressure" Hypothesis. In *The Early Mesoamerican Village*, edited by Kent V. Flannery, pp. 234–49. New York: Academic Press.

—— 1980. Specialization, Market Exchange, and the Aztec State. *Current Anthropology*, vol. 21, no. 4, pp. 459–78. Chicago, IL.

—— 1983. Aztec State Making: Ecology, Structure, and the Origin of the State. *American Anthropologist*, vol. 85, no. 2, pp. 261–84. Washington, DC.

——1987a. Consumption and Politics at Aztec Huexotla. *American Anthropologist*, vol. 89, no. 3, pp. 676–86. Washington, DC.

—— 1987b. Elite and Utilitarian Crafts in the Aztec State. In *Specialization, Exchange, and Complex Societies*, edited by Elizabeth M. Brumfiel and Timothy K. Earle, pp. 102–18. Cambridge, UK: Cambridge University Press.

—— 1991a. Weaving and Cooking: Women's Production in Aztec Mexico. In *Engendering Archaeology: Women and Prehistory*, edited by Joan M. Gero and Margaret W. Conkey, pp. 224–51. Oxford, UK: Basil Blackwell.

—— 1991b. Tribute and Commerce in Imperial Cities: The Case of Xaltocan, Mexico. In *Early State Economics*, edited by Hans J. M. Claessen and P. van de Velde. Political and Legal Anthropology, vol. 8, pp. 177–98. New Brunswick, NJ: Transaction Books.

—— 1991c. Agricultural Development and Class Stratification in the Southern Valley of Mexico. In *Land and Politics in the Valley of Mexico*, edited by H. R. Harvey, pp. 43–62. Albuquerque, NM: University of New Mexico Press.

—— 1992. Distinguished Lecture in Archaeology: Breaking and Entering the Ecosystem – Gender, Class, and Faction Steal the Show. *American Anthropologist*, vol. 94, no. 3, pp. 551–67. Washington, DC.

——1994a. Factional Competition and Political Development in the New World: An Introduction. In *Factional Competition and Political Development in the New World*, edited by Elizabeth M. Brumfiel and John W. Fox, pp. 3–13. Cambridge, UK: Cambridge University Press.

—— 1994b. Ethnic Groups and Political Development in Ancient Mexico. In *Factional Competition and Political Development in the New World*, edited by Elizabeth M. Brumfiel and John W. Fox, pp. 89–102. Cambridge, UK: Cambridge University Press.

—— 1995. Heterarchy and the Analysis of Complex Societies: Comments. In *Heterarchy and the Analysis of Complex Societies*, Robert M. Ehrenreich, Carole L. Crumley, and Janet E. Levy. Archeological Papers of the American Anthropological Association, no. 6, pp. 125–31. Arlington, VA.

—— 1998. The Multiple Identities of Aztec Craft Specialists. In *Craft and Social Identity*, edited by Cathy L. Costin and Rita P. Wright. Archeological Papers of the American Anthropological Association, no. 8, pp. 145–52. Washington, DC.

Brumfiel, Elizabeth M. and Timothy K. Earle 1987. Specialization, Exchange, and Complex Societies: An Introduction. In *Specialization, Exchange, and Complex Societies*, edited by Elizabeth M. Brumfiel and Timothy K. Earle, pp. 1–9. Cambridge, UK: Cambridge University Press.

Brumfiel, Elizabeth M. and John W. Fox, editors 1994. *Factional Competition and Political Development in the New World*. Cambridge, UK: Cambridge University Press.

Burger, Richard L. 1992. *Chavin and the Origins of Andean Civilization*. London, UK: Thames and Hudson.

Burkett, Paul 1998. A Critique of Neo-Malthusian Marxism: Society, Nature, and Population. *Historical Materialism: Research in Critical Marxist Theory*, no. 2, pp. 118–42. London, UK.

—— 1999. *Marx and Nature: Red and Green Perspectives*. New York: St. Martin's Press.

Byland, Bruce E. and John M. D. Pohl 1994. *In the Realm of 8 Deer: The Archaeology of the Mixtec Codices*. Norman, OK: University of Oklahoma Press.

Caldwell, Joseph R. 1959. The New American Archaeology. *Science*, vol. 129, no. 3345, pp. 303–7. Lancaster, PA.

Carneiro, Robert L. 1967a. Editor's Introduction. In *The Evolution of Society: Selections from Herbert Spencer's* Principles of Sociology, edited by Robert L. Carneiro, pp. ix–lvii. Chicago, IL: The University of Chicago Press.

—— 1967b. On the Relationship between Size of Population and Complexity of Social Organization. *Southwestern Journal of Anthropology*, vol. 23, no. 3, pp. 234–43. Albuquerque, NM.

—— 1970. A Theory of the Origin of the State. *Science*, vol. 169, no. 3948, pp. 733–8. Washington, DC.

—— 1978. Political Expansion as an Expression of the Principle of Competitive Exclusion. In *Origins of the State: The Anthropology of Political Evolution*, edited by Ronald Cohen and Elman R. Service, pp. 205–24. Philadelphia, PA: Institute for the Study of Human Issues.

—— 1981a. Leslie White. In *Totems and Teachers: Perspectives on the History of Anthropology*, edited by Sydel Silverman, pp. 209–54. New York: Columbia University Press.

—— 1981b. The Chiefdom: Precursor of the State. In *The Transition to Statehood in the New World*, edited by Grant D. Jones and Robert R. Kautz, pp. 37–79. Cambridge, UK: Cambridge University Press.

—— 1987. Cross-Currents in the Theory of State Formation. *American Ethnologist*, vol. 14, no. 4, pp. 756–70. Washington, DC.

—— 1991. The Nature of the Chiefdom as Revealed by Evidence from the Cauca Valley of Colombia. In *Profiles in Cultural Evolution: Papers from a Conference in Honor of Elman R. Service*, edited by A. Terry Rambo and Kathleen Gillogly. Anthropological Papers, Museum of Anthropology, University of Michigan, no. 85, pp. 167–90. Ann Arbor.

—— 1998. What Happened at the Flashpoint? Conjectures on Chiefdom Formation at the Very Moment of Conception. In *Chiefdoms and Chieftaincy in the Americas*, edited by Elsa Redmond, pp. 18–42. Gainesville, FL: University Press of Florida.

Champion, Timothy C., editor 1989. *Centre and Periphery: Comparative Studies in Archaeology*. London, UK: Unwin Hyman.

Childe, V. Gordon 1928. *The Most Ancient East: The Oriental Prelude to European Prehistory*. London, UK: Kegan Paul.

—— 1929. *The Danube in Prehistory*. Oxford, UK: Clarendon Press.

—— 1934/1953. *New Light on the Most Ancient East: The Oriental Prelude to European Prehistory*. New York: Grove Press.

—— 1935. Changing Methods and Aims in Prehistory: Presidential Address for 1935. *Proceedings of the Prehistoric Society*, vol. I, no. 1, pp. 1–15. Cambridge, UK.

—— 1936/1983. *Man Makes Himself.* New York: The New American Library.

—— 1942. *What Happened in History.* Harmondsworth, UK: Penguin Books.

—— 1946a. Archaeology and Anthropology. *Southwestern Journal of Anthropology*, vol. 2, no. 1, pp. 243–51. Albuquerque, NM.

—— 1946b. *Scotland Before the Scots, Being the Rhind Lecture for 1944.* London, UK: Methuen and Company.

—— 1947. Archaeology as a Social Science. *University of London, Institute of Archaeology, Third Annual Report,* pp. 49–60. London, UK.

——1950/1972. The Urban Revolution. In *Contemporary Archaeology: A Guide to Theory and Contributions,* edited by Mark P. Leone, pp. 43–51. Carbondale, IL: Southern Illinois University Press.

—— 1954. Early Forms of Society. In *A History of Technology,* edited by Charles Singer, E. J. Holmyard, and A. R. Hall, vol. I, *From Earliest Times to the Fall of Ancient Empires,* pp. 38–57. New York: Oxford University Press.

—— 1956. *Piecing Together the Past: The Interpretation of Archaeological Data.* New York: Fredrick A. Praeger.

Claessen, Henri J. M. and Peter Skalník, editors 1978. *The Early State.* The Hague: Mouton Publishers.

—— 1981. *The State of the State.* The Hague: Mouton Publishers.

Claessen, Henri J. M., Peter van de Velde, and M. Estellie Smith, editors 1985. *Development and Decline: The Evolution of Political Organization.* South Hadley, MA: Bergen and Garvey Publishers.

Clark, John E. and Michael Blake 1994. The Power of Prestige: Competitive Generosity and the Emergence of Rank Societies in Lowland Mesoamerica. In *Factional Competition and Political Development in the New World,* edited by Elizabeth M. Brumfiel and John W. Fox, pp. 17–30. Cambridge, UK: Cambridge University Press.

Clarke, David L. 1968. *Analytical Archaeology.* London, UK: Methuen.

—— 1969/1979. The Economic Context of Trade and Industry in Barbarian Europe till Roman Times. In *Analytical Archaeologist: Collected Papers of David L. Clarke,* edited by his colleagues, pp. 263–332. New York: Academic Press.

—— 1972/1979. Models and Paradigms in Contemporary Archaeology. In *Analytical Archaeologist: Collected Papers of David L. Clarke,* edited by his colleagues, pp. 21–82. New York: Academic Press.

—— 1973/1979. Archaeology: The Loss of Innocence. In *Analytical Archaeologist: Collected Papers of David L. Clarke,* edited by his colleagues, pp. 83–104. New York: Academic Press.

Clarke, Simon 1980. Althusserian Marxism. In *One-Dimensional Marxism: Althusser and the Politics of Culture,* by Simon Clarke, Terry Lovel, Kevin McDonnell, Kevin Roberts, and Victor J. Seidler, pp. 7–101. London, UK: Allison and Busby.

Cohen, Mark N.1977. *The Food Crisis in Prehistory: Overpopulation and the Origins of Agriculture*. New Haven, CT: Yale University Press.

—— 1981. The Ecological Basis for New World State Formation: General and Local Model Building. In *The Transition to Statehood in the New World*, edited by Grant T. Jones and Robert R. Kautz, pp. 105–22. Cambridge, UK: Cambridge University Press.

Collier, Donald 1955. Development of Civilization on the Coast of Peru. In *Irrigation Civilizations: A Comparative Study*, by Julian H. Steward, Robert M. Adams, Donald Collier, Angel Palerm, Karl A. Wittfogel, and Ralph L. Beals. Pan American Union Social Science Monographs, no. 1, pp. 19–27. Washington, DC.

Conkey, Margaret W. and Janet Spector 1984. Archaeology and the Study of Gender. In *Advances in Archaeological Method and Theory*, edited by Michael B. Schiffer, vol. 7, pp. 1–38. New York: Academic Press.

Coontz, Sydney H. 1957. *Population Theories and Their Economic Interpretation*. London, UK: Routledge and Kegan Paul.

Cowgill, George L. 1975. On Causes and Consequences of Ancient and Modern Population Changes. *American Anthropologist*, vol. 77, no. 3, pp. 505–25. Washington, DC.

—— 1988. Comment. *Current Anthropology*, vol. 29, no. 1, pp. 54–5. Chicago, IL.

—— 1992. Social Differentiation at Teotihuacan. In *Mesoamerican Elites: An Archaeological Assessment*, edited by Diane Z. Chase and Arlen F. Chase, pp. 206–20. Norman, OK: University of Oklahoma Press.

Crumley, Carole L. 1976. Toward a Locational Definition of State Systems of Settlement. *American Anthropologist*, vol. 78, no. 1, pp. 59–73. Washington, DC.

—— 1979. Three Locational Models: An Epistemological Assessment for Anthropology and Archaeology. In *Advances in Archaeological Method and Theory*, edited by Michael B. Schiffer, vol. 2, pp. 143–73. New York: Academic Press.

—— 1987. A Dialectical Critique of Hierarchy. In *Power Relations and State Formation*, edited by Thomas C. Patterson and Christine W. Gailey, pp. 155–69. Washington, DC: Archeology Division, American Anthropological Association.

—— 1995. Heterarchy and the Analysis of Complex Societies. In *Heterarchy and the Analysis of Complex Societies*, edited by Robert M. Ehrenreich, Carole L. Crumley, and Janet E. Levy. Archeological Papers of the American Anthropological Association, no. 6, pp. 1–6. Arlington, VA.

—— 2001. Communication, Holism, and the Evolution of Sociopolitical Complexity. In *From Leader to Ruler*, edited by Jonathan Haas, pp. 19–36. New York: Kluwer Academic/Plenum Publishers.

Crumley, Carole L. and William H. Marquardt, editors 1987. *Regional Dynamics: Burgundian Landscapes in Historical Perspective*. San Diego, CA: Academic Press.

d'Altroy, Terence N. and Timothy K. Earle 1985. Staple Finance, Wealth Finance, and Storage in the Inca Political Economy. *Current Anthropology*, vol. 26, no. 2, pp. 187–206. Chicago, IL.

D'Amico, Robert 1981. *Marx and the Philosophy of Culture*. University of Florida Humanities Monograph no. 50. Gainesville, FL.

DeMarrais, Elizabeth, Luis J. Castillo, and Timothy K. Earle 1996. Ideology, Materialization, and Power Strategies. *Current Anthropology*, vol. 37, no. 1, pp. 15–32. Chicago, IL.

Diakonov, Igor M., editor 1969. *Ancient Mesopotamia, Socio-Economic History: A Collection of Essays by Soviet Scholars*. Moscow, USSR: Nauka Publishing House.

Diamond, Stanley 1951/1996. Dahomey: The Development of a Proto-State. *Dialectical Anthropology*, vol. 21, no. 2, pp. 121–216. Dordrecht, NL.

—— 1974. *In Search of the Primitive: A Critique of Civilization*. New Brunswick, NJ: Transaction Books.

DiTomaso, Nancy 1982. "Sociological Reductionism" from Parsons to Althusser: Linking Action and Structure in Social Theory. *American Sociological Review*, vol. 47, no. 1, pp. 14–28. Chicago, IL.

Dobb, Maurice 1947. *Studies in the Development of Capitalism*. New York: International Publishers.

Dobres, Marcia-Anne and John Robb, editors 2000. *Agency and Archaeology*. London, UK: Routledge.

Durkheim, Émile 1885/1978. Review: Albert Schaeffle, *Bau und Leben des sozialen Körpers: Erster Band*. In *On Institutional Analysis*, edited by Mark Traugott, pp. 93–114. Chicago, IL: The University of Chicago Press.

—— 1886. Les études de science sociale. *Review Philosophique*, tome XXII, pp. 61–80. Paris, FR.

—— 1893/1964. *The Division of Labor in Society*. New York: The Free Press.

—— 1895/1938. *The Rules of Sociological Method*, edited by George. E. G. Caitlin. Glencoe, IL: The Free Press.

—— 1898. Préface. *L'Année Sociologique*, tome I, pp. i–vii. Paris, FR.

—— 1912/1965. *The Elementary Forms of Religious Life*. New York: The Free Press.

Earle, Timothy K. 1977. A Reappraisal of Redistribution: Complex Hawaiian Chiefdoms. In *Exchange Systems in Prehistory*, edited by Timothy K. Earle and Jonathon E. Ericson, pp. 213–29. New York: Academic Press.

—— 1978. *Economic and Social Organization of a Complex Chiefdom: The Halelea District, Kaua'i, Hawaii*. Anthropological Papers, Museum of Anthropology, University of Michigan, no. 63. Ann Arbor, MI.

—— 1987. Chiefdoms in Archaeological and Ethnohistorical Perspectives. *Annual Review of Anthropology*, vol. 16, pp. 279–308. Palo Alto, CA.

—— 1997. *How Chiefs Come to Power: The Political Economy in Prehistory*. Stanford, CA: Stanford University Press.

Earle, Timothy K. and Robert W. Preucel 1987. Processual Archaeology and the Radical Critique. *Current Anthropology*, vol. 28, no. 4, pp. 501–38. Chicago, IL.

Edens, Christopher 1992. Dynamics of Trade in the Ancient Mesopotamian "World System." *American Anthropologist*, vol. 94, no. 1, pp. 118–39. Arlington, VA.

Ehrenreich, Robert M., Carole L. Crumley, and Janet E. Levy, editors 1995. *Heterarchy and the Analysis of Complex Societies*. Archeological Papers of the American Anthropological Association, no. 6. Arlington, VA.

Engels, Frederick 1859/1983. Letter to Karl Marx, 11–12 December. In *Karl Marx, Frederick Engels: Collected Works*, vol. 40, pp. 550–1. New York: International Publishers.

—— 1865/1987. Letter to Friedrich Albert Lange, 29 March. In *Karl Marx, Frederick Engels: Collected Works*, vol. 42, pp. 135–8. New York: International Publishers.

—— 1873–82/1940. *Dialectics of Nature* [originally published 1925], with an introduction by J. B. S. Haldane. New York: International Publishers.

—— 1873–82/1987. Dialectics of Nature. In *Karl Marx, Frederick Engels: Collected Works*, vol. 25, pp. 313–590. New York: International Publishers.

—— 1876/1972. The Part Played by Labor in the Transition from Ape to Man [originally published 1925]. In *The Origin of the Family, Private Property and the State: In Light of the Investigations of Lewis H. Morgan*, by Frederick Engels, pp. 249–64. New York: International Publishers.

—— 1876–8/1939. *Anti-Dühring: Herr Eugen Dühring's Revolution in Science* [originally published 1878]. New York: International Publishers.

—— 1876–8/1987. Anti-Dühring: Herr Eugen Dühring's Revolution in Science [originally published 1878]. In *Karl Marx, Frederick Engels: Collected Works*, vol. 25, pp. 1–312. New York: International Publishers.

—— 1884/1972. *The Origin of the Family, Private Property and the State: In Light of the Investigations of Lewis H. Morgan* [originally published 1884], with an introduction by Eleanor B. Leacock. New York: International Publishers.

——1894/1990. The Peasant Question in France and Germany [originally published 1894–5]. In *Karl Marx, Frederick Engels: Collected Works*, vol. 27, pp. 481–502. New York: International Publishers.

Feinman, Gary M. 1995. The Emergence of Inequality: A Focus on Strategies and Processes. In *Foundations of Social Inequality*, edited by T. Douglas Price and Gary M. Feinman, pp. 255–79. New York: Plenum Publishers.

Feinman, Gary M. and Joyce Marcus, editors 1998. *Archaic States*. Santa Fe, NM: SAR Press.

Feinman, Gary M. and Jill Neitzel 1984. Too Many Types: An Overview of Sedentary Prestate Societies in the Americas. In *Advances in Archaeological*

Method and Theory, edited by Michael B. Schiffer, vol. 7, pp. 39–102. Orlando, FL: Academic Press.

Flannery, Kent V. 1965. The Ecology of Early Food Production in Mesopotamia. *Science*, vol. 147, no. 3663, pp. 1247–56. Washington, DC.

——— 1967. Culture History v. Culture Process: A Debate in American Archaeology. *Scientific American*, vol. 217, no. 2, pp. 119–22. New York.

——— 1968a. Archeological Systems Theory and Early Mesoamerica. In *Anthropological Archeology in the Americas*, edited by Betty J. Meggers, pp. 67–87. Washington, DC: Anthropological Society of Washington.

——— 1968b. The Olmec and the Valley of Oaxaca: A Model for Inter-Regional Interaction in Formative Times. In *Dumbarton Oaks Conference on the Olmec*, edited by Elizabeth P. Benson, pp. 79–110. Washington, DC: Dumbarton Oaks Research Library and Collection.

——— 1969. Origins and Ecological Effects of Early Domestication in Iran and the Near East. In *The Domestication and Exploitation of Plants and Animals*, edited by Peter J. Ucko and G. W. Dimbleby, pp. 73–100. London, UK: Gerald Duckworth and Co.

——— 1972. The Cultural Evolution of Civilizations. *Annual Review of Ecology and Systematics*, vol. 3, pp. 399–426. Palo Alto, CA.

——— 1983. Divergent Evolution. In *The Cloud People: Divergent Evolution of the Zapotec and Mixtec Civilizations*, edited by Kent V. Flannery and Joyce Marcus, pp. 1–4. San Diego, CA: Academic Press.

——— 1986. A Visit to the Master. In *Guilá Naquitz: Archaic Foraging and Early Agriculture in Oaxaca, Mexico*, edited by Kent V. Flannery, pp. 511–19. Orlando, FL: Academic Press.

——— 1988. Comment. *Current Anthropology*, vol. 29, no. 1, pp. 57–8. Chicago, IL.

——— 1999. Process and Agency in Early State Formation. *Cambridge Journal of Archaeology*, vol. 9, no. 1, pp. 3–21. Cambridge, UK.

Flannery, Kent V. and Joyce Marcus 1983a. The Origins of the State in Oaxaca. In *The Cloud People: Divergent Evolution of the Zapotec and Mixtec Civilizations*, edited by Kent V. Flannery and Joyce Marcus, pp. 79–83. San Diego, CA: Academic Press.

——— 1983b. Preface. In *The Cloud People: Divergent Evolution of the Zapotec and Mixtec Civilizations*, edited by Kent V. Flannery and Joyce Marcus, pp. xix–xxi. San Diego, CA: Academic Press.

Fluehr-Lobban, Carolyn 1986. Frederick Engels and Leslie White: The Symbol versus the Role of Labor in the Origin of Humanity. *Dialectical Anthropology*, vol. 11, no. 1, pp. 119–26. Dordrecht, NL.

Foster, John Bellamy 2000. *Marx's Ecology: Materialism and Nature*. New York: Monthly Review Press.

Foucault, Michel 1976/1994. Two Lectures. In *Culture/Power/History: A Reader in Contemporary Social Theory*, edited by Nicholas B. Dirks, Geoff Eley, and Sherry B. Ortner, pp. 200–21. Princeton, NJ: Princeton University Press.

Fried, Morton H. 1960. On the Evolution of Social Stratification and the State. In *Culture in History: Essays in Honor of Paul Radin*, edited by Stanley Diamond, pp. 713–31. New York: Columbia University Press.

—— 1967. *The Evolution of Political Society: An Essay in Political Anthropology.* New York: Random House.

—— 1975. *The Notion of Tribe.* Menlo Park, CA: Cummings.

Friedman, Jonathan 1974. Marxism, Structuralism, and Vulgar Materialism. *Man*, vol. 9, no. 3, pp. 444–69. London, UK.

—— 1975. Tribes, States, and Transformations. In *Marxist Analyses and Social Anthropology*, edited by Maurice Bloch, pp. 161–202. London, UK: Malaby Press.

Friedman, Jonathan and Michael J. Rowlands 1977. Notes Toward an Epigenetic Model of the Evolution of "Civilisation." In *The Evolution of Social Systems*, edited by Jonathan Friedman and Michael J. Rowlands, pp. 201–76. London, UK: Gerald Duckworth and Company.

Gailey, Christine W. 1983. Categories without Culture: Structuralism, Ethnohistory and Ethnocide. *Dialectical Anthropology*, vol. 8, no. 4, pp. 241–50. Amsterdam, NL.

—— 1984. Women and Warfare: Shifting Status in Precapitalist State Formation. *Culture*, vol. IV, no. 1, pp. 61–70. Montreal, PQ.

—— 1985. The State of the State. *Dialectical Anthropology*, vol. 9, nos. 1–4, pp. 65–90. Amsterdam, NL.

—— 1987a. *Kinship to Kingship: Gender Hierarchy and State Formation in the Tongan Islands.* Austin, TX: University of Texas Press.

—— 1987b. Culture Wars: Resistance to State Formation. In *Power Relations and State Formation*, edited by Thomas C. Patterson and Christine W. Gailey, pp. 35–56. Washington, DC: Archeology Division, American Anthropological Association.

—— 1988. Evolutionary Perspectives on Gender Hierarchy. In *Analyzing Gender: A Handbook of Social Science Research*, edited by Beth B. Hess and Myra M. Ferree, pp. 32–67. Newbury Park, CA: Sage Publications.

Gailey, Christine W. and Thomas C. Patterson 1987. Power Relations and State Formation. In *Power Relations and State Formation*, edited by Thomas C. Patterson and Christine W. Gailey, pp. 1–26. Washington, DC: Archeology Division, American Anthropological Association.

—— 1988. State Formation and Uneven Development. In *State and Society: The Emergence and Development of Social Hierarchy and Political Centralization*, edited by John Gledhill, Barbara Bender, and Mogens T. Larsen, pp. 77–90. London, UK: Unwin Hyman.

Gándara, Manuel 1980. La vieja "nueva arqueología" (primera parte). *Boletín de Antropología Americana*, no. 2, pp. 59–97. Mexico, DF.

—— 1981. La vieja "nueva arqueología" (segunda parte). *Boletín de Antropología Americana*, no. 3, pp. 99–159. Mexico, DF.

Gathercole, Peter 1989. Childe's Early Marxism. In *Critical Traditions in Contemporary Archaeology*, edited by Valerie Pinsky and Alison Wylie, pp. 80–9. Cambridge, UK: Cambridge University Press.

Geertz, Clifford 1973. *The Interpretation of Cultures*. New York: Basic Books.

Geras, Norman 1983. *Marx and Human Nature: Refutation of a Legend*. London, UK: Verso.

Gero, Joan M. and Margaret W. Conkey, editors 1991. *Engendering Archaeology: Women and Prehistory*. Oxford, UK: Basil Blackwell.

Giddens, Anthony 1979. *Central Problems in Social Theory: Action, Structure, and Contradiction in Social Analysis*. Berkeley, CA: University of California Press.

—— 1981. *A Contemporary Critique of Historical Materialism*, vol. 1, *Power, Property, and the State*. Berkeley, CA: University of California Press.

—— 1984. *The Constitution of Society: Outline of a Theory of Structuration*. Stanford, CA: Stanford University Press.

—— 1985. *A Contemporary Critique of Historical Materialism*, vol. 2, *The Nation-State and Violence*. Berkeley, CA: University of California Press.

Gilman, Antonio 1976. Bronze Age Dynamics in Southeast Spain. *Dialectical Anthropology*, vol. 1, no. 4, pp. 307–19. Amsterdam, NL.

—— 1981. The Development of Social Stratification in Bronze Age Europe. *Current Anthropology*, vol. 22, no. 1, pp. 1–23. Chicago, IL.

—— 1984. Explaining the Upper Palaeolithic Revolution. In *Marxist Perspectives in Archaeology*, edited by Matthew Spriggs, pp. 115–26. Cambridge, UK: Cambridge University Press.

—— 1991. Trajectories toward Social Complexity in the Later Prehistory of the Mediterranean. In *Chiefdoms: Power, Economy, and Ideology*, edited by Timothy K. Earle, pp. 146–68. Cambridge, UK: Cambridge University Press.

Gledhill, John 1978. Formative Development in the North American South West. In *Social Organisation and Settlement*, edited by David Green, Colin Haselgrove, and Matthew Spriggs. BAR International Series, no. 47, pt. ii, pp. 247–90. Oxford, UK.

—— 1981. Time's Arrow: Anthropology, History, Social Evolution and Marxist Theory. *Critique of Anthropology*, no. 16, pp. 3–30. London, UK.

—— 1984. The Transformation of Asiatic Formations: The Case of Late Prehispanic Mesoamerica. In *Marxist Perspectives in Archaeology*, edited by Matthew Spriggs, pp. 135–48. Cambridge, UK: Cambridge University Press.

Gledhill, John and Mogens T. Larsen 1982. The Polanyi Paradigm and a Dynamic Analysis of Archaic States. In *Theory and Explanation in Archaeology: The*

Southampton Conference, edited by Colin Renfrew, Michael J. Rowlands, and Barbara A. Segraves, pp. 197–230. New York: Academic Press.

Goldman, Irving 1955. Status Rivalry and Cultural Evolution in Polynesia. *American Anthropologist*, vol. 57, no. 5, pp. 580–97. Menasha, WI.

—— 1960. The Evolution of Polynesian Societies. In *Culture in History: Essays in Honor of Paul Radin*, edited by Stanley Diamond, pp. 687–712. New York: Columbia University Press.

—— 1970. *Ancient Polynesian Society*. Chicago, IL: The University of Chicago Press.

Green, Sally 1981. *Prehistorian: A Biography of V. Gordon Childe*. Wiltshire, UK: Moonraker Press.

Greene, Kevin 1999. V. Gordon Childe and the Vocabulary of Revolutionary Change. *Antiquity*, vol. 73, no. 279, pp. 97–109. Cambridge, UK.

Haas, Jonathan 1981. Class Conflict and the State in the New World. In *The Transition to Statehood in the New World*, edited by Grant D. Jones and Robert R. Kautz, pp. 80–102. Cambridge, UK: Cambridge University Press.

—— 1982. *The Evolution of the Prehistoric State*. New York: Columbia University Press.

—— 2001. Cultural Evolution and Political Centralization. In *From Leaders to Rulers*, edited by Jonathan Haas, pp. 3–18. New York: Kluwer Academic/Plenum Publishers.

Hall, Thomas D. and Christopher Chase-Dunn 1993. The World Systems Perspective and Archaeology: Forward into the Past. *Journal of Archeaological Research*, vol. 1, no. 2, pp. 121–44. New York.

—— 1996. Comparing World-Systems: Concepts and Hypotheses. In *Pre-Columbian World Systems*, edited by Peter N. Peregrine and Gary M. Feinman. Monographs in World Archaeology, no. 26, pp. 11–26. Madison, WI: Prehistory Press.

Harris, Marvin 1979. *Cultural Materialism: The Struggle for a Science of Culture*. New York: Random House.

Hart, Keith and Conrad Kottak 1999. Roy A. "Skip" Rappaport (1926–1997). *American Anthropologist*, vol. 101, no. 1, pp. 159–61. Arlington, VA.

Haupt, Georges 1982. Marx and Marxism. In *The History of Marxism*, edited by Eric J. Hobsbawm, vol. 1, *Marxism in Marx's Day*, pp. 265–90. Hemel Hempstead, UK: Harvester Press.

Haury, Emil W. 1962. The Greater American Southwest. In *Courses toward Urban Life: Archaeological Considerations of Some Cultural Alternatives*, edited by Robert J. Braidwood and Gordon R. Willey. Viking Fund Publications in Anthropology, no. 32, pp. 106–31. New York.

Heyer, Paul 1982. *Nature, Human Nature, and Society: Marx, Darwin, Biology, and the Human Sciences*. Westport, CT: Greenwood Press.

Hobsbawm, Eric J. 1984. Marx and History. *New Left Review*, no. 143, pp. 39–50. London, UK.

Howard, Michael C. and John E. King 1989. *A History of Marxian Economics*, vol. I, *1883–1929*. Princeton, NJ: Princeton University Press.

Hunley, J. D. 1991.*The Life and Thought of Friedrich Engels: A Reinterpretation*. New Haven, CT: Yale University Press.

Johnson, Gregory A. 1972. A Test of the Utility of Central Place Theory in Archaeology. In *Man, Settlement and Urbanism*, edited by Peter J. Ucko, Ruth Tringham, and G. W. Dimbleby, pp. 769–86. London, UK: Gerald Duckworth and Company.

—— 1978. Information Sources and the Development of Decision-Making Organizations. In *Social Archeology: Beyond Subsistence and Dating*, edited by Charles L. Redman, Mary J. Berman, Edward V. Curtin, William T. Langhorne, Jr., Nina Versaggi, and Jeffery C. Wanser, pp. 87–112. New York: Academic Press.

—— 1982. Organizational Structure and Scalar Stress. In *Theory and Explanation in Archaeology: The Southampton Conference*, edited by Colin Renfrew, Michael J. Rowlands, and Barbara A. Segraves, pp. 389–422. New York: Academic Press.

Jorgensen, Joseph G. 1993. Kathleen Gough's Fight against the Consequences of Class and Imperialism on Campus. *Anthropologica*, vol. XXXV, no. 2, pp. 227–34. Waterloo, ON.

Joyce, Arthur A. and Raymond G, Mueller 1997. Prehispanic Human Ecology of the Río Verde Drainage Basin, Mexico. *World Archaeology*, vol. 29, no. 1, pp. 75–94. London, UK.

Kautsky, John 1988. Introduction. In *The Materialist Conception of History*, by Karl Kautsky, pp. xxi–lxiv. New Haven, CT: Yale University Press.

Kautsky, Karl 1892/1971. *The Class Struggle*. New York: W. W. Norton and Company.

—— 1906/1918. *Ethics and the Materialist Conception of History*. Chicago, IL: Charles H. Kerr and Company.

—— 1927/1988. *The Materialist Conception of History*, edited by John H. Kautsky. New Haven, CT: Yale University Press.

Kelley, Jane H. and Marsha P. Hanen 1988. *Archaeology and the Methodology of Science*. Albuquerque, NM: University of New Mexico Press.

Kohl, Philip L. 1975. The Archeology of Trade. *Dialectical Anthropology*, vol. 1, no. 1, pp. 43–50. Amsterdam, NL.

—— 1978. The Balance of Trade in Southwestern Asia in the Mid-Third Millennium B.C. *Current Anthropology*, vol. 19, no. 3, pp. 463–92. Chicago, IL.

—— 1981. Materialist Approaches in Prehistory. *Annual Review of Anthropology*, vol. 10, pp. 89–118. Palo Alto, CA.

—— 1987a. The Use and Abuse of World Systems Theory: The Case of the "Pristine" West Asian State. *Advances in Archaeological Method and Theory*, edited by Michael B. Schiffer, vol. 11, pp. 1–35. New York: Academic Press.

—— 1987b. The Ancient Economy, Transferable Technologies and the Bronze Age World-System: A View from the Northeastern Frontier of the Ancient Near East. In *Centre and Periphery in the Ancient World*, edited by Michael Rowlands, Mogens Larsen, and Kristian Kristiansen, pp. 13–24. Cambridge, UK: Cambridge University Press.

—— 1989. The Use and Abuse of World Systems Theory: The Case of the "Pristine" West Asian State. In *Archaeological Thought in America*, edited by C. C. Lamberg-Karlovsky, pp. 218–40. Cambridge, UK: Cambridge University Press.

—— 1993. Limits to a Post-processual Archaeology (Or, The Dangers of a New Scholasticism). In *Archaeological Theory: Who Sets the Agenda?*, edited by Norman Yoffee and Andrew Sherratt, pp. 13–19. Cambridge, UK: Cambridge University Press.

Kolakowski, Leszek 1966/1969. *The Alienation of Reason: A History of Positivist Thought*. Garden City, NY: Doubleday and Company.

Krader, Lawrence 1976. *Dialectic of Civil Society*. Assen: Van Gorcum and Company.

Krieger, Alex D. 1953a. New World Culture History: Anglo-America. In *Anthropology Today: An Encyclopedic Inventory*, edited by Alfred L. Kroeber, pp. 238–65. Chicago, IL: The University of Chicago Press.

——1953b. Basic Stages of Cultural Evolution. In *An Appraisal of Anthropology Today*, edited by Sol Tax, pp. 247–50. Chicago, IL: The University of Chicago Press.

Kristiansen, Kristian 1991. Chiefdoms, States, and Systems of Social Evolution. In *Chiefdoms: Power, Economy, and Ideology*, edited by Timothy K. Earle, pp. 16–43. Cambridge, UK: Cambridge University Press.

Larco Hoyle, Rafael 1948. *Cronología arqueológica del norte del Perù*. Buenos Aires: Sociedad Geografíca Americana.

Larrain, Jorge 1991. Base and Superstructure. In *A Dictionary of Marxist Thought*, 2nd edn., edited by Tom Bottomore, pp. 45–8. Oxford, UK: Basil Blackwell

Larsen, Mogens T.1987. Commercial Networks in the Ancient Near East. In *Centre and Periphery in the Ancient World* edited by Michael Rowlands, Mogens T. Larsen, and Kristian Kristiansen, pp. 47–56. Cambridge, UK: Cambridge University Press.

Leacock, Eleanor B. 1972. Introduction. In *The Origin of the Family, Private Property and the State*, by Frederick Engels, pp. 7–67. New York: International Publishers.

—— 1982. Relations of Production in Band Society. In *Politics and History in Band Societies*, edited by Eleanor B. Leacock and Richard B. Lee, pp. 159–70. Cambridge, UK: Cambridge University Press.

—— 1993. Being an Anthropologist. In *From Labrador to Samoa: The Theory and Practice of Eleanor Burke Leacock*, edited by Constance R. Sutton, pp. 1–32.

Arlington, VA: Association for Feminist Anthropology/American Anthropological Association.

Leacock, Eleanor B. and Richard B. Lee, editors 1982. *Politics and History in Band Societies*. Cambridge, UK: Cambridge

Lee, Richard B. and Karen Brodkin Sacks 1993. Anthropology, Imperialism and Resistance: The Work of Kathleen Gough. *Anthropologica*, vol. XXXV, no. 2, pp. 181–95. Waterloo, ON.

Leone, Mark 1982. Some Opinions about Recovering Mind. *American Antiquity*, vol. 47, no. 4, pp. 742–60. Washington, DC.

—— 1995. A Historical Archaeology of Capitalism. *American Anthropologist*, vol. 97, no. 2, pp. 251–68. Washington, DC.

Levins, Richard and Richard Lewontin 1985. *The Dialectical Biologist*. Cambridge, MA: Harvard University Press.

Liverani, Mario 1988. *Antice Oriente: Storia Società Economia*. Rome: Editori Laterza.

Llobera, Josep R. 1981. Durkheim, the Durkheimians and Their Collective Misrepresentation of Marx. In *The Anthropology of Pre-Capitalist Societies*, edited by Joel S. Kahn and Josep R. Llobera, pp. 214–40. London, UK: The Macmillan Press.

Logan, Michael H. and William T. Sanders 1976. The Model. In *The Valley of Mexico: Studies in Pre-Hispanic Ecology and Society*, edited by Eric R. Wolf, pp. 33–58. Albuquerque, NM: University of New Mexico Press.

Lukes, Steven 1977. *Émile Durkheim: His Life and Work: A Historical and Critical Study*. Harmondsworth, UK: Penguin Books.

Lukács, Georg 1923/1971. *History and Class Consciousness*. Cambridge, MA: The MIT Press.

McGuire, Randall H. 1996. The Limits of World-Systems Theory for the Study of Prehistory. In *Pre-Columbian World Systems*, edited Peter N. Peregrine and Gary M. Feinman. Monographs in World Archaeology, no. 26, pp. 51–64. Madison, WI: Prehistory Press.

McGuire, Randall H. and Robert Paynter, editors 1991. *The Archaeology of Inequality*. Oxford, UK: Basil Blackwell.

McGuire, Randall H. and Dean J. Saitta 1996. Although They Have Petty Captains, They Obey Them Badly: The Dialectics of Prehispanic Western Pueblo Social Organization. *American Antiquity*, vol. 61, no. 2, pp. 197–216. Washington, DC.

McIntosh, Susan K. 1999. Pathways to Complexity: An African Perspective. In *Beyond Chiefdoms: Pathways to Complexity in Africa*, edited by Susan K. McIntosh, pp. 1–30. Cambridge, UK: Cambridge University Press.

McLellan, David 1973.*Karl Marx: His Life and Thought*. New York: Harper & Row Publishers.

McMurtry, John 1978. *The Structure of Marx's World-View*. Princeton, NJ: Princeton University Press.

MacNeish, Richard S.1958. *Preliminary Archaeological Investigations in the Sierra de Tamaulipas, Mexico*. Transactions of the American Philosophical Society, vol. 48, pt. 6, pp. 1–210. Philadelphia.

—— 1964. Origins of New World Civilization. *Scientific American*, vol. 211, no. 5, pp. 29–37. New York.

—— 1967. A Summary of the Subsistence. In *The Prehistory of the Tehuacan Valley* edited by Douglas S. Byers, vol. 1, *Environment and Subsistence*, pp. 290–309. Austin, TX: University of Texas Press.

—— 1978. *The Science of Archaeology?* North Scituate, MA: Duxbury Press.

Malthus, Thomas R. 1798/1926. *An Essay on the Principle of Population: As It Effects the Future Improvement of Society, with Remarks on the Speculations of Mr. Godwin, Mr. Condorcet, and Other Writers*. 1st edn. London, UK: Macmillan and Company.

Mao Zedong 1937/1975. On Contradiction. In *Selected Works of Mao Tse-tung*, vol. I, pp. 311–47. Peking, PRC: Foreign Language Press.

Marcus, Joyce 1976. *Emblem and State in the Classic Maya Lowlands: An Epigraphic Approach to Territorial Organization*. Washington, DC: Dumbarton Oaks.

—— 1983. Summary and Conclusions. In *The Cloud People: Divergent Evolution of the Zapotec and Mixtec Civilizations*, edited by Kent V. Flannery and Joyce Marcus, pp. 355–60. San Diego, CA: Academic Press.

—— 1989. From Centralized Systems to City-States: Possible Models for the Epiclassic. In *Mesoamerica after the Decline of Teotihuacan*, edited by Richard Diehl and Janet C. Berlo, pp. 201–8. Washington, DC: Dumbarton Oaks Research Library and Collection.

—— 1992. Political Fluctuations in Mesoamerica: Dynamic Cycles of Mesoamerican States. *National Geographic Research and Exploration*, vol. 8, no. 4, pp. 392–411. Washington, DC.

—— 1993. Ancient Maya Political Organization. *Lowland Maya Political Organization in the Eighth Century A.D.*, edited by Jeremy A. Sabloff and John S. Henderson, pp. 111–84. Washington, DC: Dumbarton Oaks Research Library and Collection.

—— 1998. The Peaks and Valleys of Ancient States: An Extension of the Dynamic Model. In *Archaic States*, edited by Gary M. Feinman and Joyce Marcus, pp. 59–94. Santa Fe, NM: SAR Press.

Marcus, Joyce and Kent V. Flannery 1996. *Zapotec Civilization: How Urban Society Evolved in Mexico's Oaxaca Valley*. London, UK: Thames and Hudson.

Márkus, George 1978. *Marxism and Anthropology*. Assen, NL: Van Gorcum and Company.

Marquardt, William H. 1987. The Calusa Social Formation in Protohistoric South Florida. In *Power Relations and State Formation*, edited by Thomas C. Patterson and Christine W. Gailey, pp. 98–116. Washington, DC: Archaeology Division, American Anthropological Association.

—— 1992. Dialectical Archaeology. In *Archaeological Method and Theory*, edited by Michael B. Schiffer, vol. 4, pp. 101–40. Tucson, AZ: University of Arizona Press.

Marx, Karl 1840–1/1975. Difference between the Democritean and Epicurean Philosophy of Nature [originally published 1902]. In *Karl Marx, Frederick Engels: Collected Works*, vol. 1, pp. 25–105. New York: International Publishers.

—— 1844/1964. *The Economic and Philosophic Manuscripts of 1844* [originally published 1932]. New York: International Publishers.

—— 1844/1975a. The Economic and Philosophic Manuscripts of 1844. In *Karl Marx, Frederick Engels: Collected Works*, vol. 3, pp. 229–348. New York: International Publishers.

—— 1844/1975b. Economic and Philosophical Manuscripts. In *Marx: Early Writings*, pp. 279–400. Harmondsworth, UK: Penguin Books.

—— 1845/1976. Theses on Feuerbach [originally published 1888]. In *Karl Marx, Frederick Engels: Collected Works*, vol. 5, pp. 3–5. New York: International Publishers.

—— 1852/1978. The Eighteenth Brumaire of Louis Bonaparte [originally published 1852]. In *Karl Marx, Frederick Engels: Collected Works*, vol. 11, pp. 99–197. New York: International Publishers.

—— 1853/1979. The Indian Question – Irish Tenant Right [originally published 1853]. In *Karl Marx, Frederick Engels: Collected Works*, vol. 12, pp. 157–62. New York: International Publishers.

—— 1857–8/1964. *Pre-Capitalist Economic Formations* [=*Grundrisse*, pp. 471–514], with an introduction by Eric J. Hobsbawm. New York: International Publishers.

—— 1857–8/1973. *Grundrisse: Foundations to the Critique of Political Economy* [originally published in 2 vols., 1939, 1941]. New York: Vintage Books.

—— 1859/1970. *A Contribution to the Critique of Political Economy* [originally published 1903]. New York: International Publishers.

—— 1860/1985. Letter to Frederick Engels, 19 December. In *Karl Marx, Frederick Engels: Collected Works*, vol. 41, pp. 231–3. New York: International Publishers.

—— 1861/1985. Letter to Ferdinand Lassalle, 16 January. In *Karl Marx, Frederick Engels: Collected Works*, vol. 41, pp. 245–7. New York: International Publishers.

—— 1861–3/1968. *Theories of Surplus Value* [originally published 1905–10], pt. II. Moscow, USSR: Progress Publishers.

——— 1861–3/1971. *Theories of Surplus Value* [originally published 1905–10], pt. III. Moscow, USSR: Progress Publishers.

——— 1863–7/1977. *Capital: A Critique of Political Economy*, vol. 1 [originally published 1867]. New York: Vintage Books.

——— 1863–7/1981. *Capital: A Critique of Political Economy*, vol. 3 [originally published 1894]. New York: Vintage Books.

——— 1868/1988. Letter to Frederick Engels, 23 May. In *Karl Marx, Frederick Engels: Collected Works*, vol. 43, pp. 38–40. New York: International Publishers.

——— 1875/1989. Critique of the Gotha Programme [originally published 1891]. In *Karl Marx, Frederick Engels: Collected Works*, vol. 24, pp. 75–99. New York: International Publishers.

——— 1880–2/1974. *The Ethnological Notebooks of Karl Marx*, edited by Lawrence Krader. Assen: Van Gorcum and Company.

Marx, Karl and Frederick Engels 1845–6/1976. The German Ideology [originally published 1932]. In *Karl Marx, Frederick Engels: Collected Works*, vol. 5, pp. 19–452. New York International Publishers.

——— 1848/1976. Manifesto of the Communist Party [originally published 1848]. In *Karl Marx, Frederick Engels: Collected Works*, vol. 6, pp. 477–519. New York: International Publishers.

Meek, Ronald, editor 1953/1971. *Marx and Engels on the Population Bomb*. Berkeley, CA: The Ramparts Press.

Mészaros, István 1991. Totality. In *A Dictionary of Marxist Thought*, 2nd edn., edited by Tom Bottomore, pp. 537–8. Oxford, UK: Basil Blackwell.

Millon, René 1954. Irrigation at Teotihuacan. *American Antiquity*, vol. XX, no. 2, pp. 177–80. Salt Lake City, UT.

——— 1955. Trade, Tree Cultivation, and the Development of Private Property in Land. *American Anthropologist*, vol. 57, no. 4, pp. 698–712. Menasha, WI.

——— 1976. Social Relations in Ancient Teotihuacán. In *The Valley of Mexico: Studies in Pre-Hispanic Ecology and Society*, edited by Eric R. Wolf, pp. 205–48. Albuquerque, NM: University of New Mexico Press.

——— 1981. Teotihuacan: City, State, and Civilization. *Supplement to the Handbook of Middle American Indians*, edited by Victoria R. Bricker, vol. 1, *Archaeology*, edited by Jeremy A. Sabloff, pp. 198–243. Austin, TX: University of Texas Press.

——— 1988. The Last Years of Teotihuacan Dominance. In *The Collapse of Ancient States and Civilizations*, edited by Norman Yoffee and George L. Cowgill, pp. 102–64. Tucson, AZ: University of Arizona Press.

——— 1992. Teotihuacan Studies: From 1950 to 1990 and Beyond. In *Art, Ideology, and the City of Teotihuacan: A Symposium at Dumbarton Oaks, 8th and 9th October 1988*, edited by Janet C. Berlo, pp. 339–429. Washington, DC: Dumbarton Oaks Research Library and Collection.

Moret, Alexandre and Georges Davy 1926. *From Tribe to Empire: Social Organization among Primitives in the Ancient East.* London, UK: Kegan Paul.

Morgan, Lewis H. 1877/1963. *Ancient Society: Or, Researches in the Lines of Human Progress from Savagery through Barbarism to Civilization.* Cleveland, OH: The World Publishing Company.

Neale, R. S. 1985. *Writing Marxist History: British Society, Economy and Culture since 1700.* Oxford, UK: Basil Blackwell.

Nichols, Deborah L. and Thomas H. Charlton, editors 1997. *The Archaeology of City-States.* Washington, DC: Smithsonian Institution Press.

Nonini, Don 1985. Varieties of Materialism. *Dialectical Anthropology*, vol. 9, nos. 1–4, pp. 7–64. Dordrecht, NL.

Olivé Negrete, Julio C. 1958. Estructura y dinámica de Mesoamérica. *Acta Antropológica*, epoca 2, vol. 1, no. 3. Mexico, DF.

———— 1987. The Presence of Vere Gordon Childe in Mexican Archaeology. In *Studies in the Neolithic and Urban Revolutions: The V. Gordon Childe Colloquium, Mexico, 1986*, edited by Linda Manzanilla. BAR International Series, no. 349, pp. 9–17. Oxford, UK.

Ollman, Bertell 1993. *Dialectical Investigations.* New York: Routledge.

Olmstead, Albert T. 1948. *A History of the Persian Empire.* Chicago, IL: The University of Chicago Press.

Orser, Charles E., Jr. 1988. Toward a Theory of Power for Historical Archaeology: Plantations and Space. In *The Recovery of Meaning: Historical Archaeology in the Eastern United States*, edited by Mark P. Leone and Parker B. Pottery, Jr., pp. 313–43. Washington, DC: Smithsonian Institution Press.

———— 1990. Archaeological Approaches to New World Slavery. In *Archaeological Method and Theory*, edited by Michael B. Schiffer, vol. 2, pp. 111–54. Tucson, AZ: University of Arizona Press.

———— 1991. The Continued Pattern of Dominance: Landlord and Tenant on the Post-Bellum Plantation. In *The Archaeology of Inequality*, edited by Randall H. McGuire and Robert Paynter, pp. 40–54. Oxford, UK: Basil Blackwell.

———— 1994. Toward a Global Historical Archaeology: An Example from Brazil. *Historical Archaeology*, vol. 28, no. 1, pp. 5–22. Tucson, AZ.

———— 1996. *A Historical Archaeology of the Modern World.* New York: Plenum Press.

———— 1999. Archaeology and the Challenges of Capitalist Farm Tenancy in America. In *Historical Archaeologies of Capitalism*, edited by Mark P. Leone and Parker B. Potter, Jr., pp. 143–68. New York: Kluwer Academic/Plenum Publishers.

Outhwaite, William 1975. *Understanding Social Life: The Method Called Verstehen.* London, UK: George Allen and Unwin.

Parsons, Talcott 1951. *The Social System.* New York: The Free Press.

———— 1964. *Social Structure and Personality.* New York: The Free Press.

Parsons, Talcott, Robert F. Bales, James Olds, Morris Zedlitch, and Philip E. Slater 1955. *Family, Socialization and Interaction Process*. New York: The Free Press.

Patterson, Thomas C. 1981. *Archaeology: The Evolution of Ancient Societies*. Engelwood Cliffs, NJ: Prentice-Hall.

—— 1983a. Archaeological Systems Theory and the Origin of the State: A Critique. Paper presented at the annual meeting of the Canadian Ethnological Society, May 6–9, 1983, Hamilton, ON.

—— 1983b. The Historical Development of a Coastal Andean Social Formation in Central Peru: 6000 to 500 B.C. In *Investigations of the Andean Past: Papers from the First Annual Northeast Conference on Andean Archaeology and Ethnohistory*, edited by Daniel Sandweiss, pp. 21–37. Ithaca, NY: Latin American Studies Program, Cornell University.

——1983c. *The Theory and Practice of Archaeology: A Workbook*. Englewood Cliffs, NJ: Prentice-Hall.

—— 1985. Culture and Ideology: Distinct Concepts or Alternate Metaphors? Paper presented at the annual meeting of the Regional Archaeology Theory Symposium, November 16, 1985, Binghamton, NY.

—— 1986a. The Last Sixty Years: Toward a Social History of Americanist Archaeology in the United States. *American Anthropologist*, vol. 88, no. 1, pp. 7–26. Washington, DC.

—— 1986b. Some Postwar Theoretical Trends in U.S. Archaeology. *Culture*, vol. 6, no. 1, pp. 43–54. Montreal, PQ.

—— 1988/1998. The Creation of Culture in Pre-State and Non-State Social Formations. *Journal of Theoretical Archaeology*, vol. 5–6, pp. 81–98. Glasgow, UK.

—— 1989. History and the Postprocessual Archaeologies. *Man*, vol. 24, no. 4, pp. 555–66. London, UK.

—— 1991. *The Inca Empire: The Formation and Disintegration of a Pre-Capitalist State*. Oxford, UK: Berg Publishers.

—— 1992. *Archaeology: The Historical Development of Civilizations*. Englewood Cliffs, NJ: Prentice-Hall.

—— 1997a. *The Invention of Western Civilization*. New York: Monthly Review Press.

—— 1997b. *Las sociedades nucleares de Mesoamérica*. Caracas, VE: Historia General de America. Academic de Historia Nacional.

—— 1999a. *Change and Development in the Twentieth Century*. Oxford, UK: Berg Publishers.

—— 1999b. The Development of Agriculture and the Emergence of Formative Civilization in the Central Andes. In *Pacific Latin America in Prehistory: The Evolution of Archaic and Formative Cultures*, edited by Michael Blake, pp. 181–8. Pullman, WA: Washington State University Press.

—— 2000. Social Theory and Interdisciplinary Archaeology: A Perspective on the Work of Richard S. MacNeish. Paper presented at the annual meeting of the Society for American Archaeology, April 8, Philadelphia, PA.

—— 2001. *A Social History of Anthropology in the United States*. Oxford, UK: Berg Publishers.

Paynter, Robert 1985. Surplus Flows between Frontiers and Homelands. In *The Archaeology of Frontiers and Boundaries*, edited by Stanton W. Green and Stephen M. Perlman, pp. 163–211. Orlando, FL: Academic Press.

—— 1988. Steps to an Archaeology of Capitalism: Material Change and Class Analysis. In *The Recovery of Meaning: Historical Archaeology in the Eastern United States*, edited by Mark P. Leone and Parker B. Pottery, Jr., pp. 407–34. Washington, DC: Smithsonian Institution Press.

—— 1999. The Archaeology of Equality and Inequality. *Annual Review of Anthropology*, vol. 18, pp. 369–99. Palo Alto, CA.

—— 2000. Historical Archaeology and the Post-Columbian World of North America. *Journal of Archaeological Research*, vol. 8, no. 3, pp. 169–217. New York.

—— 2001. The Cult of Whiteness in Western New England. In *Race and the Archaeology of Identity*, edited by Charles E. Orser, Jr., pp. 125–42. Salt Lake City, UT: University of Utah Press.

Paynter, Robert and John W. Cole 1980. Ethnographic Overproduction, Tribal Political Economy and the Kapauku of Irian Jaya. In *Beyond the Myth of Culture: Essays in Cultural Materialism*, edited by Eric B. Ross, pp. 61–99. New York: Academic Press.

Peace, William J. 1992. *The Enigmatic Career of Vere Gordon Childe: A Peculiar and Individual Manifestation of the Human Spirit*. Ph.D. Dissertation in Anthropology, Columbia University, New York. Ann Arbor, MI: University Microfilms International, no. 9421386.

—— 1993. Leslie White and Evolutionary Theory. *Dialectical Anthropology*, vol. 18, no. 2, pp. 123–52. Dordrecht, NL.

Peel, John D. Y. 1971. *Herbert Spencer: The Evolution of a Sociologist*. London, UK: Heinemann.

Peregrine, Peter N. and Gary M. Feinman, editors 1996. *Pre-Columbian World Systems*. Monographs in World Archaeology, no. 26. Madison, WI: Prehistory Press.

Plunket, Patricia 1983. *An Intensive Survey in the Yucuita Sector of the Nochixtlan Valley, Oaxaca, Mexico*. Ph.D. Dissertation in Anthropology, Tulane University. Ann Arbor, MI: University Microfilms International.

Preucel, Robert 1995. The Postprocessual Condition. *Journal of Archaeological Research*, vol. 3, no. 2, pp. 147–75. New York.

Price, Barbara J. 1971. Prehistoric Irrigation Agriculture in Nuclear America. *Latin American Research Review*, vol. VI, no. 3, pp. 3–60. Austin, TX.

—— 1977. Shifts in Production and Organization: A Cluster-Interaction Model. *Current Anthropology*, vol. 18, no. 2, pp. 209–34. Chicago, IL.

—— 1982. Cultural Materialism: A Theoretical Review. *American Antiquity*, vol. 47, no. 4, pp. 709–41. Washington, DC.

Pyburn, K. Anne 1997. The Archaeological Signature of Complexity in the Maya Lowlands. In *The Archaeology of City-States: Cross-Cultural Perspectives*, edited by Deborah L. Nichols and Thomas H. Charlton, pp. 155–68. Washington, DC: Smithsonian Institution Press.

Rai, Milan 1995. *Chomsky's Politics*. London, UK: Verso.

Rapp, Rayna 1977. Gender and Class: An Archaeology of Knowledge Concerning the Origin of the State. *Dialectical Anthropology*, vol. 2, no. 4, pp. 309–16. Amsterdam, NL.

Redfield, Robert 1934/1962. Culture Changes in Yucatan. In *Human Nature and the Study of Society: The Papers of Robert Redfield*, edited by Margaret P. Redfield, vol. 1, pp. 160–72. Chicago, IL: The University of Chicago Press.

—— 1953. *The Primitive World and Its Transformations*. Ithaca, NY: Cornell University Press.

—— 1954/1962. The Cultural Role of Cities. In *Human Nature and the Study of Society: The Papers of Robert Redfield*, edited by Margaret P. Redfield, vol. 1, pp. 326–50. Chicago, IL: The University of Chicago Press.

Redmond, Elsa M. 1998. In War and Peace: Alternative Paths to Centralized Leadership. In *Chiefdoms and Chieftaincy in the Americas*, edited by Elsa Redmond, pp. 68–103. Gainesville, FL: University Press of Florida.

Renfrew, Colin 1969. Trade and Culture Process in European Prehistory. *Current Anthropology*, vol. 10, no. 2–3, pp. 151–96. Chicago, IL.

—— 1972/1984. Cultural Systems and the Multiplier Effect. In *Approaches to Social Archaeology*, by Colin Renfrew, pp. 258–82. Edinburgh, UK: Edinburgh University Press.

—— 1973. Monuments, Mobilisation and Social Organisation in Neolithic Wessex. In *The Explanation of Culture Change: Models in Prehistory*, edited by Colin Renfrew, pp. 539–58. London, UK: Gerald Duckworth and Company.

—— 1974. Beyond a Subsistence Economy: The Evolution of Prehistoric Social Organisation in Europe. In *Reconstructing Complex Societies: An Archaeological Colloquium*, edited by Charlotte B. Moore. Supplement to the Bulletin of the American Schools of Oriental Research, no. 20, pp. 69–95. Cambridge, MA.

—— 1975. Trade as Action at a Distance: Questions of Integration and Communication. In *Ancient Civilization and Trade*, edited by Jeremy A. Sabloff and C. C. Lamberg-Karlovsky, pp. 3–59. Albuquerque, NM: University of New Mexico Press.

—— 1977. Space, Time and Polity. In *The Evolution of Social Systems*, edited by Jonathan Friedman and Michael J. Rowlands, pp. 89–112. London, UK: Gerald Duckworth and Company.

—— 1978. Trajectory Discontinuity and Morphogenesis: The Implications of Catastrophe Theory for Archaeology. *American Antiquity*, vol. 43, no. 2, pp. 203–22. Washington, DC.

—— 1979a. Transformations. In *Transformations: Mathematical Approaches to Culture Change*, edited by Colin Renfrew and K. L. Cooke, pp. 1–44. New York: Academic Press.

—— 1979b. Systems Collapse as Social Transformation: Catastrophe and Anastrophe in Early State Societies. In *Transformations: Mathematical Approaches to Culture Change*, edited by Colin Renfrew and K. L. Cooke, pp. 481–506. New York: Academic Press.

—— 1982a. Socio-economic Change in Ranked Societies. In *Ranking, Resource and Exchange: Aspects of the Archaeology of Early European Society*, edited by Colin Renfrew and Stephen Shennan, pp. 1–8. Cambridge, UK: Cambridge University Press.

—— 1982b. Polity and Power: Interaction, Intensification and Exploitation. In *An Island Polity: The Archaeology of Exploitation in Melos*, edited by Colin Renfrew and Malcolm Wagstaff, pp. 264–90. Cambridge, UK: Cambridge University Press.

—— 1984. Societies in Space: The Landscape of Power. In *Approaches to Social Archaeology*, by Colin Renfrew, pp. 24–9. Edinburgh: Edinburgh University Press.

—— 1986. Introduction: Peer Polity Interaction and Socio-political Change. In *Peer Polity Interaction and Socio-political Change*, edited by Colin Renfrew and John F. Cherry, pp. 1–18. Cambridge, UK: Cambridge University Press.

Renfrew, Colin and Eric V. Level 1979. Exploring Dominance: Predicting Polities from Centres. In *Transformations: Mathematical Approaches to Culture Change*, edited by Colin Renfrew and K. L. Cooke, pp. 145–69. New York: Academic Press.

Roseberry, William 1988. Political Economy. *Annual Review of Anthropology*, vol. 18, pp. 161–85. Palo Alto, CA.

Rostow, Walter W. 1960. *The Stages of Economic Growth: A Non-Communist Manifesto*. Cambridge, UK: Cambridge University Press.

Rothman, Mitchell S., editor 2001. *Uruk Mesopotamia and Its Neighbors: Cross-Cultural Interactions in the Era of State Formation*. Santa Fe, NM: SAR Press.

Rowe, John H. 1962. Stages and Periods in Archaeological Interpretation. *Southwestern Journal of Anthropology*, vol. 18, no. 1, pp. 40–54. Albuquerque, NM.

—— 1963. Urban Settlements in Ancient Peru. *Ñawpa Pacha*, no. 1, pp. 1–28. Berkeley, CA.

Rowlands, Michael, Mogens Larsen, and Kristian Kristiansen, editors 1987. *Centre and Periphery in the Ancient World.* Cambridge, UK: Cambridge University Press.

Sacks, Karen Brodkin 1975. Engels Revisited: Women, the Organization of Production, and Private Property. In *Toward an Anthropology of Women,* edited by Rayna Rapp Reiter, pp. 211–34. New York: Monthly Review Press.

—— 1976. State Bias and Women's Status. *American Anthropologist,* vol. 78, no. 3, pp. 565–9. Washington, DC.

—— 1979/1982. *Sisters and Wives: The Past and Future of Sexual Equality.* Urbana, IL: The University of Illinois Press.

Sahlins, Marshall D. 1960. Evolution: Specific and General. In *Evolution and Culture,* edited by Marshall D. Sahlins and Elman R. Service, pp. 12–44. Ann Arbor, MI: The University of Michigan Press.

—— 1961. The Segmentary Lineage: An Organization of Predatory Expansion. *American Anthropologist,* vol. 63, no. 2, pp. 322–45. Menasha, WI.

—— 1963. Poor Man, Rich Man, Big-Man, Chief: Political Types in Melanesia and Polynesia. *Comparative Studies in Society and History,* vol. 5, no. 3, pp. 285–303. The Hague, NL.

Ste Croix, Geoffrey E. M. de 1981. *The Class Struggle in the Ancient Greek World from the Archaic Age to the Arab Conquest.* Ithaca, NY: Cornell University Press.

—— 1984. Class in Marx's Conception of History, Ancient and Modern. *New Left Review,* no. 146, pp. 94–111. London, UK.

Saitta, Dean J.1988. Marxism, Prehistory, and Primitive Communism. *Rethinking Marxism,* vol. 1, no. 4, pp. 146–68. New York.

—— 1994a. Agency, Class, and Archaeological Interpretation. *Journal of Anthropological Archaeology,* vol. 13, no. 2, pp. 201–27. San Diego, CA.

—— 1994b. Class and Community in the Prehistoric Southwest. In *The Ancient Southwestern Community: Models and Methods for the Study of Prehistoric Social Organization,* edited by Wirt Wills and Robert Leonard, pp. 25–43. Albuquerque, NM: University of New Mexico Press.

—— 1997. Power, Labor, and the Dynamics of Change in Chacoan Political Economy. *American Antiquity,* vol. 62, no. 1, pp. 7–26. Washington, DC.

—— 2001. Marxist Theory and Tribal Political Economy. Paper presented at the annual meeting of the American Anthropological Association, November 30. Washington, DC.

Sanders, William T. 1956. The Central Mexican Symbiotic Region: A Study in Prehistoric Settlement Patterns. In *Prehistoric Settlement Patterns in the New World,* edited by Gordon R. Willey. Viking Fund Publications in Anthropology, no. 23, pp. 115–27. New York.

—— 1962. Cultural Ecology of Nuclear America. *American Anthropologist,* vol. 64, no. 1, pt. 1, pp. 34–43. Menasha, WI.

—— 1968. Hydraulic Agriculture, Economic Symbiosis and the Evolution of States in Central Mexico. In *Anthropological Archeology in the Americas*, edited by Betty J. Meggers, pp. 88–107. Washington, DC: The Anthropological Society of Washington.

—— 1972. Population, Agricultural History, and Societal Evolution in Meso-america. In *Population Growth: Anthropological Implications*, edited by Brian Spooner, pp. 101–49. Cambridge, MA: The MIT Press.

—— 1974. Chiefdom to State: Political Evolution at Kaminaljuyu, Guatemala. In *Reconstructing Complex Societies: An Archaeological Colloquium*, edited by Charlotte B. Moore. Supplement to the Bulletin of the American Schools of Oriental Research, no. 20, pp. 97–112. Cambridge, MA.

Sanders, William T. and Deborah L. Nichols 1988. Ecological Theory and Cultural Evolution in the Valley of Oaxaca. *Current Anthropology*, vol. 29, no. 1, pp. 33–80. Chicago, IL.

Sanders, William T., Jeffrey R. Parsons, and Robert S. Santley 1979. *The Basin of Mexico: Ecological Processes in the Evolution of a Civilization*. New York: Academic Press.

Sanders, William T. and Barbara J. Price 1968. *Mesoamerica: The Evolution of a Civilization*. New York: Random House.

Sanders, William T. and David Webster 1978. Unilinealism, Multilinealism, and the Evolution of Complex Societies. In *Social Archaeology: Beyond Subsistence and Dating*, edited by Charles L. Redman, Mary J. Berman, Edward V. Curtin, William T. Langhorne, Jr., Nina M. Versaggi, and Jeffery C. Wanser, pp. 249–302. New York: Academic Press.

Saunders, Tom 1990. Prestige and Exchange: Althusser and Structuralist Marxist Archaeology. In *Writing the Past in the Present*, edited by Frederick Baker and Julian Thomas, pp. 90–8. Lampeter, UK: Saint David's University College.

Sayer, Derek 1979. *Marx's Method: Ideology, Science and Critique in* Capital. Hassocks, UK: The Harvester Press.

Sayers, Sean 1998. *Marxism and Human Nature*. London, UK: Routledge.

Schneider, Jane 1977. Was There a Pre-Capitalist World-System? *Peasant Studies*, no. 6, pp. 20–9. Salt Lake City, UT.

Schortman, Edward M. and Patricia A. Urban, editors 1992. *Resources, Power, and Interregional Interaction*. New York: Plenum Publishers.

Schwartz, Glenn M. and Steven E. Falconer 1994. Rural Approaches to Social Complexity. In *Archaeological Views from the Countryside: Village Communities in Early Complex Societies*, edited by Glenn M. Schwartz and Steven E. Falconer, pp. 1–9. Washington, DC: Smithsonian Institution Press.

Seccombe, Wally 1992. *A Millennium of Family Change: Feudalism to Capitalism in Northwestern Europe*. London, UK: Verso.

—— 1993. *Weathering the Storm: Working-Class Families from the Industrial Revolution to the Fertility Decline*. London, UK: Verso.

Service, Elman R. 1962/1971. *Primitive Social Organization: An Evolutionary Perspective*, 2nd edn. New York: Random House.

—— 1975. *Origins of the State and Civilization: The Process of Cultural Evolution*. New York: W. W. Norton.

Silverblatt, Irene 1976. Principios de organización femenina en el Tawantinsuyu. *Revista del Museo Nacional*, tomo XLII, pp. 299–340. Lima, PE.

—— 1987. *Moon, Sun, and Witches: Gender Ideologies and Class in Inca and Colonial Peru*. Princeton, NJ: Princeton University Press.

—— 1991. Interpreting Women in States: New Feminist Ethnohistories. In *Gender at the Crossroads of Knowledge: Feminist Anthropology in the Postmodern Era*, edited by Micaela di Leonardo, pp. 140–74. Berkeley, CA: University of California Press.

Smith, Michael E. 1994. Social Complexity in the Aztec Countryside. In *Archaeological Views from the Countryside: Village Communities in Early Complex Societies*, edited by Glenn M. Schwartz and Steven E. Falconer, pp. 143–59. Washington, DC: Smithsonian Institution Press.

Southall, Aidan 1988. The Segmentary State in Africa and Asia. *Comparative Studies in Society and History*, vol. 30, no. 1, pp. 52–82. New York.

—— 1991. The Segmentary State: From the Imaginary to the Material Means of Production. In *Early State Economics*, edited by Henri J. M. Claessen and Pieter van de Velde. Political and Legal Anthropology Series, vol. 8, pp. 75–96. New Brunswick, NJ: Transaction Books.

—— 1999. The Segmentary State and the Ritual Phase in Political Economy. In *Beyond Chiefdoms: Pathways to Complexity in Africa*, edited by Susan K. McIntosh, pp. 31–8. Cambridge, UK: Cambridge University Press.

Spector, Janet 1983. Male/Female Task Differentiation among the Hidatsa: Toward the Development of an Archaeological Approach to the Study of Gender. In *The Hidden Half: Studies of Plains Indian Women*, edited by Patricia Albers and Beatrice Medicine, pp. 77–99. Washington, DC: University Press of America.

Spencer, Charles S. 1988. Comment. *Current Anthropology*, vol. 29, no. 1, pp. 65–6. Chicago, IL.

—— 1990. On the Tempo and Mode of State Formation: Neoevolutionism Reconsidered. *Journal of Anthropological Archaeology*, vol. 9, no. 1, pp. 1–30. San Diego, CA.

—— 1993. Human Agency, Biased Transmission, and the Cultural Evolution of Chiefly Authority. *Journal of Anthropological Archaeology*, vol. 12, no. 1, pp. 41–74. San Diego, CA.

Spencer, Herbert 1851/1995. *Social Statics: The Conditions Essential to Human Happiness Specified, and The First of Them Developed*. New York: Robert Schalkenbach Foundation.

—— 1852. A Theory of Population, Deduced from the General Law of Animal Fertility. *The Westminister Review*, vol. LVII, pp. 250–68. London, UK.

—— 1857. Progress: Its Law and Cause. *The Westminister Review*, vol. LXVII, pp. 244–67. London, UK.

—— 1862/1880. *First Principles*. New York: A. L. Burt.

—— 1874–96/1898. *Principles of Sociology*, 3 vols. New York: Appleton.

—— 1887. *The Factors of Organic Evolution*. London, UK: Williams and Norgate.

—— 1904. *An Autobiography*, 2 vols. London, UK: Williams and Norgate.

Spores, Ronald 1983. Ramos Phase Urbanization in the Mixteca Alta. In *The Cloud People: Divergent Evolution of the Zapotec and Mixtec Civilizations*, edited by Kent V. Flannery and Joyce Marcus, pp. 120–3. San Diego, CA: Academic Press.

Spriggs, Matthew, editor 1984. *Marxist Perspectives in Archaeology*. Cambridge, UK: Cambridge University Press.

Steenson, Gary P. 1978. *Karl Kautsky, 1854–1938: Marxism in the Classical Years*. Pittsburgh, PA: University of Pittsburgh Press.

Stein, Gil J. 1990. On the Uruk Expansion. *Current Anthropology*, vol. 31, no. 1, pp. 66–7. Chicago, IL.

—— 1999. *Rethinking World-Systems: Diasporas, Colonies, and Interaction in Uruk Mesopotamia*. Tucson, AZ: University of Arizona Press.

Steponaitis, Vincas P. 1978. Location Theory and Complex Chiefdoms: A Mississippian Example. In *Mississippian Settlement Patterns*, edited by Bruce D. Smith, pp. 417–53. New York: Academic Press.

Steward, Julian H. 1948. A Functional-Developmental Classification of American High Cultures. In *A Reappraisal of Peruvian Archaeology*, edited by Wendell C. Bennett. Memoirs of the Society for American Archaeology, no. 4, pp. 103–4. Menasha, WI.

—— 1949. Cultural Causality and Law: A Trial Formulation of the Development of Early Civilizations. *American Anthropologist*, vol. 51, no. 1, pp. 1–27. Menasha, WI.

—— 1950. *Area Research: Theory and Practice*. Social Science Research Council Bulletin 63. New York.

—— 1953. Evolution and Process. In *Anthropology Today: An Encyclopedic Inventory*, edited by Alfred L. Kroeber, pp. 313–26. Chicago, IL: The University of Chicago Press.

—— 1955a. *Theory of Culture Change: The Methodology of Multilinear Evolution*. Urbana, IL: University of Illinois Press.

—— 1955b. Some Implications of the Symposium. In *Irrigation Civilizations: A Comparative Study*, by Julian H. Steward, Robert McC. Adams, Donald Collier, Angel Palerm, Karl A. Wittfogel, and Ralph L. Beals. Pan American Union Social Science Monographs, no. 1, pp. 58–78. Washington, DC.

Sweezy, Paul 1952/1976. A Critique. In *The Transition from Feudalism to Capitalism*, edited by Rodney H. Hilton, pp. 33–56. London, UK: New Left Books.

Terray, Emmanuel 1975. Classes and Class Consciousness in the Abron Kingdom of Gyaman. In *Marxist Analyses and Social Anthropology*, edited by Maurice Bloch. ASA Studies 2, pp. 85–125 London, UK: Malaby Press.

Thompson, Edward P. 1978. *The Poverty of Theory and Other Essays*. New York: Monthly Review Press.

Trigger, Bruce G. 1967. Engels on the Part Played by Labour in the Transition from Ape to Man: An Anticipation of Contemporary Anthropological Theory. *Canadian Review of Sociology and Anthropology*, vol. 4, no. 2, pp. 165–76. Ottawa, ON.

—— 1970. Aims in Prehistoric Archaeology. *Antiquity*, vol. XLIV, no. 173, pp. 26–37. Cambridge, UK.

—— 1971. Archaeology and Ecology. *World Archaeology*, vol. 2, no. 3, pp. 321–36. London, UK.

—— 1972. Determinants of Urban Growth in Pre-Industrial Centres. In *Man, Settlement and Urbanism*, edited by Peter J. Ucko, Ruth Tringham, and G. W. Dimbleby, pp. 575–600. London, UK: Gerald Duckworth and Company.

—— 1973. The Future of Archeology is the Past. In *Research and Theory in Current Archeology*, edited by Charles L. Redman, pp. 95–111. New York: John Wiley and Sons.

—— 1978. *Time and Traditions: Essays in Archaeological Interpretation*. New York: Columbia University Press.

—— 1980. *Gordon Childe: Revolutions in Archaeology*. New York: Columbia University Press.

—— 1982. If Childe Were Alive Today. *Bulletin of the Institute of Archaeology, University of London*, no. 19, pp. 1–20. London, UK.

—— 1984a. Childe and Soviet Archaeology. *Australian Archaeology*, vol. 18, no. 1, pp. 1018. Sydney, AU.

—— 1984b. Marxism and Archaeology. In *Marxist Perspectives in Anthropology: Essays in Honor of Harry Hoijer*, edited by Jacques Maquet and Nancy Daniels, pp. 59–96. Malibu, CA: Undena Publications.

—— 1986. The Role of Technology in V. Gordon Childe's Archaeology. *Norwegian Archaeological Review*, vol. 19, no. 1, pp. 1–14. Oslo, NO.

—— 1987. V. Gordon Childe: A Marxist Archaeologist. In *Studies in the Neolithic and Urban Revolutions: The V. Gordon Childe Colloquium, Mexico, 1986*, edited by Linda Manzanilla. British Archaeological Reports, International Series, no. 349, pp. 1–8. Oxford, UK.

—— 1989. *A History of Archaeological Thought*. Cambridge, UK: Cambridge University Press.

—— 1990. Maintaining Economic Equality in Opposition to Complexity: An Iroquoian Case Study. In *The Evolution of Political Systems: Sociopolitics in*

Small-Scale Sedentary Societies, edited by Steadman Upham, pp. 119–45. Cambridge, UK: Cambridge University Press.

—— 1993a. *Early Civilizations: Ancient Egypt in Context*. Cairo, EG: The American University in Cairo Press.

—— 1993b. The State-Church Reconsidered. In *Configurations of Power: Holistic Anthropology in Theory and Practice*, edited by John S. Henderson and Patricia J. Netherly, pp. 74–111. Ithaca, NY: Cornell University Press.

—— 1993c. Marxism in Contemporary Western Archaeology. In *Archaeological Method and Theory*, edited by Michael B. Schiffer, vol. 5, pp. 159–200. Tucson, AZ: University of Arizona Press.

—— 1998. Archaeology and Epistemology: Dialoguing Across the Darwinian Chasm. *American Journal of Archaeology* vol. 102, no. 1, pp. 1–34. Boston, MA.

—— 2003. Introduction: Understanding the Material Remains of the Past. In *Artifacts and Ideas: Essays in Archaeology*, by Bruce G. Trigger, pp. 1–30. New Brunswick, NJ: Transaction Publishers.

Turner, Jonathan 1985. *Herbert Spencer: A Renewed Appreciation*. Beverly Hills, CA: Sage Publications.

Wallerstein, Immanuel 1974. *The Modern World-System: Capitalist Agriculture and the Origins of the European World-Economy in the Sixteenth Century*. New York: Academic Press.

Watson, Patty Jo, Steven A. LeBlanc, and Charles L. Redman 1971. *Explanation in Archaeology: An Explicitly Scientific Approach*. New York: Columbia University Press.

—— 1984. *Archaeological Explanation: The Scientific Method in Archaeology*. New York: Columbia University Press.

Weber, Max 1894/1989. Developmental Tendencies in the Situation of East Elbian Rural Labourers. In *Reading Weber*, edited by Keith Tribe, pp. 158–87. London, UK: Routledge.

—— 1922/1947. *The Theory of Social and Economic Organization*, edited with an introduction by Talcott Parsons. New York: The Free Press.

—— 1923/1981. *General Economic History*. New Brunswick, NJ: Transaction Books.

Webster, David L. 1975. Warfare and the Evolution of the State: A Reconsideration. *American Antiquity*, vol. 40, no. 4, pp. 464–70. Washington, DC.

Wheatley, Paul 1971. *The Pivot of Four Quarters: A Preliminary Inquiry into the Origins and Character of the Ancient Chinese City*. Edinburgh: Edinburgh University Press.

White, Joyce C. 1995. Incorporating Heterarchy into Theory on Socio-Political Development: The Case from Southeast Asia. In *Heterarchy and the Analysis of Complex Societies*, edited by Robert M. Ehrenreich, Carole L. Crumley, and

Janet E. Levy. Archeological Papers of the American Anthropological Association, no. 6, pp. 100–24. Arlington, VA.

White, Leslie A. 1943/1949. Energy and the Evolution of Culture. In *The Science of Culture: A Study of Man and Civilization*, by Leslie A. White, pp. 363–96. New York: Grove Press.

—— 1945a. "Diffusion vs. Evolution": An Anti-Evolutionist Fallacy. *American Anthropologist*, vol. 47, no. 3, pp. 339–56. Menasha, WI.

—— 1945b. History, Evolutionism, and Functionalism: Three Types of Interpretation in Culture. *Southwestern Journal of Anthropology*, vol. 1, no. 2, pp. 221–48. Albuquerque, NM.

—— 1946. Kroeber's "Configurations of Culture Growth." *American Anthropologist*, vol. 48, no. 1, pp. 78–93. Menasha, WI.

——1959. *The Evolution of Civilization: The Development of Civilization to the Fall of Rome*. New York: McGraw-Hill Book Company.

—— 1976. A Materialist Interpretation of Culture. *Critique of Anthropology*, no. 6, pp. 38–43. London, UK.

Wilk, Richard 1985. The Ancient Maya and the Political Present. *Journal of Anthropological Research*, vol. 41, no. 4, pp. 307–26. Albuquerque, NM.

Willey, Gordon R. 1946. The Chiclin Conference for Peruvian Archaeology. *American Antiquity*, vol. XII, no. 1, pp. 49–56. Menasha, WI.

—— 1953. Archeological Theories and Interpretation: New World. In *Anthropology Today: An Encyclopedic Inventory*, edited by Alfred L. Kroeber, pp. 361–85. Chicago, IL: The University of Chicago Press.

—— 1955. The Prehistoric Civilizations of Nuclear America. *American Anthropologist*, vol. 57, no. 3, pt. 1, pp. 571–93. Menasha, WI.

—— 1960a. New World Prehistory. *Science*, vol. 131, no. 3393, pp. 73–86. Washington, DC.

—— 1960b. Historical Patterns and Evolution in Native New World Cultures. In *Evolution after Darwin*, edited by Sol Tax, vol. 2, *The Evolution of Man*, pp. 111–42. Chicago, IL: The University of Chicago Press.

—— 1964. An Hypothesis on the Process of Mesoamerican Agricultural Development. In *Homenaje a Fernando Márquez-Miranda: arqueológo e historiador de América*. Seminario de Estudios Americanistas, Universidad Central, pp. 378–87. Madrid, ES: Castilla.

—— 1967. *An Introduction to American Archaeology*, vol. 1, *North and Middle America*. Englewood Cliffs, NJ: Prentice-Hall.

—— 1971. *An Introduction to American Archaeology*, vol. 2, *South America*. Englewood Cliffs, NJ: Prentice-Hall.

Willey, Gordon R. and Philip Phillips 1958. *Method and Theory in American Archaeology*. Chicago, IL: The University of Chicago Press.

Williams, Raymond 1981. *The Sociology of Culture*. New York: Schocken Books.

Wilmsen, Edwin 1989. *Land Filled with Flies: A Political Economy of the Kalahari*. Chicago, IL: The University of Chicago Press.

Wilson, David J. 1997. Early State Formation on the North Coast of Peru: A Critique of the City-State Model. In *The Archaeology of City-States: Cross-Cultural Perspectives*, edited by Deborah L. Nichols and Thomas H. Charlton, pp. 229–44. Washington, DC: Smithsonian Institution Press.

Wilson, H. T. 1991. *Marx's Critical/Dialectical Procedure*. London, UK: Routledge.

Winter, Marcus C. 1988. Comment. *Current Anthropology*, vol. 29, no. 1, pp. 67–8. Chicago, IL.

Wittfogel, Karl A. 1955. Developmental Aspects of Hydraulic Societies. In *Irrigation Civilizations: A Comparative Study*, by Julian H. Steward, Robert McC. Adams, Donald Collier, Angel Palerm, Karl A. Wittfogel, and Ralph L. Beals. Pan American Union Social Science Monographs, no. 1, pp. 43–52. Washington, DC.

Wolf, Eric 1959. *Sons of the Shaking Earth*. Chicago, IL: The University of Chicago Press.

—— 1982. *Europe and the People without History*. Berkeley, CA: University of California Press.

Woolfson, Charles 1982. *The Labour Theory of Culture: A Re-examination of Engels's Theory of Human Origins*. London, UK: Routledge and Kegan Paul.

Wright, Eric O. 1983. Giddens's Critique of Marxism. *New Left Review*, no. 138, pp. 11–35. London, UK.

Wright, Henry T. 1977a. Toward an Explanation of the Origin of the State. In *Explanation of Prehistoric Change*, edited by James N. Hill, pp. 215–30. Albuquerque, NM: University of New Mexico Press.

—— 1977b. Recent Research on the Origin of the State. *Annual Review of Anthropology*, vol. 6, pp. 379–97. Palo Alto, CA.

—— 1978. Towards an Explanation of the Origin of the State. In *Origins of the State: The Anthropology of Political Evolution*, edited by Ronald Cohen and Elman K. Service, pp. 49–68. Philadelphia, PA: Institute for the Study of Human Issues.

—— 1984. Prestate Political Formations. In *On the Evolution of Complex Societies: Essays in Honor of Harry Hoijer,* edited by Timothy K. Earle, pp. 41–77. Malibu, CA: Udena Publications.

—— 1986. The Evolution of Civilizations. In *American Archaeology Past and Future: A Celebration of the Society for American Archaeology, 1935–1985*, edited by David J. Meltzer, Don D. Fowler, and Jeremy A. Sabloff, pp. 323–65. Washington, DC: Smithsonian Institution Press.

—— 1998. Uruk States in Southwestern Iran. In *Archaic States*, edited by Gary M. Feinman and Joyce Marcus, pp. 173–99. Santa Fe, NM: SAR Press.

Wright, Henry T. and Gregory A. Johnson 1975. Population, Exchange, and Early State Formation in Southwestern Iran. *American Anthropologist*, vol. 77, no. 2, pp. 267–89. Washington, DC.

Wylie, Alison 1982. *Positivism and the New Archaeology*. Ph.D. Dissertation in Philosophy, State University of New York at Binghamton. Ann Arbor, MI: University Microfilms International no. 8201043.

Yoffee, Norman 1979. The Decline and Rise of Mesopotamian Civilization: An Ethnoarchaeological Perspective on the Evolution of Social Complexity. *American Antiquity*, vol. 44, no. 1, pp. 1–35. Washington, DC.

—— 1993. Too Many Chiefs? (Or, Safe Texts for the '90s). In *Archaeological Theory: Who Sets the Agenda?*, edited by Norman Yoffee and Andrew Sherratt, pp. 60–78. Cambridge, UK: Cambridge University Press.

—— 1995. Political Economy in Early Mesopotamian States. *Annual Review of Anthropology* vol. 24, pp. 281–311. Palo Alto, CA.

—— 1997. The Obvious and the Chimerical: City-States in Archaeological Perspective. In *The Archaeology of City-States: Cross-Cultural Perspectives*, edited by Deborah L. Nichols and Thomas H. Charlton, pp. 255–64. Washington, DC: Smithsonian Institution Press.

Young, Robert 1963. The Development of Herbert Spencer's Concept of Evolution. *Actas du XIᵉ Congrès International d'Histoire des Sciences, Varsovie 24–31 Août 1963*, vol. II, pp. 273–8. Cracow: Maison d'Edition de l'Académie Polonaise des Sciences.

Zagarell, Allen 1986a. Structural Discontinuity – A Critical Factor in the Emergence of Primary and Secondary States. *Dialectical Anthropology*, vol. 10, no. 2, pp. 155–77. Amsterdam, NL.

—— 1986b. Trade, Women, Class, and Society in Ancient Western Asia. *Current Anthropology*, vol. 27, no. 5, pp. 415–30. Chicago, IL.

Zeidler, James A. 1987. The Evolution of Prehistoric "Tribal" Systems as Historical Process: Archeological Indicators of Social Reproduction. In *Chiefdoms in the Americas*, edited by Robert D. Drennan and Carlos A. Uribe, pp. 325–44. Lanham, MD: University Press of America.

Index

Index

exchange, 78
exploitation, 21–3
forces of production, 20–1
form of surplus extraction, 22–3
human nature, 13–15
human sociality, 15–18
labor, 15
laws of motion, 24–5
metabolic exchange, 28ff.
mode of production, 18, 24
on Darwin, 14
population, 30–2
relations of production, 20–3
social class structures, 20–3
state, 23–4
state formation, 26–7
theory of society and history, 13–27
totality, 8
Marxist social thought, 92, 122, 123–5, 132
critique of structural Marxism, 125–6,
131–2, 134, 159n6
structural Marxism, 97–8, 118–19
Millon, René, 101–2, 127
relation to Marx and Weber, 127
resistance, 102
mode of production, 4, 18–27, 43–4, 89
articulation, 99–100
asiatic, 99
capitalist, 24–6
Germanic, 118, 133
Lineage, 133
primitive communist (see also kin-
communal), 25–6, 45–6, 95–7, 117,
152n7
relation to concepts of culture and society,
18–20
tributary, 25, 45, 49–51
modernity, 148
Morgan, Lewis Henry, 1–2, 63

nature, 27
neo-Kantianism, 37ff, 40, 42–4
Neolithic Revolution, 44
new archaeology
see processual archaeology

origin of the state, 82, 96–7
Orser, Charles, 121, 146–7

Patterson, Thomas, 95–7, 99–100, 132, 137–8,
152n8
articulation of modes of production, 99–100
class and state formation, 96–7
critique of systems theory approaches, 95–6
kin-communal societies, 95–7
Paynter, Robert, 121, 134, 146
Peregrine, Peter, 140
Phillips, Philip, 65–71
historical causality, 65–6
stages of development, 65–71
uneven development, 67
population, 4, 30–2, 34–5, 79–84, 103–4,
152n9, 160n8
positivism, 43, 74, 91, 111–12
power, 76, 117, 135–6
Preucel, Robert, 162n8
Price, Barbara, 79–82, 161n13
primitive communism, 25–6, 45–6, 95–6, 97,
117, 158n4
processual (new) archaeology, 3–4, 72–9, 91–2,
103–12, 122–3
use of Marxist analytical categories, 122–3

Redfield, Robert, 53–5, 63
critique of Childe, 53–4
moral v. technical order, 54
reductionism, 4
relations of production, 20–2, 78, 94, 97
see also division of labor, social
Renfrew, Colin, 77–9, 93–4, 107–12, 157n3
chiefdoms, group-oriented v. individualizing,
107–8
early state module 110–12
exchange as motor of change, 76–9, 109
peer polity interaction, 109–10
relation to Durkheim, 108–9
rise of civilization, 76
systems theory, 74, 77
resistance, 23, 88, 102
see also class conflict
rise of civilization, 3–4, 55, 57–8, 68–9, 75–6,
79, 97–8
see also origin of the state
Robin, Cynthia, 130
Rothman, Mitchell, 144
Rowe, John
on rise of cities, 70–1

– 202 –

Index